Rocky Mountain Heartland

The Modern American West
Richard W. Etulain and David M. Wrobel, Editors

Carl Abbott
The Metropolitan Frontier: Cities in the Modern American West

Richard W. Etulain
*Re-imagining the Modern American West:
A Century of Fiction, History, and Art*

Gerald D. Nash
*The Federal Landscape: An Economic History of the
Twentieth-Century West*

Ferenc Morton Szasz
Religion in the Modern American West

Oscar J. Martínez
Mexican-Origin People in the United States: A Topical History

Duane A. Smith
*Rocky Mountain Heartland: Colorado, Montana, and
Wyoming in the Twentieth Century*

Rocky Mountain Heartland

Colorado, Montana, and Wyoming
in the Twentieth Century

DUANE A. SMITH

The University of Arizona Press   Tucson

Dedicated to
Kay and Jack Eberl, Don and Linda

The University of Arizona Press
© 2008 The Arizona Board of Regents
All rights reserved

www.uapress.arizona.edu

Library of Congress Cataloging-in-Publication Data
Smith, Duane A.
  Rocky Mountain heartland : Colorado, Montana,
and Wyoming in the twentieth century / Duane A. Smith.
     p. cm. — (The modern American West)
  Includes bibliographical references and index.
  ISBN 978-0-8165-2456-3 (hardcover : alk. paper) —
  ISBN 978-0-8165-2759-5 (pbk. : alk. paper)
  1. Rocky Mountains Region—History—20th century.
2. Colorado—History—20th century. 3. Montana—
History—20th century. 4. Wyoming—History—20th
century. I. Title.
F721.S646   2008
978'.03—dc22   2008012516

Publication of this book is made possible in part by the proceeds of
a permanent endowment created with the assistance of a Challenge
Grant from the National Endowment for the Humanities, a federal
agency.

13   12   11   10   09   08   6   5   4   3   2   1

Book composition: Alcorn Publication Design

Contents

Illustrations

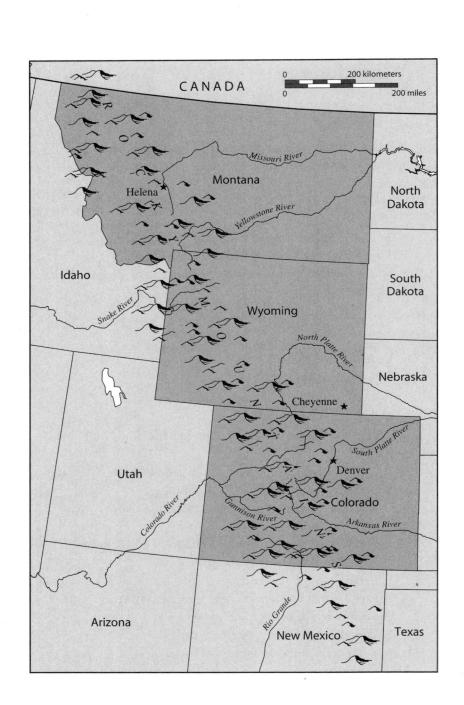

CANADA

0   200 kilometers

0   200 miles

Missouri River

Montana

North
Dakota

Helena★

Yellowstone River

Idaho

South
Dakota

Snake River

Wyoming

North Platte River

Nebraska

Cheyenne ★

South Platte River

Utah

Denver ★

Colorado

Colorado River

Gunnison River

Arkansas River

Arizona

Rio Grande

New Mexico

Texas

Preface

PHILOSOPHER GEORGE SANTAYANA emphasized in 1906 that "those who cannot remember the past are condemned to repeat it." In that quotation, he echoed what the fourth-century BC Greek historian Thucydides maintained. In his history of *The Peloponnesian War*, Thucydides avowed, "I shall be content if it is judged useful by those inquirers who desire an exact knowledge of the past as an aid to the interpretation of the future."

Considering that people read history in various ways and therefore may draw thoroughly different conclusions, it remains a noble goal to work toward understanding the past and its influence on the present and the future. This is the goal of this study of Wyoming, Montana, and Colorado in the twentieth century. This is a West of the most modern of American places, while at the same time a West of hallowed traditions and captivating heritage.

With no natural boundaries, the three states were creatures of the whims of nineteenth-century promoters and politicians. These states constitute the Rocky Mountain heartland, a place that has intrigued and fascinated Americans and others for well over two centuries.

What they have in common geographically are the Rocky Mountains running down their backbones and the Great Plains pushing up against those majestic mountains from the east. Rainfall, except in the mountains, is a rare commodity, and water is treasured everywhere. Indeed, water, or lack thereof, holds the key to the twenty-first century.

Vast and full of spectacular natural wonders, this heartland attracted visitors, artists, and explorers—along with its first natural-resource exploiters, the fur trappers and traders—long before settlers emerged on the horizon. These latecomers came because of gold and the opportunity to get rich without working, which mining since the California gold rush had seemingly promised. Others came, thanks to that nineteenth-century transportation wonder the railroad, to plow the fields, mine the coal, and dream of making their way in a prosperous community. Tourists started arriving with ease and comfort unknown to any previous generation. It did not take long for locals to take advantage of this economic windfall, a windfall that grew with each passing year.

With mineral wealth, agricultural riches, and seemingly unlimited opportunities awaiting them, these settlers represented the nineteenth-century American dream of going west to exploit the promised land. Abraham Lincoln captured this vision in comments he reportedly made to Schuyler Colfax as the latter prepared to travel west in the late spring of 1865. Colfax delivered the remarks to an appreciative crowd in Denver: "I have very large ideas of the mineral wealth of our nation. It abounds all over the western country, from the Rocky Mountains to the Pacific. . . . [The miners'] prosperity is the prosperity of the Nation, and we shall prove in a very few years that we are indeed the *treasury of the world*."

And indeed Montanans, Wyomingites, and Coloradans did just that in the nineteenth century. They were joined by investors and a variety of outside exploiters, and the words of historian Patricia Limerick in her *The Legacy of Conquest* ring true: "The history of the West is a study of a place undergoing conquest and never fully escaping its consequences."

It did not stop there. Others read about this "wondrous land" and vicariously went west as well through photographs, literature, and Wild West shows. The West became a treasured spot in the national consciousness.

There was the West of imagination, a West vividly captured by Owen Wister in *The Virginian* (1902). A West that *High Noon* and *Gunsmoke* kept alive for later generations. A West that literature, movies, and television found so lucrative in the twentieth century. A West that intrigued and fascinated generations of outsiders more than it did those living the experience.

In many ways, these three Rocky Mountain states lived up to that dream, that image. The variety of mineral wealth from gold to copper had benefited the whole country. Western beef and grains had graced eastern tables; and the towns and villages, mines and farms had provided eastern manufacturers, stores, and investors a tempting market. Settlers from all walks of life and countries had come west to participate in their development by means limited only by their imaginations. Politically, as new and weakly populated states, their impact had been marginal except

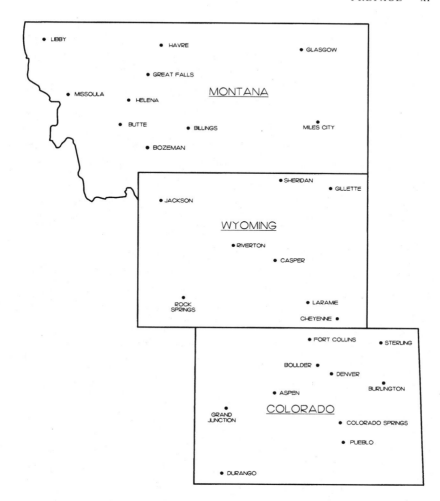

in 1896 when the silver issue aroused them to a new frenzy that frightened some easterners nearly to death.

As the twentieth century dawned, Colorado, Montana, and Wyoming were much alike, former frontiers maturing in some ways in spite of themselves. For nearly half the next century, the Rocky Mountain heartland states were followers among their sister states. All this changed after World War II. By the dawn of the twenty-first century, great changes and transformations had come from within and without the Rocky Mountains.

Changes had come because of a continuing current in the history of the Rocky Mountains and the entire region: the role of Uncle Sam.

As Limerick stated vigorously, "the involvement of the federal government in the economy and the resulting dependence, resentment, and deficit have become major issues in American history and in contemporary politics, and the American West was the arena in which an expanded role for the federal government first took hold."

The New West was for some less new than old; for others, it was an exciting vision of what had just transpired and what was yet to come. Urbanization had always been part of this region from the earliest mining camp, making it very different from earlier eastern and midwestern frontiers. Although urbanization ebbed and flowed throughout the western region in the post–World War II years, it took on new meaning and significance.

Montana, Wyoming, and Colorado once had been nearly equal in potential and opportunity, but that changed as the twentieth century advanced. Colorado now dominated, marching to an urban, twenty-first-century tempo—professional sports teams; a highly urbanized Front Range from Fort Collins to Pueblo; a diversified economy, from space engineering to tourism to an old standby—coal mining; a transportation and communication network that tied it to the whole world; a broad-based higher education system; and the region's leading city, Denver. It left its two longtime neighbors far behind.

Montana and Wyoming still reflected much of an earlier, more earthy era, a West that once had dominated this Rocky Mountain heartland. To some people this reflected a legendary West where one could do what one wanted, when one desired, and where one decided. To others it meant only heartbreak and dismay. Less urbanized, more rural, and depending on natural resources from coal to ranch- and farmland, these states would have seemed very familiar to a resident from a century before. Pioneers of that earlier age would have seen, however, that tourism was adding a new dimension and playing a much greater role than ever before. They might have been amazed at how their lives, typically full of hard times and tribulations, had become a romantic and sanitized attraction for visitors.

These three states do have a common story to tell, a story of twentieth-century optimism, development, and change. As they were shaped by the nineteenth century, so would they help shape the twenty-first century.

There is a continuity in western history, as Earl Pomeroy and others have stressed, not just a legendary frontier and that which followed.

Westerner, historian, and novelist Bernard DeVoto defended his native region as though it was the most positive element in developing the American character. However, in his essay "The West: A Plundered Province," he insisted, "The mountains and the high plains, which had seen the end of the frontier movement and had caused the collapse of the pioneer culture, thus also set the first full stop to the American dream." Although perhaps too pessimistic, DeVoto was right in focusing attention on the American dream — that hope of a fresh start, a prosperous life, and the freedom to be an individual.

These seasons of the past have so much to tell us today. Theirs is a story well worth telling, remembering, contemplating, and learning from as the twenty-first century moves along into history. Perhaps the old baseball wizard and breaker of the color line in baseball in 1947, Branch Rickey, said it most clearly. If fans walking into Denver's Coors Field pause for a moment at the statue of the baseball player, they may read Rickey's words: "It is not the honor that you take with you but the heritage you leave behind."

For most people, January 1, 1900, marked the start of a new century, although there were those who argued for January 1, 1901. Regardless, Rocky Mountain westerners entered the year 1900 confident, optimistic, and seemingly with a bright future stretching before them and an exciting, epic heritage stretching out behind them. This is their story and that of their children, their grandchildren, and their great-grandchildren.

Acknowledgments

The author owes a deep debt of gratitude to a large group of people who helped with this project. Richard Gilbert provided photographs, thoughts on Wyoming, and some of the Wyoming legwork. John Ninnemann climbed a "mountain" to capture just the right photo, while Patrick Saunders found some other photographs for me. Duane Hampton worked through some Montana issues. Todd Ellison was his usual professional self in finding material.

The staffs of the Colorado Historical Society, the Wyoming Archives, the Montana Historical Society, the Durango Public Library, the Fort Lewis Library, and the Southwest Center Library did stalwart work on behalf of the author. Along the way, in the past years, others have assisted in a variety of ways, and their contributions are also appreciated.

My wife, Gay, provided her usual well-thought-out editorial advice and encouragement. Fort Lewis College supported the endeavor in a variety of much-appreciated ways. Richard Etulain and David Wrobel offered excellent guidance and ideas as editors of the series in which this book appears. Patti Hartmann and the professional staff of the University of Arizona Press turned the manuscript into a book and offered many outstanding suggestions for improvements along the way. An author could not have asked for any better support.

Rocky Mountain Heartland

Prologue

1900

OPENING THEIR NEWSPAPERS on the brisk January days as the new century opened, Rocky Mountain readers found a variety of topics to tempt their interest.

> The sugar, cotton and tobacco cultivated by Asiatic coolie labor will soon drive the Southern product [sugar, cotton, tobacco] out of the market, and, as the American laborer cannot compete with the Oriental coolie, . . . he will have to look for work somewhere else.
>
> It looks now as if Great Britain will stand to experience much more disappointment and sad experience from the unjustified war in South Africa than it expected in the beginning.
>
> —*Denver Evening Post*, January 1, 1900

> For this country the [nineteenth] century has been a remarkable one. What it still has in store for us, or what the coming century will bring are matters of speculation.
>
> —*Rocky Mountain News*, January 1, 1900

> A happy New Year, all year is the wish of the *Independent* for its friends. May 1900 be an improvement over 1899 in every good respect.
>
> We read with much comfort the dispatch from Washington setting forth that the European powers interested have agreed [in] full to all of our demands for a guarantee of our rights to trading in China [Open Door Policy]. With these rights secured there is absolutely no need of holding Manila and the Philippine Islands as a naval base.
>
> —*Helena Independent*, January 2, 1900

> To the people of Montana the *Miner* wishes a happy New Year. As a people, they are entitled to a little more recompense for their efforts in the up building of a magnificent commonwealth against some of the odds that nature has opposed against them.
>
> —*Butte Daily Miner*, January 1, 1900

> Wyoming's New Era. The year 1899 was one of progress for Wyoming and in fact marks the commencement of a new era—one of development and prosperity in a very substantial manner. Even our neighbors are noticing what is going on in this state.
> —*Cheyenne Daily Sun-Leader*, January 2, 1900

The news was encouraging for the readers as crisp, cold weather settled over the Rockies at the New Year's dawning. Not only did local and state news interest them but the world scene was sneaking into their lives whether they were ready or not.

Montanans, Coloradans, and Wyomingites could enjoy with a sense of pleasure and relief; they had survived the worst decade in their history. The 1890s had featured disheartening farm prices, the horrific crash of 1893, a nearly decade-long depression, and their hopes crushed with the defeat of silver and William Jennings Bryan in the traumatic 1896 election. It seemed to folks in the Rockies that they had suffered more than any other section of the country. Now 1900 dawned with renewed hope and optimism for most if not all.

Not everything had been gloom and despair for the westerners. They, like their countrymen, felt great pride as the United States easily defeated Spain in the 1898 Spanish-American War, which in many ways hardly deserved to be called a war. Rocky Mountain men had enthusiastically volunteered, and some had charged up San Juan Hill with that hero of the day, Theodore Roosevelt. In American eyes, the United States had emerged a world power, equal to "super power" England.

As the newspaper stories indicated that January day, U.S. citizens had pride in their country as well as a concern about their role in this new world and what it meant to be a player on the larger scene. They did not totally comprehend the world situation in China or the former parts of the Spanish empire they now controlled—Cuba and the Philippine Islands.

They well understood that the West was part of the larger world. Montana and Colorado were major silver mining states, and residents watched angrily as international monetary issues depressed the price of their economic pillar and helped slide them into a crash and a depression. Copper prices and, to a lesser degree, cattle prices hinged on the international situation. Still, the world scene generally proved of more interest than personal concern.

In this, westerners were not alone, but it seems doubtful that many worried about what transpired beyond their state. The United States would be able to handle international matters as it had dealt with Spain in 1898. To them it seemed more important to wish one and all a happy New Year than to ponder foreign affairs.

Realizing that they stood on the threshold of a new century, westerners assessed the old as well as the changes already here and those still to come that would forever transform the Rocky Mountain heartland. Being perched on such a threshold was both gratifying and threatening. They could look back to where they had been with a certain amount of pride. After all, the oldest of them, Colorado, had only last year reached the fortieth birthday of the now legendary Pike's Peak Rush, which gave it life, and yet they had already survived the ups and downs of the late nineteenth century and could now look ahead with renewed confidence.

Looking ahead to an unknown future, the Rocky Mountain dwellers had a strong sense of progress and buoyancy. That future would be challenging, it would be exciting, and it would have good days and bad. With renewed western optimism, residents of Montana, Wyoming, and Colorado stood ready to enter that era.

Meanwhile, the *New York Times* had asked state governors to send a brief "state of the state" summary. Not too many did, but, fortunately, all three Rocky Mountain executives responded confidently. Montana's Gov. Robert Smith soared in his evaluation: "The mining industry is prosperous and will continue so. Stock interests look better than for many years at this season, and our stockmen expect even better times next year than the past one." Not stopping there, he continued that "farming and all other industries are doing well. In fact, Montana cannot well be affected by changed conditions elsewhere." Nor did Colorado's and Wyoming's governors languish a step behind. "The outlook for 1900 is particularly bright; considerable railroad building will be done, mines will be developed, and other important steps taken in the direction of advancement and progress," enthusiastically declared Wyoming's Gov. Richard DeForest. Charles Thomas continued in the same vein. "We are a great, growing, and loyal commonwealth prosperous because of our bountiful resources and our energetic and indefatigable citizens. Colorado begins the new year with bright hopes and with brighter prospects than ever before."[1]

Montana's governor missed his guess about the state not being affected by "conditions elsewhere." It already had been and would be even more so. Governor DeForest looked to the past in hopes that the future would produce more of the same, and Governor Thomas saw that future much more clearly.

Wyomingites, Coloradans, Montanans, and Americans in general toasted the arrival of the new century with speeches, articles, and books that declared a firm faith in their nation's future. Many were the praises and promises—and other observations—made in New Year's editorials in Colorado, Wyoming, and Montana and by the governors. The future, they were confident, would surpass the past.

Times appeared better than they had for years. Inventions, high farm income, more jobs in the cities, and expanding educational opportunities made possible prosperity only dreamed of in the past. A belief in progress heralded the advent of the twentieth century.

Americans had a right to expect that wonders loomed just around the corner. The previous generation had seen the invention of the telephone, the electric light, the skyscraper, railroads that crossed the continent in a matter of days, and the miracle medicine, aspirin. A few eastern city dwellers watched with amazement as the automobile chugged by, as did startled cattle and horses in the nearby hinterland. With pride, the West could point to eight territories becoming states, including Colorado (1876), Montana (1889), and Wyoming (1890). They were now part of the sisterhood of states.

These Americans were the best educated in the country's history, with only a 10.7 percent illiteracy rate. Nearly half the youth of high school age were in school, and one out of every twenty-five young men between ages eighteen and twenty-one continued on to college. Job opportunities seemed unprecedented, particularly as they bounced back after the 1890s depression. Americans also had the highest per capita income in the world—$569—with real wages on the rise and prices declining steadily. Twenty percent of women over age fifteen worked outside the home, but growing numbers of urban middle-class women had the leisure time to become involved in a widening range of activities.

As Jacob Riis pointed out in his 1890 classic, *How the Other Half Lives*, America also contained an underclass—a fact evident in the Rockies' largest community, Denver, population 133,800. They lived crowded into filthy tenements in the cities and in hovels in the country. The technological, educational, and other improvements so highly praised at the century's turn did not reach them. For these folks, the American dream of rising beyond one's status in life proved almost entirely illusionary.   •

Nevertheless, William McKinley, with the Republican promise of the full dinner pail seemingly being achieved, sat comfortably and conservatively in the White House. The Republicans indeed appeared enthroned there, having lost only two presidential elections in the past forty years if one discounts the controversial ending of the 1876 election. (The GOP lost the popular vote, contested the electoral college vote, and finally won by the decision of an electoral commission.)

Colorado was particularly significant because it gained statehood that year and cast its electoral-college vote for candidate Rutherford Hayes, without which Democrat Samuel Tilden would have won without any dispute. The Rockies, however, had been stubbornly Democratic for nearly a decade, except for Wyoming, which slipped back into the Republican presidential column in 1900.

The early nineties, uproar and hearsay of farmers' revolts, reform, and the hullabaloo of Populism receded into the "distant" past. William Jennings Bryan and his "Cross of Gold" ideas echoed yesterday, not today. The 1896 presidential election seemingly put the end to such radicalism. America seemed to have safe, conservative business leadership, and the Republican Party planned to do everything in its power to keep it that way.

Yes, some complained loudly about monopolies, the widening gulf between rich and poor, wretched working conditions, urban blight, and political corruption. Fewer complained about racial discrimination and the ravaging of the country's natural resources. Most Americans thought such problems were permanent and irresolvable.

As the two national parties convened for their quadrennial national gathering in 1900, they renominated the 1896 warhorses, McKinley and Bryan. The Republicans made one change that proved monumental for the United States. The party selected that Spanish American War hero, "damned cowboy," noted author and advocate of the strenuous life, Theodore Roosevelt, as McKinley's running mate, to the horror of some old-guard Republicans (with Roosevelt being a heartbeat away from the

White House). To others it provided a way to put him "out to pasture," so to speak, and reduce his growing political power.

The issues in 1900 failed to generate the excitement of 1896. The silver issue created little stir this time around (although mining states Montana and Colorado stayed loyal to the faith), and the Populist Party had nearly disappeared, except in a few states. Its idealism and reform platform, fortunately, remained far from dead. Imperialism and the sudden emergence of American colonies, scattered from the Caribbean to the Philippines, aroused some, and pride in the "grand" victory over Spain in 1898 still glowed. The "splendid little war," all three months of it, had helped dispel the depression's gloom and revive the buoyancy and optimism of earlier years. The American spirit had rebounded magnificently.

That slogan of the war days, "Remember the Maine, to Hell with Spain," ushered the country into its twentieth-century issues, which, unfortunately, proved less easy to solve than the war had been to win. The high-tariff and the low-tariff advocates hissed and sputtered a bit, but most Americans did not rush to the barricades.

Imperialism was becoming an issue after all. America had become a world power, although most Americans did not understand what that entailed. A nasty little war had exploded in the Philippines, because our "Little Brown Brothers," as we often patronizingly referred to them, seemed less than enamored with their new overlord. The United States was about to get more involved in China in a sticky situation called the Boxer Rebellion. Indiana senator Albert Beveridge declared boldly that God "has made us [United States] the master organizers of the world to establish system where chaos reigns. He has made us adept in government that we may administer government among savages and senile peoples."[2]

McKinley again triumphed, with a larger electoral college majority and popular vote than four years before. Both houses of Congress also contained substantial Republican majorities. Insofar as an election could decide anything, the country had given its approval to imperialism, the gold standard, and a high protective tariff.

While rural America held tenuously to the nineteenth century, its urban cousins surged ahead. The trend was clearly emerging of people moving from farm to village to town and city. Once called the backbone of America, the farmer did not appreciate his new comedic status as the rube, the rural hick.

The farmer did gain some benefits from technological improvements, however. Labor time and costs declined, and production dramatically increased. At the same time, farms grew larger, and one person could easily handle more acreage. Commercial, specialized farming clearly loomed in the future. The less skilled, the underfunded, and the unfortunate, those hanging on to the old ways, found themselves forced to the sidelines.

By 1900, more Americans lived in cities than ever before, and almost 40 percent resided in communities with over 2,500 people. Here was found the technology that promised a better tomorrow. Rural Americans eagerly left the shrinking agriculture opportunities for the bright lights, the job opportunities, and the better life beckoning them away from the farm.

In the cities, too, was found the developing urban middle class — salaried professionals, technicians, college graduates, government employees, business leaders, clerical workers — people with optimism, faith, and growing prosperity, who were about to change the country.

The cities could be looked upon as centers of progress, business, and the good life, but they had their share of troubles. Not the least of these problems were poverty and slums, polluted air, noise, poor drinking water, corrupt political machines and bosses, crime, lack of sanitation, and transportation tribulations. Furthermore, agricultural counties often carried disproportionate political weight in the state legislatures. When legislative districts were created, agriculture often prevailed, giving rural representatives dominance in many legislatures. Rural representatives were now trying to solve unfamiliar urban problems.

The industrial city, with its business and industrial center, and its poorest residents clustered nearby, heralded the new era. Next geographically were the workers' neighborhoods, the middle-class residential area, and the "pure air, peaceful" suburbs. The structure was already drawing comments and concern. In these industrial cities people were sorted by class, income, occupation, and race. This produced economic and social polarization, with the middle class moving ahead faster than those below it.

For middle- and upper-class Americans, life was better than it had been in their parents' and grandparents' day. They had more leisure time and a higher standard of living. They enjoyed more comforts, and, as Lord Bryce observed in his classic book *American Commonwealth* back in 1888, "the average [American's] knowledge is higher, the habit of reading and thinking more generally diffused, than in any other country." While pulling oneself up by the bootstraps had never been as easy as the popular Horatio Alger books proclaimed, it could and did happen. Unlimited and equal opportunity for upward advancement proved much easier for native-born, middle-class whites, who tended to have the skills, resources, and connections that opened up the most desirable jobs. This situation highlighted the gap between rural and urban America. The cities, for example, made greater strides than did rural areas in the quality of education, physical plants, and equipment. The best libraries, hospitals, newspapers, cultural events, financial institutions, parks, and variety and quality of stores were found in metropolitan areas.

It was also in the cities that reforms germinated, after the rural Populists had planted the seeds. The problems and concerns could be seen right next door, or at least on the way to work. Middle-class women had more leisure time to devote to causes, and they jumped to the forefront. Women's suffrage became a touchstone for the new era.

Yet in 1900, as had been true since the government first took a census, more Americans lived in rural than in urban areas. Until the gap between the two could be bridged economically, culturally, and in a host of other ways, the promise of America could not be attained.

At least one movement, Chautauqua, partly bridged the cultural gap. It became a nationwide phenomenon that drew hundreds of thousands of people to local clubs and summer Chautauqua lecture series. Farmers and their families, as well as small town and village folk, found their cultural isolation—if not broken down, at least breached. Steel baron Andrew Carnegie's philanthropic donation of library buildings to communities that gave sites and pledged maintenance also helped to bridge the cultural gap, at least for small towns if not all villages.

However, even the turn-of-the century intellectual fervor separated farmer and city dweller. The theory of evolution took hold in the "godless" cities, according to many country dwellers, while they hung on to that "old-time religion." To make matters worse, progressive education, under the leadership of John Dewey, threatened the hallowed, familiar "three Rs" so popular in nineteenth-century America.

Meanwhile, the new year found Colorado, Wyoming, and Montana basking in the glow of the war's aftermath, the closing of the frontier, and high expectations for the upcoming century. They had been centers of

Populism and support for Bryan, neither of which had faded. Colorado, particularly, had espoused the cause and had become quite radical. However, such radicalism masked Colorado's underlying conservatism on most matters.

Wyoming, Colorado, and Montana in 1900 had both similarities and differences—more of the former than the latter. The population densities in large portions of all three states were fewer than two inhabitants per square mile, with only Denver urbanized to ninety people per square mile. Each was an economic colony for outside influences, including transportation, economics, and federal policy. Agriculture in each state had not rebounded as much as hoped for, but that did not hinder people from coming to try their faith against an unforgiving environment. Politically, except in their own estimation, the states carried little national weight.

Geographically, both Montana and Colorado had profoundly different regions. Montana's plains to the east and mountains in the west were matched by Colorado, which included several more divisions within its larger regions. The two states' needs, environments, and settlement patterns were different. However, Wyoming offered less of a split between east and west, except in the northwest corner, where the country's first national park—Yellowstone—was located. Land and space provided the one common denominator.

Often the various mountain and plains regions did not understand one another and had conflicting goals. These facts would influence their history. Drawn on a map, the states had no natural boundaries, with Montana crunching up against Canada in the north.

The 1900 census found the United States just shy of a population of 76 million. The Rocky Mountain states contributed only a small share, with Coloradans numbering 539,000, Montanans topping 243,000, and Wyomingites trailing with 92,000. Already obvious signs that the new America truly was on its way could be seen in the Centennial State, as Coloradans referred to their territory. There were 29,599 of them working in manufacturing; 24,078 in metal mining (5,427 coal miners); 18,235 in transportation, communication, and other public utilities; and 3,625 in education. Agriculture still led in numbers, with 44,302, but trailed badly in generating revenue for the state's economy. New urban/industrial America was on its way in Colorado.

Montana's mines had 15,250 laborers, with the largest percentage digging copper at Butte. Farming and ranching had 27,177 workers, and 12,293 Montanans were involved in transportation, communication, and public utilities. Agriculture dominated Wyoming's smaller work force, with nearly 30 percent of its labor force involved in ranching or farming.

These statistics provide plenty of hints about the future. Colorado surged far in front of Wyoming and Montana in professional and related classifications, finance and clerical positions, and wholesale and retail trade. Public-service jobs (federal, state, and local governments and the military) were also dominated by Colorado, although less than the other categories.

Each state retained its economic colonial status, trapped or so it seemed, by dark forces beyond their control. Investments generally came from eastern or foreign sources, outside interests dominated transportation, and mining and agricultural prices were established elsewhere — except for gold, which secured an international price of just over $20 per ounce. The three states from the Rocky Mountain region furnished raw materials, while higher-priced manufactured products usually arrived from elsewhere, further draining money away. Finally, overexpansion, optimism, and an abiding faith in themselves and their efforts caused many to go into debt.

All this provided the bedrock of the 1890s turmoil. Easterners often pictured westerners as radical malcontents who little appreciated what others had done for them. Sometimes they wondered what had happened to their cousins who had migrated to the promised land. Rocky Mountain westerners, however, thought of themselves as the backbone of solid American virtues and the hope for the future.

The three states showed to different degrees what was transpiring on the larger U.S. scene. Agricultural Wyoming, with little manufacturing, had only two small urban centers, Cheyenne (population 14,100) and Laramie (6,400). Montana, while agricultural, included one mining and industrial center, Butte (30,500), and a fine capital city, Helena (10,800).

Colorado was by far the most urbanized and industrialized of the three states. While the eastern plains and parts of the Western Slope (beyond the Continental Divide) were rural and agricultural, they were not dominating, except in the legislature, in which they held an unfair advantage because of the original districting that had favored rural over urban counties. Indeed, in 1876 most of the state's counties had been rural, except for Denver and a few of its neighbors. Crucial votes often went against urban interests.

Denver, "the Queen City of the Mountains and Plains," dominated the region. Its population of 133,859 was larger than Wyoming's and over half the size of Montana's. Mining had given birth to Denver, had nurtured it, developed it, and made it ready for the new century. With an economy based solidly on mining—having evolved through gold, silver, and then again gold excitements—the city had become the smelting, banking, transportation, mining, and commercial heart of the Rocky Mountains.

Rural agriculture in the state had grown; however, it played a minor role in the capital city. Denver served as a regional agricultural center but was no "cow town," as some easterners degradingly described it.

In fact, Denver was a favorite destination for tourism and a rail hub for the region. After sampling its variety of attractions, tourists could travel into the mountains, to the mining communities, and even beyond to the Western Slope. Depending on their imaginings of what it was, they could sample the "real" West along the way. All this augured well for Denver's future.

Socially and culturally, Denver endeavored to emulate its older, established eastern cousins, and, in fact, its Tabor Grand Opera House—a gift of Colorado's legendary silver king Horace Tabor—was the finest between St. Louis and San Francisco. Even though easterners might have chuckled over the adventures of the nouveau riche, like Mrs. J. J. Brown, better known as Molly, Denver countered with its own "sacred 100" who established its social pace.

In addition, Denver became known as a health mecca for those with respiratory ailments, the "one-lunged army," as they were called. In fact, Colorado as a whole, with its dry climate, healthful "ozone," and "medical miracle" mineral springs, had long been a destination for those suffering from a variety of illnesses. Its neighbors were only a step or two behind.

Sufferers could find sanitariums in a variety of Colorado, Wyoming, and Montana towns. Each promised a cure for at least one disease, maybe several, that afflicted mankind. Mineral springs owners claimed to cure, among other things, "lost manhood," "lost womanhood," sour stomachs,

cancer, tuberculosis, baldness, and a wide variety of other ailments, not
to mention weight problems. They raised more hopes than they produced cures. Nevertheless, at least the patient felt a little better (though
not quite twenty-one again!) after treatments in the warm mineral water.
The same could not be said for those who drank the mineral water, with
its often unsavory taste and its habit of "flushing out" the drinker.

Denver's "queen" status aroused envy, both at home and abroad.
Cheyenne, Laramie, Butte, and Helena, as well as nearby Salt Lake
City, might hope or even think they rivaled Denver, but their wishes far
exceeded reality at the turn of the twentieth century.

Denver faced a number of potential rivals in Colorado with the state's
growing urbanization. Pueblo (34,448 population), the industrial center;
Leadville (12,455) and Cripple Creek (10,147), the mining centers;
Boulder (6,150), the educational center; and Colorado Springs (21,086),
with a variety of attractions, were all urban centers. Some had only started
their climb up the urbanization ladder. The mining areas, scattered
about the mountains, depicted the boom-and-bust aspects of the nineteenth-century, urban mining West. Only one other mining region, far
down in the San Juans, still prospered. There Silverton, Telluride, and
Ouray formed a prosperous mining triangle. Gold, though, had replaced
silver as the primary metal in these high mountains.

Still much more rural than urban, many parts of the three states
looked just as they had when their pioneering ancestors arrived a generation before. Only the cities had such modern conveniences as electricity
and the telephone. In the rural Rockies it could have been 1860 as easily
as 1900.

To many easterners the three states still represented the Wild West,
where life reflected what they had read about in popular dime novels or
dreamed about as they went through their workaday lives. They might
have seen that life reenacted in the Buffalo Bill Wild West show or one of
its imitators. Already those visitors were coming, with an ease unknown to
the pioneers of a generation before, to see this vanishing frontier before it
rode into a western sunset. On they came to Denver, the largest railroad
hub in the Rockies. From there they could venture off to wherever their
wishes or dreams might take them.

An abandoned mining camp might entice them, or a booming mining town such as Butte or Cripple Creek. With Indian reservations in all

three states, they could see a segment of curiously fascinating Americana. A trip into the mountains for an easterner or a midwesterner might be the thrill of a lifetime. Then there were the health-giving mineral springs, as well as fishing and hunting.

Visitors might take the "Swing around the Circle" as the Denver & Rio Grande Railroad described the ride from Denver to Durango to Ouray and back to Denver. Colorado's baby railroad, now grown up, would take them through mountains, mining camps, and a variety of amazing scenery. A side trip, via the Rio Grande Southern, took the visitors to Mesa Verde and its "Aztec" cliff dwellings. They could visit a ranch in Wyoming or Montana for a different kind of adventure at what became known as dude ranches.

Yellowstone National Park, the country's oldest, lured many now that the railroad made travel so comfortable and easy. Fishing, hunting, mountain climbing, and a stay at one of the hot springs spas in search of health or relaxation brought more visitors. Tourism, alive and well, promised even more in the future.

As January 1, 1900, dawned, Rocky Mountain westerners had much to be optimistic about. As they sang or recalled those immortal words of Robert Burns, "Should auld acquaintance be forgot, and auld lang syne!" they looked back at the receding nineteenth century with a mix of good riddance and nostalgia, and ahead with hopefulness and excitement.

In their New Year's resolutions, they probably wished for a variety of individual things for themselves and their families and good times for the future. If Montana, Wyoming, and Colorado could also have made resolutions, they would have been pleased to continue the prosperity, growth, and development that had become more common over the past year or so.

That crusty relic of another age, Mark Twain, did not think too highly of New Year's resolutions: "Now is the accepted time to make your regular annual good resolutions. Next week you can begin paving hell with them as usual." Whether or not his Rocky Mountain contemporaries planned just that, they might have agreed with another observation he made at a New Year's party. Asked if he had made a resolution, he resolutely replied, "Indeed, I'm going to live within my income this year even if I have to borrow money to do it."[3] Out in the Rockies, many planned to follow his plan.

CHAPTER 1

The Heart of the West

From Century's Turn to 1914

The achieved West had given the United States something that no
people had ever had before, an internal, domestic empire.
— Bernard DeVoto, *The Year of Decision*

"THE WEST IS DEAD, MY FRIEND," remonstrated the famous Montanan
Charlie Russell in 1917. A generation before, amid the variety of attractions
at Chicago's 1893 World's Fair, a young academic from the University of
Wisconsin, Frederick Jackson Turner, had pointed out what his research
and the 1890 census indicated. A great historical movement had ended:
"Up to our own day American history has been in a large degree the history of the colonization of the Great West."[1]

Ironically, Turner was speaking at the Columbian Exposition, as its
promoters called it, to honor Columbus's arrival in the West Indies 401
years before. Montana, Colorado, and Wyoming all had exhibits of their
agricultural and mining products, plus photographs of their abundant
natural wonders. They beckoned people to come visit and stay. Colorado
also featured a Mesa Verde exhibit allowing visitors to wander through
a one-tenth-scale replica of several cliff dwellings. They could also see
mummies, which were in a separate exhibit room so as not to offend any
genteel souls.

The organizers of this wondrous exhibition had not been sufficiently
organized to celebrate it correctly in 1892. Yet the exhibition hailed the
same amazing accomplishments and advancements of industrial and
modern America that in Turner's thesis had ended the very frontier that
had shaped America since Europeans arrived back in the early seven-
teenth century. Within a decade of the Columbian Exposition, that West
had become legendary in art and literature.

Paradoxically, Russell was painting and writing about his adored
Montana just as western movies emerged to further shape the public's

image of that departed romantic, and seemingly simpler, time. He hoped that writers held the seed to preserving his beloved West. Even in the literary West, a new image was growing stronger. Dime novels had started to portray that image, but they were not acceptable to many parents and teachers. Then came Owen Wister's *The Virginian*, which was acceptable. Wyoming had never enjoyed better publicity than Wister gave it in this novel. The "gunsmoke and gallop" West, alive and well, had captured America's heart and imagination.

Russell, whose paintings and sketches did much to preserve—and romanticize—that vanished pioneering West, bemoaned the changing times. Turner, meantime, spent the rest of his life examining the West, first as a frontier, then as a section, and what it meant to America and Americans.

Yet that very West, in a less idealized manner, was still alive and well, as Americans bade farewell to the nineteenth century and the Rocky Mountain West that was and entered the new century along with the birth of the New West. What the West still offered, in theory, was what had lured their ancestors to cross the continent—opportunity and land. That might not be true in all areas, but certainly the eastern prairies of Montana and Colorado and, to a lesser degree, Wyoming still beckoned.

Thus, they came—the unprepared, the believers, the desperate, the dreamers, and some who knew what was before them and still gambled. They were all gambling on nature, for did not rain follow the plow, the telegraph line, or whatever hope they had? To their dismay, it did not, and they found that the region offered little moisture. Fortunately for them, however, many arrived during one of the region's periodic wet cycles, when the rains came, and often just at the right moment.

All this beckoning land lay, however, beyond the 100th meridian, where it rained typically from eight to twenty inches per year. Here, unforgiving winter came early and might stay while humans and animals hunkered down awaiting better days. The scorching, seemingly unending summers might finish a homestead before it came of age.

The optimistic gambled that national and international markets for their crops would bless them. They wagered that they would learn the necessary survival skills. They had the wherewithal to hold out until the land started to produce the bountiful crops they hoped would blossom on the prairies. It was a race of education versus dwindling resources, of hope against harsh reality. Unfair? Certainly. Did that make these twentieth-century pioneers lose their dream? No.

The land they yearned to develop was semiarid at best, unless one proved fortunate enough to find a parcel along a stream or a readily available water source near a railroad or town. To help even the odds, the windmill could pump sufficient water for home consumption, animals, and a garden. The water might be alkaline enough to nearly take off one's skin, but it was wet and, in some places, fairly plentiful.

Dry-land farming, with its special techniques of tillage and cultivation of certain crops, had been slowly developing over the past generation. The point was to store up precious water for times of drought—not in reservoirs but in the soil, just beneath the growing crops. Deep plowing broke up the soil (a sandy loam proved best) and increased its capacity to hold water.

Because of the plains' winds and hot sun, the dry-land farmers needed to cultivate after every rain. Neglecting to do this could result in soil too hard to break up and untold damage to crops. The Industrial Revolution providentially produced powerful machines to allow farmers to cultivate acreage quickly, but they were expensive to acquire.

Along with methods and machinery, crops that required relatively little water needed to be found. The answer appeared quickly; wheat became the leading dry-land crop, particularly in the northern states.

When initially ballyhooed, dry-land farming appeared to herald once and for all a solution for agriculture beyond the 100th meridian. Despite the trials and tribulations of the last quarter of the nineteenth century, which showed it not to be a cure-all, land speculators and promoters continued to pitch their spiel. And the ever hopeful continually believed it, so on they came to eastern Montana and Colorado.

These prewar years proved exciting and compelling for long-ignored eastern and central Montana. The cattlemen had been there before the homesteader; now everyone could come and fulfill the American dream of owning land, being one's own master, and prospering. Cattlemen were not particularly happy with their new neighbors who plowed the open range. Furthermore, they had an idea of the weather cycles that hit the prairies.

Montana needed these homesteaders to grow and prosper. They, in turn, needed the land to fulfill their destiny. The railroads (which owned

large segments of the land), promoters, local newspaper editors, politicians, and, along with Anaconda mining, nearly Montana itself heralded
this wonderland. The Great Northern Railroad offered a one-way ticket
for only $12.50 and told of flowery meadows, fertile, lush grasslands,
and a healthy climate awaiting everyone. The Northern Pacific and the
Chicago, Milwaukee, St. Paul, and Pacific railroads also did their best
to carry settlers and their supplies. For $22.50 a homesteader could buy
space on a freight car to bring family, belongings, and livestock from St.
Paul. Huge billboards appeared along railroad rights-of-way, and alluring
ads were placed in newspapers and magazines.

Soon green fields would blossom, needing only hard work to turn a
profit. The farm family would be comfortably settled in its little white
house with a nearby barn. The neighborhood would offer the American
icon, the little red schoolhouse, and a nearby village with stores, a church,
and railroad connections.

Agricultural display trains toured the country, carrying leaflets and
brochures. The same material was sent over to Europe to tempt folks
to come. Speakers did their best to further spread the information. The
news of prizes for bountiful crops and livestock, already awarded at farm
exhibits, showed what could be accomplished.

James J. Hill, the railroad pioneer who largely controlled three of
the five regional railroads, obviously marketed the area. The railroads
needed to profitably sell the land the government had given them for
building westward. Still, as a Jeffersonian, Hill believed the small farmer
was the backbone of America. He energetically and sincerely promoted
the idea of small family farms and yeoman farmers.

So the honest, the hopeful, and the huckster joined together to paint an
alluring picture. They succeeded—1913 was the peak year of homesteading in the entire West, and the following years proved good ones too. They
came—foreigners, midwesterners, westerners, the experienced, the nov-
ices, the poor, the moderately financed, the dreamers, the practical—overall, a determined, optimistic group. A surprising number of single women
joined the rush as well. In some areas, they neared 20 percent of those filing claims. "Honyockers" or "scissorbills" the newcomers were nicknamed,
rather disparagingly, but most did not care—they had a vision.

The promised land lured them in large numbers. The Miles City,
Montana, land office averaged 1,200 homestead entries per month in

1909, and Havre had a similar experience. On one spring evening alone, the railroad disembarked 250 homesteaders. Honyockers jammed Elder, Big Sandy, Conrad, and other communities during their peak rushes. In the first two decades of the twentieth century, Montana farm acreage jumped over 2,300 percent, and wheat acreage soared from 200,000 to 3.4 million acres during the same period. Homestead claims totaled over 25 million acres by the early 1920s.

Much to the amazement of old-timers, in 1910 agriculture surpassed mining as the state's major source of income. The dramatic rush cooled somewhat after that, then surged again in the war years.

Everything seemed to be in the newcomers' favor. Grain prices climbed steadily, faster than the cost of farming. Montana's high-quality, high-protein spring and winter wheat captured a strong ranking on the flourishing international market. The federal government expanded the Homestead Act (1909) by doubling the size of a homestead to 320 acres. Subsequently, the government reduced the residence requirement to gain ownership from five to three years and permitted homesteaders to be absent five months out of the year. That would allow them to take another job to earn needed cash.

A generous Congress also passed the Newlands Reclamation Act (1902) to construct large-scale irrigation projects. The projects started in Montana, much to Montanans' pleasure, but they left much of eastern Montana unwatered. Pessimists still wondered if the Great American Desert, as it had once been called, would bloom like a rose, because there seemed to be too little water for too much land.

The farmers, too, enjoyed a positive development: modern equipment. By 1900, stores and catalogs offered the steel moldboard plow, grain drills, steam-powered threshers, combines, and other effective machinery—if farmers had the money or were willing to go into debt. With the techniques of dry-land farming better understood, even the rawest honyockers had the potential to succeed.

Nature contributed blessings. Rainfall averaged sixteen inches annually during the early decades of the century, and it showered down at the right time—in late spring and early summer. The new Montanans naively thought this was typical.

Although rain came in plentiful amounts during those years, a concern still lurked that nature might need help in the future. To the rescue rode the rainmakers, a group not new to the West. These individuals promised to somehow tickle the clouds to release their moisture for a price. They shot electricity upward or sent up balloons filled with mysterious concoctions. They tried noise, sent acid to the heavens (oblivious as to what might come down!), and tried various other techniques that came to mind. The gullible or desperate sometimes fell victim despite warnings from the federal government and others. No miracles occurred before the war; nature would not be fooled.

With everything going well, it was no wonder eastern Montana boomed and the farmers saw a rosy future. Mabel Lux's family became one of those that homesteaded. She grew up in a homesteader's "shack," "plainly, usually meagerly furnished." Her mother, like most other women, proved "ingenious in making them [the shacks] into cozy if not beautiful homes."[2]

Mabel recalled her sketchy first schooling, with her mother teaching her to read and write. School was too far away to attend until a young neighbor woman offered to open one in her home: "About a dozen of us received early schooling seated around her kitchen table." That worked well until "Miss Collins 'proved up,' and left to get married." Mabel estimated she "only had about one good term," and that was during the warm summer months.

"Homesteaders were not hard pressed by social life," Mabel recalled, because such "gatherings were well spaced." July 4 was always eagerly anticipated. In fact, looking back, those childhood "picnics were more meaningful than ever [they] seemed to me in adulthood." She added: "It often seems to me that home and family life in those log and frame houses with the warped floors, kerosene lamps, ill-fitting doors and windows . . . were far richer in natural beauty and human association than they are today with all the comforts and conveniences that we have come to prize so highly." Mabel remembered the life of the homesteader a bit brighter than it was. Still, the closeness of family and the social gatherings, such as box socials, Saturday night dances, and even summer baseball games, broke the monotony.

The small sod houses and rough tar paper shacks had only pot-bellied stoves to keep out winter's frigid wind. Perhaps some valuable farm animals were crowded in to help the family keep warm on the desperately cold Montana winter nights. With wood scarce and coal expensive, twisted bunches of grass and anything else that burned stuffed the stoves. The climate proved little better in the hot summer, with its windblown dust.

Water, that most precious commodity, proved hard to find; and drilling for wells was expensive, difficult, and unpredictable. Rainwater could be trapped in cisterns and waterholes cleared of frogs, dead mice, and whatever else floated in them, but diseases lurked everywhere. Typhoid, diarrhea, and childhood diseases terrorized isolated families. Even the best-quality water often had a high mineral content, making laundering difficult, bathing a chore, and drinking a risk.

Occasionally, the homesteaders got to go to town. As in the Midwest, small communities sprouted along the railroads, every ten miles or so. They tried to appear like transplanted villages from across the Missouri, but with little success. The dusty main street, with its clapboard buildings, the absence of trees, and the handful of houses, a school, and a church or two, did not remind visitors of a midwestern farm town. Nor did these small communities become great railroad centers. Fortunate indeed were those who secured that county seat designation.

As World War I neared, Montana agriculture prospered as never before, and settlement grew in an unprecedented fashion. Neither arid eastern Wyoming nor Colorado witnessed a similar event. Colorado had previously gone through a smaller prosperous period in the late 1870s and early 1880s, during a wet cycle. Then a bust came, and "busted by God," the homesteaders fled back to the folks or wherever they came from. Buoyed by false hopes about shifting rain belts and other impossible dreams, back came some of them, along with newcomers, to try again after the new century. Like Montanans, these Coloradans, with the new dry-land farming methods, would again test their luck.

Some eastern plains Colorado counties resembled Montana. The populations of Washington and Yuma counties increased 313 percent, and Cheyenne county increased an amazing 635 percent between 1900 and 1910. Out west they came, among them Clara Hilderman's family. She recalled her childhood in eastern Colorado:

Frame houses were proper to the East and to that civilized region, so as soon as necessary money was available a more commodious wooden building was added to the south side of the old sod house.

The farm work was always given first attention, and when planting or harvesting time was at hand, it was only the fields that counted. We came in at the end of the day, heavy with fatigue and content with work well done.

There were special days for shopping trips to Orchard. They offered "an interesting break in the everyday routine of the farm," and in a little girl's eyes they constituted "events of importance": "On the way home he [father] would entertain us with an account of all the news he had gleaned, of the birth of a new baby or of the birth of an especially lively colt, or a family moving away or a new one moving in."[3]

Colorado farmers also had a new cash crop: sugar beets. The crop spread from the Western Slope to irrigated or well-watered farmland along the eastern foothills near Loveland, Fort Collins, and other towns. German-Russian families arrived to work in the fields and factories. An exciting "sugar vision" infected the area. It was a fine cash crop, but it faced international competition and needed Uncle Sam to offer tariff protection. As it had been earlier, the federal government remained an active player in the Rocky Mountain states.

Ranching continued to build on the lessons of the previous century. Now that the pioneering range days were gone, progressive cattlemen seized the reins. Blooded stock, hay, fenced pastures, bookkeeping to show profit or loss, and winter shelter replaced the freewheeling open-range days that had disappeared during the disastrous blizzards and drought in the mid-1880s.

The end of fencing of public land dealt another blow, as did oncoming federal regulations regarding conservation. The rushing of new farmers did not help either, and old-time cattlemen often blamed them, fairly or not, for a host of troubles.

The sodbusters and the cowboys might not have liked each other, but few turned to violence. Tom Horn's activities in turn-of-the-century Wyoming, as a hired gun for the Cattlemen's Association, however, provided an example of how far the cattlemen might go to drive homesteaders out. Nonetheless, the West was getting calmer, and Horn was hanged for murder.

Examples of sheep men and cattlemen squaring off could be found in both Colorado and Wyoming. Usually the sheep men suffered the most, with hundreds of sheep sometimes being killed, and herders and occasionally owners killed or beaten up. Despite these problems, sheep continued to make inroads and, along with the farmers, set a new agricultural pattern for the three Rocky Mountain states.

Wyoming and Montana ranchers called upon strong stock growers' associations to protect their "turf." Particularly in Wyoming, they wielded strong political clout. Brand inspection and promotion of their interests against federal government grazing laws represented two areas they watched closely. Colorado ranchers ran second to miners until World War I, so they did not dominate the political scene; in Montana, farmers and ranchers ran second to Anaconda and its copper interests.

As farmers and ranchers continued to live the great western dream, miners saw their vision of making a strike and living happily ever after slip away before their eyes. This vision had been noticeably on the wane for a decade or so before the new century. Corporations, with absentee stockholders and mine managers charged with making a profit or else, replaced the legendary prospector and the eternally optimistic small mine owner in most Rocky Mountain districts.

A classic example of this trend came to Butte, Montana, and its great copper mines. Backed by Rockefeller oil money, the giant Amalgamated Copper (it became Anaconda Copper Mining Company in 1915) finally won a fight that had stretched out over nearly two decades both in and out of courts. The end came in 1906, with a triumph over the company's last aggressive rival, Fritz Heinze and his Butte properties. When William Clark sold his mines in 1910, Anaconda enjoyed a near monopoly in Butte.

The victors, who in the eyes of many western Montanans were out-of-state robber barons, emerged as the world's greatest copper mining company as the world slipped into war. Bothered little by the name calling, the company purchased more property, expanded beyond Montana, and set about enlarging and upgrading the smelting and refining complex at its town of Anaconda. The future looked rosy for the company.

Meanwhile, Butte—Montana's largest community—became *the* company town, with Anaconda involved gently or firmly in just about everything. Anaconda was the political force in this thinly populated state. Its lobbyists were ubiquitous in Helena during legislative sessions. In fact, Montana almost became Anaconda's political and economic fiefdom with its "pet" legislators and political supporters.

Southward in Colorado, Cripple Creek, the last major gold rush in the state, followed a path similar to Butte's in the 1890s, the difference being that no one company dominated mining and it was not a company town. Winfield Scott Stratton, who discovered the first rich mine, the Independence, became the district's largest owner, but he had worked as a miner and had little desire to place his workers in an untenable situation. His fellow owners, however, were guided solely by profit.

Earlier an individual could savor the potential of working for a while, then prospecting, making a strike, and emerging from the working class into ownership. Not any more. These two districts, Butte and Cripple Creek, were locked in, and, as a result, miners turned to unionism to give them leverage and some voice in developments. Before 1895, Butte had hosted the organizational meeting of the Western Federation of Miners, and Cripple Creek had been the site of their first great victory, a strike that the union won. From 1894 through 1914, Colorado was rocked with labor violence in its hard-rock and coal districts. That image wasn't attractive to investors and settlers.

Cripple Creek owners waited for a rematch against the union. In the headiness of the victory, the Western Federation tried a power play at declining silver-ribbed Leadville and lost in 1896. Both sides braced for another round. Wages, hours, recognition, and the closed shop were major issues for the union, whereas the owners wanted no group tampering with their control.

The inevitable came in 1903 and 1904 in the two booming districts of Cripple Creek and Telluride, located far to the west in the beautiful and elevated San Juan Mountains. It became a struggle for control between the union and the operators, organized in a Mine Owners' Association. Behind them stood the ardently anti-union Gov. James Peabody, the whole state government, many newspapers, and the courts.

The battle started when the Western Federation attempted to organize the smelter workers and called out its 3,500 Cripple Creek miners in a sympathetic strike to force union recognition at the mills. Although briefly settled, this episode eventually led to another strike over wages, which closed down everything in the district by the end of October 1903. Meanwhile, in Telluride, which had been tense since violence erupted there in 1902, the union miners marched out in support of the eight-hour day for mill men in the fall of 1903. As a result, both of Colorado's major mining districts quickly were shut down.

Violence soon erupted in both districts, with people beaten, some killed, many more falsely charged and imprisoned or driven from the district, and both sides liberally spreading propaganda. The two leading towns, as well as Cripple Creek's satellite communities, split into two factions, as the terror-filled strike dragged on. Mine owners stood firm and asked the governor to send in the Colorado militia to quell the violence, which he did enthusiastically. It proved a one-sided conflict, with power, money, and the courts lined up on the owners' side and the soon dispirited, blacklisted strikers on the other. The union did not have the wherewithal to fight a long battle, and winter settled in, bringing further hardships.

By spring, the owners had won a Pyrrhic victory. The Western Federation was broken. Colorado had gained a violent image, and the state found itself $750,000 in debt (even with the owners having paid part of the cost of stationing troops around their mines). Individuals' civil rights had been violated, and the camaraderie and spirit of an earlier time departed forever.

The union emerged even more violent and radical; the owners were more determined and conservative than ever, and the general public was stunned and shocked by the turn of events. The battle would continue in other states at other times, but never again to this degree in Colorado.

In the midst of all this, and generally overlooked by Coloradans, the United Mine Workers had tried to organize the coal miners in the state's leading coalfields. Unfortunately, the coal miners' organization had a reputation for violence that went back to the 1870s and included violence in the Pennsylvania coalfields.

Colorado had quickly emerged as one of the dominant coal regions in the Rocky Mountains. Coal mining had arrived at around the same time as the Fifty-niners searching for gold. As early as 1861, coal had appeared in the Denver market. The real development, however, awaited the arrival of the railroad there, as elsewhere. The trains soon arrived, and with easier transportation coal mining and coal camps increased in the 1870s.

Coal mining had never seemed as glamorous or exciting as gold, nor had it seemed the doorway to instant wealth. Furthermore, it was company-controlled, highly dangerous, and generally staffed with a cosmopolitan group of immigrants. As long as the coal arrived on time for cooking and winter, the public seemed little concerned about how it was mined, by whom, and at what human cost. Two dominant companies controlled most of the major southern field (the Trinidad-Walsenburg area)—the Colorado Fuel and Iron Company and the Victor Coal Company. They managed their mines and operated their company towns with a firm hand.

Unsafe working conditions, paternalistic coal companies, and substandard living conditions in many coal camps made coal districts ripe for labor trouble. The worst camps had families crowded together in ugly, jerry-built houses (cold in the winter, hot in the summer), with little sanitation and no running water—and the residents paid the company for the privilege of living there. The mine managers and other officials lived in separate sections in better homes with more amenities. The contrast proved all too clear.

The companies, intentionally or not, countered union solidarity, hiring as many nationalities as possible to work in their mines. That made it difficult for union organizers to gain support. Furthermore, some of the new immigrants appeared happy to have jobs that were better than those in their native lands; thus, they did not appreciate how bad their situation was. Also, joining a union was a sure way to lose one's job.

In Wyoming, and to a lesser degree in Colorado, Japanese joined the international mix. In light of racism against Asians of the era, this might seem unusual; however, the companies counted on using the Japanese to break strikes. That intensified racist attitudes. Generally marginalized by their neighbors, the Japanese did not readily join unions and simply wanted to work.

Everything was stacked against the miners. The companies insisted on using the long ton (2,200 pounds) rather than the usual 2,000-pound short ton. They also hired the weigh man, who officially weighed each car coming out of the mines and credited miners for the day's work. Complaints surfaced everywhere about unfair practices, from short-weighing miners' cards, with credit for fewer tons than mined, to favoritism. Each shift of miners was also assigned veins for mining; the miners found sometimes that bribery or other favors led to better and easier diggings. Since miners were paid by the ton, all of these factors impacted their income.

To make matters worse, in both Colorado and Wyoming mechanization was setting in. Cutting and drilling machines, undercutting

machines, and a host of other kinds of machinery made skilled coal miners less valuable. While machines sped up work and cut expenses, they
also added more danger to already dangerous work.

The Colorado commissioner of labor statistics, in his 1902 report,
starkly summarized the situation in the mines: "The workmen employed
have been looked upon as so many machines, useful for the purpose of
grinding out profits, but worthless from any other point of view."[4] The
paternalistic companies simply did not care.

By 1903, nevertheless, the eastern-born United Mine Workers of
America had infiltrated the mines sufficiently to believe it could win a
strike. The union called one and the miners went out, but the press and
public focused on Cripple Creek and Telluride paid little attention. The
all-powerful companies triumphed and emerged more determined than
ever to keep the radical, un-American, "foreign-dominated" unions out
of their districts.

Given the owners' strength and determination, the strike was doomed
from the start. With the host of unified legal, press, government, and
private entities, the unity of the railroads, and state government backing
the companies, a miracle would have been needed to save the strikers
from defeat. Further, their plight gained little press coverage against the
violent strikes in the hard-rock districts. The vast majority of Colorado's
press stood strongly antiunion or lukewarm at best toward unions. The
public just wanted coal to warm their homes and businesses.

Colorado had two major fields, the southern and the northern
(Boulder and Weld counties). Scattered about were smaller districts,
such as those at Crested Butte and Durango. Throughout the period of
strife, the southern coalfield set the pace for developments.

The United Mine Workers eventually hoped to gain concessions that
would make life more rewarding monetarily, safer in the mines, and bear-
able in the coal mining camps. The union's goals typified those of earlier
confrontations back East. It wanted an increase in wages; no child labor;
payment in legal tender, not company script; and workers' right to select
their own living quarters and doctors (company towns and company doctors garnered little popularity). The union also wanted stricter enforcement
of Colorado's eight-hour workday law and health and safety regulations.

Despite the companies' best efforts, including placing informants in
the workforce and firing any known union members, the United Mine

Workers rebounded in the district. Companies continued hiring crews of many nationalities to try to check interaction regarding problems and concerns, and spies lurked about, reporting on anything suspicious or seemingly anticompany. It did no good even though the workers risked dismissal and being thrown out of their company homes if they organized.

Feeling amply strong, the union's southern field miners struck in September 1913. A familiar saga unfolded. Colorado and Wyoming had been through this before.

The mine operators struck back in the usual manner, kicking the miners out of the camps and bringing in company guards. Backed by the national organization, the union local organized tent colonies to house the strikers, who armed themselves as best they could. The skilled John Lawson led the strike aided by some of the union's national leaders. None gained more notoriety than the eighty-two-year-old, fire-eating activist Mary Harris, better known as Mother Jones, the union's most famous organizer. Sometimes referred to as the "most dangerous woman in America," she had been rallying strikers in Butte, Montana, in 1909 when she punched a photographer and left town. Colorado already knew her when she appeared during the 1903–4 coal strike. The owners hated her.

On she came once again to help her "boys" when the strike broke out. Mother Jones rallied the women and children for parades and protests and then took on the owners in action and in the press. Ordering Mother Jones out of the district in January 1914 by a special commission, on charges of inciting a riot, the coal barons solved nothing and found themselves facing a public outcry. Such action wasn't going to stop her; she returned in a week.

Management found itself in a publicity quandary. The owners finally had Mother Jones committed to a hospital for "her health" and to be on the safe side placed her on the top floor. That did not stop her; she yelled out the windows, rallying her followers and calling attention to her plight and theirs. Worse publicity occurred when a women's march in Trinidad, protesting the treatment of Harris, was broken up by saber-waving cavalry. Finally let out, Harris traveled to Washington to gain support there and was gone when all hell broke out.

Colorado Fuel and Iron (CF&I), acting as spokesman, presented its side of the story and quickly attempted to bring in strikebreakers. The strikers just as quickly made every effort to keep the scabs out or, if they arrived, to talk them into quitting. Violence soon erupted, and the owners appealed to the governor. The militia marched in. Uneasy guards and militia watched the tent colonies, protected the mines, and, if possible, helped the strikebreakers continue working. Neither side trusted the other. Hatred left little margin for compromise.

Tension mounted that winter especially at Ludlow Station, a colony eighteen miles north of Trinidad. On April 20, 1914, the inevitable exploded. Someone fired a shot, each side accusing the other, and machine-gun and rifle fire scattered the camp's 900 men, women, and children. Adding to the horror, tents and buildings caught on fire—smoke, fire, bullets, cries, and panic shattered the spring day. Five miners, one militia man, two women, and eleven children died that day in what the press and union called the Ludlow Massacre.

Infuriated, the miners took over the district in a ten-day rampage seeking vengeance. More property was destroyed, people were killed, and Colorado's reputation sank even lower. Finally, President Woodrow Wilson sent in troops, as a horrified country watched with revulsion.

This classic tragedy at long last brought everybody to their senses. Hearings were held that dragged the famous Rockefeller family—which still owned CF&I—into the limelight. The testimony about the company's attitudes toward its workers made it appear that horses and mules were valued more than people.

Desperately trying to stem the unfavorable tide, the company responded with the Rockefeller Plan, a form of welfare capitalism. The miners gained some concessions in work conditions, higher pay, and shorter hours but not in union recognition. A company-sponsored union was supposed to help but lacked the power to do so. Annual conferences between management and workers' spokesmen, as well as numerous welfare benefits, completed the package for the miners. Improvements were also made to company camps and living quarters. This achievement lessened some of the antagonism for the short run but did not totally eliminate grievances.

Ludlow ended Colorado's two decades of labor violence and dramatic social and political changes, as is discussed in chapter 2. These years marked the transition era between the riotous closing and the expectant birth of two periods. The free-wheeling days of the nineteenth century closed, and the industrial-urban twentieth opened. Unfortunately, the transition between two centuries had been bitter and violent.

Montana witnessed a similar convulsion at Butte, as owners and workers squared off in a familiar fashion. Here the battle was even more one-sided. The all-powerful Anaconda held political and economic power unequaled by any company in Colorado, and it also controlled most of the state's newspapers. Opposed to Anaconda stood two unions, the Western Federation of Miners and the Wobblies, the radical Industrial Workers of the World, formed in 1905. Once the single most powerful union in the West, the now weakened WFM had become more conservative and right-leaning after the disaster in Colorado.

The IWW attempted to be an all-inclusive industrial union, with a motto of "Solidarity" and the long-range goal of a working-class revolution. Like the WFM, it too worked for better wages, hours, and working conditions, generally in a nonviolent manner. However—and that was a huge "however"—it gained a violent reputation through a series of strikes throughout the West.

Butte had long been a union-sympathetic town, particularly among the large Irish contingent that dominated the community; now it became a battle ground between the unions. Butte, unlike many of its contemporaries, grew into a large stable mining town. The Western Federation of Miners had been organized there, and local unions answered other workers' needs. Butte proudly called itself the "Gibraltar of Unionism." The Butte Miners' Union, Number 1, of the WFM, reached a peak membership of 6,200 by 1910.

After the turn of the century, however, Anaconda tightened its control and presented the most formidable obstacle to unionism in the Rocky Mountains. Butte's miners' and smeltermen's unions did not stand unified, in a common cause. Conservatives squared off against "progressives" (some called them militants) over what approach to take in a division that haunted industrial workers for the next century. Yet compared to other western metal-mining districts, Butte enjoyed a relatively peaceful labor situation early in the new century.

The cautious leadership of Butte's Local #1, however, was becoming out of step with its more leftist members. The split in the ranks became open in March 1912, when Anaconda and other companies fired about 500 "socialist" miners. The militants called for a strike, but a referendum found a four-to-one majority opposed.

Seizing control of the local, the conservatives negotiated a contract that tied wages to a sliding scale, based on the copper price. That move did not please the militant members. Then the copper price fell and, along with it, wages, resulting in unhappy miners. Rumors that the company had somehow influenced the union leadership did not help the situation, nor did the mounting struggle between the WFM and the IWW.

In December 1912, the Butte copper companies started issuing a permit, or "rustling card," to prospective workers, which posed yet another threat, because the system could be used to blacklist undesirables. Opposition quickly mounted within the union rank and file toward its own leadership. Again the militants called for a strike, but the conservative union leaders did nothing.

Conflict between the two groups continued, with protest meetings and angry speeches. In 1914 the militants boycotted the traditional Miners' Union Day and disrupted the annual parade. Then they sacked the Miners' Union Hall. Faced with such turmoil, the WFM executive board took control of the local, but peace did not follow. On June 19 the rebels formed a rival Butte Mine Workers' Union, seceding from the WFM. Four days later someone dynamited the Miners' Union Hall.

The militants, willing to strike for recognition, struggled with the conservatives for control. After an Anaconda employment office was dynamited in late August, the governor sent in the National Guard and declared the city under martial law. Troops arrived in September, and an enforced peace took hold. On September 8 Anaconda and other operators announced that they would not deal with the miners' union. The Gibraltar of unions lived no more, buried in broken dreams. But, within its neighborhoods, the spirit of unionism still flickered.

WFM supporters, convinced that the IWW aimed to crush them, also faced that union. The latter, in turn, blamed the conservative WFM leadership for all the union's problems. Amid such suspicion and entrenched company control, the Anaconda workers labored under unjust wages and harsh conditions.

Meanwhile, the declining Western Federation of Miners, trying to lay to rest its radical past, changed its name at its 1916 convention. The now International Union of Mine, Mill, and Smelter Workers rewrote its preamble. It went from advocating class struggle to more conservative bread-and-butter goals, with pay and job security the overriding concerns.

Anaconda Copper clearly dominated Montana's economy and its politics. With an annual copper production capacity of 300 million pounds, it was a giant, and Montana became almost a one-company state. Anaconda owned lumber operations, coalfields, hotels, and other businesses, along with its newspapers. No company in the state hired more workers, paid more wages, or purchased more goods.

Wyoming had nothing to compare with Anaconda. In fact, its small mining production, except for coal, sank to new lows. The Encampment copper area continued to hold a spark of promise. A smelter was built, and a sixteen-mile tramway (the longest in the world at the time) carried ore from mine to mill. Optimists soon called the district the "Pittsburgh of the West" (more truthfully, that label applied to Pueblo's steel mills in Colorado). Hundreds rushed into the Encampment area, with little camps seeking to make it the new El Dorado. The area had promise, but bad luck dogged it, including a series of fires and a drop in the price of copper that affected Butte in a minor way but bankrupted the Wyoming operations.

Between 1898 and 1915, the district produced only slightly more than $3 million in ore. The situation had become so bad that the *Engineering & Mining Journal*, the country's leading mining reporter, did not even mention Wyoming in its 1914 summary. The year 1915 proved no better, with only two mentions in weekly reports—and those dealt with oil. The federal government's report that year listed production totals of $14,000 in gold, $426 in silver, and $78,000 in copper—hardly a day's production in Butte.

Older mining districts in Colorado, Montana, and even Wyoming lived on hope and often "died a-starving," as Ben Franklin had written a century and a half before. Montana's famed Alder Gulch, Bannack, and Helena districts mined a little and prospected some. Colorado had even more districts seeking promised salvation. Most, however, lived only on hope. Three notable exceptions maintained Colorado's mining reputation—the San Juans, Leadville (now more lead and zinc rather than the silver that had brought it fame in the late 1870s), and Cripple Creek.

Most Colorado districts, however, resembled St. Elmo in Chaffee County. Signs of a declining town loomed everywhere by 1916 in a camp that was not very prosperous to start with. The trustees held no meetings throughout the winter and often skipped them at other times, with apparently no business to capture their attention. Trustees resigned regularly, and the mayor and his wife (the city clerk) became the de facto government. Money collected from business licenses, taxes, and renting the city hall declined steadily, along with salaries. Soon no real need existed for a town government, but some residents hung on, awaiting a better future.

That optimism seemed almost universal in the old districts. Commenting about mining at South Pass, once a large producer and the site of Wyoming's first gold rush fifty years before, L. W. Trumbull wrote in his "Atlantic City" report, "The district will again become a steady and probably a relatively large producer."[5] That hope was never realized.

If hard-rock mining did not sparkle in Wyoming, the black diamonds coming out of the coal mines did. The Union Pacific, as it wound its way across Wyoming in the late 1860s, watched out for coal for fuel and as a product to transport to market. The company found it; coal gave the new territory an economic boost. Wyoming beat Colorado to railroad transportation, and its coalfields developed faster. Rock Springs, Carbon, and Almy coal districts eventually opened. Indeed, coal became Wyoming's major economic pillar for a decade.

By 1900, Wyoming's coal mining had entered a prosperous era that lasted to 1920. The over 3 million tons produced at the century's turn had more than doubled by 1910. The railroads shipped coal east and west to growing markets. Company camps came and went, depending on the coal deposits in their neighborhood, but for every closure, new prospects seemed to emerge and new camps appeared. Large mines opened near Sheridan, Kemmerer, and Rock Springs, each of which soon gained new neighbors as the company built and controlled new camps.

With much of Wyoming unsettled, a company town provided a quick and easy way to bring development to the state and put mining on a firm foundation. Both the towns and mines needed a railroad connection, which eased and speeded up development. Besides the basic industrial plant, the company usually built boardinghouses, homes, a schoolhouse, a hospital, a company store, perhaps a church, and in some cases a small "opera house." Built posthaste, the structures were not models of permanency, beauty, or health, as water and sanitation needs were not always carefully planned. Miners rented houses based on the number of rooms and traded at the company store.

The company town obviously returned profit to the company. After rent and items purchased at the store were deducted from their paychecks, the miners were often left with little take-home pay. It was possible for someone to be born in the company hospital, to be educated in the company school, to marry in the company-sponsored church, to live in company housing, to work in the company's mine, to be treated by the company doctor, and to be buried in the company cemetery.

Life expectancy was not too long for the coal miners. An old saying about coal mining states: "God made the coal, then he hid it. Then some fool found it, and we've been in trouble ever since." That proved true in both Colorado and Wyoming. Highly dangerous coal mining took a terrible death toll every year, and the domination of the companies, as shown in Colorado, made the situation even worse.

The odds were good that you would not be buried in the company cemetery because of old age or natural causes. "All night, women and children walked the streets or hovered around the entrance to the mine. Many were inconsolable." Thus did the *Rock Springs Miner*, July 2, 1903, describe the aftermath of Wyoming's worst coal mining disaster. One hundred sixty-nine miners lost their lives in an explosion at the Hanna No. 1 mine. The *Denver Times* (June 30) honestly, if bluntly, called the victims "martyrs not to our civilization, but to our ignorance, thoughtlessness and greed!" That sentiment applied to Colorado and every coal-producing state.

The Hanna Mine explosion was one of five major disasters in Wyoming during the century's first decade. A total of 448 men died, making it the worst decade in the state's history. In his report, Wyoming's Coal Mine Inspector described the situation: "At the end of the second day we abandoned all hope of finding anyone alive. The explosion had been so destructive, causing enormous caves and filling every space with a flood of afterdamp, that it was impossible for any human being to have survived in it [for] 48 hours. All we could hope to accomplish was to recover bodies."[6] Seventy-five miners died in that explosion west of Trinidad, Colorado, adding significantly to the record carnage of 319 killed in the state in 1910. Compounding the tragedy, the men left behind 163 widows and 303 children.

Colorado and Wyoming were not the only states to experience coal mine disasters. About 3,000 miners died in 1907 across the United States. Why was there not an outburst of protest over such slaughter?

One reason was likely the men's nationality. The Starkville, Colorado, explosion in October 1910 killed five Americans, one of whom was black, and fifty immigrants, including twenty-three Poles. Hungarians,

Croatians, Mexican, Italians, Russians, and Austrians lost their lives that year, with few Americans killed. They died politically powerless and little known or appreciated by the majority of Coloradans, Montanans, and Wyomingites.

Of course, the companies blamed the workers for the disasters. Since the companies usually controlled local law enforcement and the judicial system, the hearings and juries called to investigate the accidents regularly supported that contention. Excuses and placing blame on carelessness and other noncompany factors could not cover up the obvious, however. Coal mining, as conducted at the time, proved dangerous, and safety laws on the books were more often ignored than enforced.

Some Wyoming and Colorado coal miners looked to politics to improve their situation. Neither mainline party offered much support, but the Socialist Party did. In 1908, at the Wyoming state convention, the party adopted a platform that included election of coal mine inspectors by miners, the eight-hour workday, state-funded insurance, and old-age pensions. Locally, the party nominated candidates with little success, but its pressure may have aided passage of an eight-hour workday for coal miners by the legislature.

The long-popular Socialist presidential candidate Eugene Debs drew votes every time he ran in the Rocky Mountain states. In the midst of the 1903 Telluride turmoil, the party elected a few local candidates, which convinced conservatives of how bad the situation there had become.

Montanans, who upheld the virtues of individualism and a simpler America, were shocked when socialism took root in their state. By 1902, twenty-five local branches had been organized. The state party's platform reflected Wyoming's, with the eight-hour workday, workmen's compensation, and other reforms. It went even further and called for outlawing anti-union blacklists, companies' favorite devices for culling union supporters.

Anaconda gained a measure of fame in 1902, when it became the first city west of the Mississippi to elect a Socialist government. The working-district wards carried the party to victory. For those workers, socialism promised an alternative to the stark capitalism affecting their lives.

The shocked company reacted promptly by firing every Socialist or alleged Socialist on its employment rolls. That action, in addition to irate public reaction, took its toll, and two years later voters crushed the party. Butte voters also elected a Socialist mayor and city government in 1911, giving Montana the dubious notoriety, from conservatives' point of view, of having the most Socialist successes in the Rocky Mountain states.

In none of the three states did the Socialists dominate the coal communities. Only in Montana, in the two hard-rock/smelter communities, did it achieve success. What encouragement the party received prior to World War I came from its support for labor and labor issues. Although socialism offered little or no appeal for most Americans, this period represented the high tide of its political efforts in the United States. Even the small successes convinced eastern conservatives that the radical, wild westerners could not be completely trusted, and that such heresy needed to be wiped out before its contamination spread.

Attention was naturally focused on the major mining districts and developments, but other fascinating events foreshadowed the future. In Colorado, oil production dated from the 1860s, but production had declined by 1900. The excitement over the 1901 discovery of Texas's astonishing Spindletop oil field encouraged further exploration, which led to the opening of the Boulder field the next year. It all came together. The new automobiles needed gasoline and oil, and the oil business needed an exciting, expanding market.

Never in the same league as Spindletop, by 1914 the Boulder field had seen better days, as had Colorado oil, except in western Colorado. Both De Beque and Rangely showed promise, but at the time, neither had adequate transportation connections or an exciting promise.

Wyoming, too, had oil hopes. In October 1908 the Salt Creek field, north of Casper, was blown in with a gusher. The well, 1,050 feet deep, proved that oil existed there if only the drillers were patient. Unfortunately, lawyers reaped the biggest benefits, because of overlapping vague claims. Wyoming would have to wait for its oil boom.

A more exotic item, oil shale, caused a brief flurry of activity in western Colorado. Of course, it was not oil in the typical sense of the word. It was shale carrying hydrocarbons, capable of yielding oil with distillation. Therein lay the challenge for the new century: to find a means to profitably release that oil. Still, by 1906, oil shale was being tested as a road-building material.

Colorado seemed full of discoveries as the new century dawned. Molybdenum had been identified only in 1900; ten years passed before an industrial use was found. Near Leadville, Climax perched on the largest deposit in the United States. Used to toughen alloy steels, moly, as miners called it, proved valuable in the construction industry, to the fledging automobile factories, and in manufacturing military armaments. All of these industries held great potential, particularly with war breaking out in Europe in August 1914.

Uranium (found in pitchblende and carnotite) was also discovered in Colorado. Not until Marie Curie unlocked radium's secret, however, did it create more than passing interest. Medical and scientific research provided the prime markets, as mines opened in the far western part of the state. A few small mills produced radium for the limited market, primarily in the United States and Germany. The outbreak of the war in 1914 ended uranium's first era and left the industry in a weak condition.

Less exotic but more important at the time was zinc, which had various industrial uses and which all three states produced. Hard-rock miners cursed it because it caused smelting problems, until experiments found a profitable way to separate zinc from the ore. Miners also despised tungsten, known as "black iron," which hampered precious metal production.

When industry finally recognized tungsten alloys for their extreme hardness and wear resistance (particularly in steel), swearing stopped and a search for the metal ensued. Boulder County, Colorado—particularly Nederland—suddenly enjoyed a tungsten boom and quickly emerged as America's leading source. By 1910, nearly 80 percent of the entire country's production came from its mines. Tungsten was a vital component in war-related industries manufacturing weapons, and it flourished into the World War I years. The price per pound jumped from 45 cents in peacetime to $4.16 in 1916. A rush ensued to Nederland with cars, buses, trucks, telephones, and movie houses bringing the twentieth century to a mining town, along with such nineteenth-century favorites as gambling, prostitution, and stock speculation.

The Rocky Mountain states may have made significant strides in the changing world of mining, but the same could not be said for the region's industrial component. In the late nineteenth century the United States had emerged as one of the world's industrial giants. One of the key factors had been the rise of the steel industry, which in the 1880s began overtaking British leadership. By 1900 it ranked as the most technologically advanced industry in the country and, for the first time, accepted orders from British customers. The mechanical efficiency of American mills became an international byword.

In the isolated Rocky Mountains the excitement focused on Pueblo, Colorado, with its Colorado Fuel and Iron works. The company, organized through a merger in 1892, included 69,000 acres of coal lands in several states, including Colorado and Wyoming. It also owned coal camps, coking ovens, iron and limestone lands, and the West's only integrated Bessemer steel plant. To make it competitive in the steel industry, the firm promptly hired experienced personnel.

At the turn of the century, CF&I launched an ambitious expansion and modernization program at its Pueblo Minnequa works designed to make it the best plant in the region. Along with its mines and quarries, CF&I operated nine up-to-date coking plants and its major plant, thus controlling everything from raw materials to the finished product ready for sale.

Colorado Fuel and Iron was in better shape in the early twentieth century than it had ever been. The company's predominance in the fuel trade placed it at the forefront within the region, and its industrial development was unrivaled in the three states. Within years, however, it was shaken to its foundation. The collapse of silver mining derailed the smelting industry and hurt the coke market early in the century. The development, as weak as it appeared at the moment, of natural gas and petroleum threatened the traditional coal market. Also, old coal mines closed (twelve in the century's first two decades) and had to be replaced, and options for further expansion were running out. Finally, strong outside steel and iron competitors continued pressing for advantages in the local market with cheaper products.

Further, CF&I's image had not been helped by the disastrous 1913–14 coal strike. Despite its best efforts to refute its public perception, the company, like the rest of the region, found itself in the new world of the twentieth century. How well it adapted would tell the story and determine the future of Pueblo, the state's second-largest city.

Economically, Colorado, Wyoming, and Montana still relied on the twin pillars of agriculture and mining, as the World War neared. Coal mining set production records despite the turmoil. The three states also relied on the federal government, in spite of a love-hate relationship (they desired federal assistance but not the strings that came with it) to help them open up this land and maintain themselves.

Urbanization, industrialization, and evolving times for mining and agriculture put the three states right in step with the rest of the country and into the twentieth-century mold. The times were changing and the new world did not always sit well with the old-timers. Mark Twain understood this when he observed, "What, then, is the true Gospel of consistency? Change."[7] A new chord had been struck in what had been the refrain of the Rocky Mountains for generations.

CHAPTER 2

Setting the Scene for the Future

1900 to 1916

It was a stunning little century, for sure, that nineteenth! But it's a
poor thing compared to what the twentieth is going to be.
— Mark Twain

AMERICA'S FAVORITE AUTHOR, the one-time riverboat pilot and Nevada
miner Samuel Clemens, better known as Mark Twain, looked ahead
with crystal-clear vision. He knew the nineteenth century well, having
seen most of it, and peered forward, with some trepidation, to a century
in which he would entertain and influence people, if not participate in
for long.

Wyoming, Montana, and Colorado would prove that Twain's predic-
tion about the twentieth century would be stunning. Before it was over,
the three states would far outshine in almost all respects both the developments of their birth century and their neighbors as well as the older
states. In some ways they marched to their own drumbeat; in others they
reflected the trends of the country as a whole.

Even in the years prior to the American entry into the "Great War,"
the trends that would dominate their century had appeared. The continued involvement, and increasing involvement, of Uncle Sam in easterners' and westerners' lives as well as their states did not please everyone.
The old love-hate bond did not go away.

The heartland states increasingly found themselves drawn into the
larger U.S. picture. They reflected the trends of progressivism, national-
ism, and growing internationalism their cousins back East heralded. At
the same time, a reactionary attitude captured some. The region's two
large cities — Butte and Denver — saw to a degree many of the same problems reformers worried about in Boston and St. Louis.

Tourism continued to increase as Americans' love affair with the
automobile matured. What better place to go than the Rocky Mountain

West, where they could recapture a simpler America? But what about roads, better roads than the dirt and sometimes gravel ones that led from city to ranch and farm? They too reflected a simpler America!

Those roads stretched to the scenic wonders that represented the goal of many visitors. More national parks were created, although some Rocky Mountain residents did not want the land removed from their "right" to develop it in any manner they saw fit.

The three states began to realize that they held a heritage worth promoting and exploiting. And Americans were ready to come and see the Old West. Robert Athearn in his *The Mythic West* made several observations relevant to the Montana, Colorado, and Wyoming West. "This plains-and-Rockies region was the last frontier, and as time passed, it was here that the fluidity of the westward surge ground to a halt." He also pointed out, "But not just the West of geography. It was also the West of the mind, of the spirit, a place to go, even though most of them [Americans] would choose not to move."[1] The growing fascination of Americans with the Old West could become another boom, perhaps a lasting one. Chambers of commerce and others had already started to take advantage of the possibilities.

Colorado moved ahead at a faster pace than its two mountain neighbors. Wyoming and Montana continued, with a few exceptions, to march to a more nineteenth-century rural tempo. Colorado left its mining heritage behind and temporarily relied on its agriculture, although the state soon developed a more broad-based economy than the other two states.

The twentieth century would belong to the urbanite, not the rural dweller in the Rocky Mountain heartland. The 1896 election brought that fate, and the 1900 election confirmed it. The new world of electricity, telephones, automobiles, airplanes, motion pictures, job variety, streetcars, indoor plumbing, and a host of other conveniences and inventions belonged to the cities, with Butte, Cheyenne, and Denver leading the way. Eventually, these developments would spread to the towns, while villages and agricultural folk generally looked on with dismay and a dash of envy.

Conflicts between rural and urban America had been going on for generations. The loathsome, sinful city and the rural country bumpkin were already stereotypes before the Civil War. The conflicts intensified even more with the birth of a modern, industrial, urban America in the postwar years.

Now, as the first decade of the twentieth century began, the triumph of urbanization was clear, even in the young Rocky Mountain states. Denver stood preeminent, followed by two mining towns, Butte and Cripple Creek; the child of the Denver & Rio Grande Railroad, Colorado Springs; industrial Pueblo; and one predominantly cattle town, Cheyenne.

As mentioned earlier, Denver, with its industrial, banking, transportation, and social/cultural advantages, had, crowded into its city limits, a population larger than Wyoming's and over half again as large as Montana's. No other city in the extended Rocky Mountain region or the neighboring Southwest even came close to rivaling Colorado's capital. Denver was the largest city between the Missouri River and the West Coast. In this world of dog-eat-dog urban fights, Denver had fought off Leadville and its silver millions and had too much of a head start for Colorado Springs, backed by Cripple Creek gold. The crown rested easily on the "Queen of the Mountains and Plains." Denverites basked optimistically in their city's Rocky Mountain significance.

People journeyed to Denver for the region's best hospitals, schools, entertainment, variety of businesses, opportunities for advancement, modern conveniences, and opportunities to get in on the ground floor of business prospects. Real estate glittered as a major prospect and a road to wealth. The city offered the region's transportation hub, and it had the area's strongest financial institutions, the largest group of investors, and a variety of industrial enterprises. Its economic hinterland (proud Denverites called it their "empire"), encompassed the agricultural plains to the east, the coal mines and steel town Pueblo to the south, Cheyenne to the north, and the mountain mining towns to the west. Some might object to the label "empire," out of community pride, but no rational person could deny Denver's regional dominance. Denver was poised to boom as the twentieth century opened.

As a big city, though obviously not as large, important, or powerful as New York or Chicago, Denver reflected the highs and lows of America's urban heartland. These were the years when urbanization overwhelmed rural America, just as Denver had done in its own small region.

North of Denver, only the copper town of Butte, with approximately 60,000 people, could claim the title of city. An industrial workers' community, with about a third of the population made up of immigrants and another third of first-generation Americans, Anaconda and the copper jobs on the "richest hill on earth" dominated the city. Butte's undercurrent of labor unrest made headlines, and the town did not offer the variety of attractions and possibilities that Denver did. Conservatives and progressives squared off regarding Butte's present and future, but in reality Anaconda controlled its fate.

Butte did have the largest red-light district in the region, and reformers were unable to close it down. The red-hot, hatchet-toting Carrie Nation tried to do so and managed to get herself thrown out of a brothel by an irate madam. Butte continued with its "sinful" ways without missing a beat. Carrie had no better luck in trying to reform Denver's equally infamous Market Street.

These years, 1901 to 1916, came to be known as the Progressive Era. It started in the cities and spread over the prairies and mountains and throughout the country. Discontented middle-class Americans, joined by others of all classes, shared a fundamental belief—America needed a new social consciousness. The enormous rush of economic and social change in recent decades created problems that needed to be faced and if possible resolved. While not a unified movement, the progressives set out to reform America. They optimistically took on a wide variety of twentieth-century challenges, both locally and nationally, but their roots went back to an earlier America where rural folks rose in protest.

It was the farmers and small-town Americans who rose up in protest against the changing, challenging world around them. What they saw in the future was an America dominated by its cities. Clearly, the farmers and townspeople were dropping behind, with little hope of catching up unless they marched together. Thus, the Populist Party emerged and held its first national convention in Omaha, Nebraska, in July 1892. Actually, it was more of a revival than a political gathering. While singing one of their favorite songs, "Good-be, My Party, Good-bye," they prepared to march to their "Zion."

They had managed to delineate themes for the next generation during those exciting days in Omaha. From a relatively narrow base, they would expand into a movement that would echo throughout the twentieth century.

The Populists did well in 1892 for a new party, only to die with the 1896 defeat of Democratic presidential candidate William Jennings

Bryan, who had appropriated their platform. The Populists might have died, but their cause did not. A broader, urban-based, middle-class group of reformers picked up the banner and marched forward as progressives. The radicalism of the Western Federation of Miners, which adopted some of the Populist ideas, did not please many progressives, who did not approve of the violence of unionism.

What were they concerned about? What solutions did they present? Simply put, the Populists had protested urban-industrial America's rising dominance. Instead of being the "backbone of America," as Thomas Jefferson believed, they had become the rube, the hick, the butt of vaudeville jokes. Economically, the world seemed to be passing them by, their fate and future out of their grasp. Politically, eastern states and the wealthy seemed to be charting the course of the United States. Socially and culturally, the hinterlands found themselves left in the dust of racing urbanization.

To counter this, the rural uprising wanted power back in the hands of the people. Montana, Colorado, and Wyoming stood in the forefront of the fight. This was, after all, the People's Party, even though *Populist* became the more popular label. To protect the status quo, its members became radical. They pushed for government ownership of railroads, the local symbol of the oppressive eastern business clique. For good measure, they believed the telegraph and telephone systems should also be placed under government control.

Coloradans, Montanans, and Wyomingites of the progressive stripe also advocated a graduated income tax, direct election of senators by vote of the people, the secret ballot to overturn the power of political machines, and shorter working hours for laborers. The initiative and referendum, or the right of the people to pass their own laws and vote on those passed by their legislators, demonstrated the way power would pass to the people. The Populists also wanted the expansion of currency, as shown in an issue that so appealed to Colorado and Montana silver miners: the free and unlimited coinage of silver at a ratio of sixteen to one.

The Populists, despite talking and voting, still lost. Nonetheless, they became the prophets for the Progressive movement that took up their reforms. Urban, urbane progressives seemed less radical than the "wild-eyed" farmers and miners from the mountains and plains. No more of those Populist firebrands, such as "sockless" Jerry Simpson or Mary Lease and her "raise less corn and more hell" rallying cry. The American public had also had time to read about, discuss, and reflect upon their world. As a result, by the turn of the century, Populist demands seemed less radical and threatening.

The Progressive movement slowly gained momentum, then suddenly it received a huge, exhilarating boost. When President McKinley died from an assassin's bullet in September 1901, Theodore Roosevelt, at age forty-two, became the youngest president in American history. No one loved being president more. The "bully pulpit," he called the presidency. With his love for the job, an exuberant personality, his zest for life, and a sparkling sense of humor, Roosevelt was a good subject for the new mass-market newspapers and magazines.

The public called him Teddy, a name he despised (he preferred TR or The Colonel), and adopted him as their favorite American. An outdoorsman and westerner at heart, a younger TR had ranched in the Dakota Badlands, an experience he never forgot. He had wanted to raise a cowboy army to rid eastern Montana and the Dakota region of rustlers and thieves. Fortunately, cooler heads prevailed, but eventually the deed was accomplished in secret. Roosevelt never forgot those days.

An advocate of the "strenuous life," partly to overcome a sickly childhood, he doggedly pursued his interests with a driving energy unmatched by most of his contemporaries. Roosevelt loved hunting in the West and had done so in Colorado and Wyoming.

When this whirlwind, unstoppable, determined individual took up a cause, it was, in the phrase of the day, "Katy, bar the door." President Roosevelt publicized his current cause, and the public could not help but read about it. Mark Twain, who did not particularly like him, still caught a major essence of the man. TR was, Twain decided, "the Tom Sawyer of the political world of the twentieth century; always showing off; always hunting for a chance to show off." Another observer simply remarked, after one of his exuberances, "The president is really only six years old."[2]

Most Rocky Mountain residents, however, did not mind; they generally admired and loved him. He in turn loved the Rocky Mountain West. Perhaps no American president before or since had more enthusiasm for the lifestyle and adventure that could be found there.

TR made the office of the presidency popular and strengthened its power. And he took what some considered a dangerous, radical step.

Roosevelt promoted the idea that the federal government had the responsibility to regulate, control, and promote social justice. There existed, though, something many rural westerners did not appreciate — his enthusiasm for national forests and parks. That sparked fear and in some cases outright revolt.

He proved just what the Progressives needed as the country slipped into the Progressive Era, which lasted until just before the United States entered the war in 1917. The war altered the Progressive movement, but it survived and influenced the Rocky Mountain states and the rest of the country through much of the century. Roosevelt, who did not approve of everything the movement encompassed, still became one of its champions and focused Americans' attention on it in a singular way.

Progressivism, a broad, diverse, and sometimes contradictory movement, grew from its 1890s roots to dominate the early part of the twentieth century. Starting with many local activists, it attained state and then national significance. Women played an increasingly important role, reflecting the change in their status beyond the home. They also played an increasing role in politics, thanks to the Populist Party, which included some outstanding and outspoken women among its leadership. The women proved they had the ability, fortitude, and stamina not only to be involved but also to lead.

Colorado stood in the vanguard, having been the first state to give women, by the decision of its male voters, the long overdue suffrage right in 1893. Prior to this, several western legislatures had given women the vote, the first being Wyoming in 1869.

The kaleidoscope of the Progressive movement's reforms and causes touched urbanite and ruralist alike in the mountains, foothills, prairies, and everywhere else. These Progressives built on the Populists' ideas and goals.

Both movements held the innate belief that the people, if informed, would right the matters that were wrong. "All power to the people" became the cry. Progressives reached out across the country and shaped the new century. Child labor, slums, juvenile delinquency, education, women's suffrage, adulterated foods (when the public found out what was really in some of their milk and meat, they were sick and horrified), a graduated income tax, and big business (those evil trusts) all caught their attention. Workmen's compensation, limiting women's work hours, public assistance to mothers with dependent children, and minimum-wage laws were enacted in some states.

Corrupt cities and politicians quickly captured the Progressives' ire. They hoped to extend democracy by pushing for the initiative and referendum and recall. These advances would give the public more power than it had ever had to become involved in politics and government. Colorado even voted to allow its citizens to recall judicial decisions, the only state to take this step. Conservatives could not believe anyone would take such a radical step.

Municipal reform movements varied from city to city, but reformers everywhere fought to limit the power of city bosses. Out of this came the city manager, or commissioner, system. Urban progressives also took to heart the City Beautiful movement, strongly influenced by the 1893 Chicago World's Fair. Playgrounds, parks, museums, new public buildings, libraries, and tree-lined boulevards made the cities more attractive, livable, and meaningful for the middle and upper classes. The working classes also benefited, albeit in a trickle-down manner. Some of these attractions had been closed on Sundays, generally the only day the working class had off. Some were too far away from home for a day trip.

Montana and Colorado stood in the forefront of helping juveniles. Colorado's dynamic little crusader Ben Lindsey gained national attention in trying to help young women and men "gone wrong." His juvenile court system became a pacesetter, and Montana adopted the idea in 1907.

Colorado, among the most reform-minded of the states, was so progressive in 1912 that it passed a judicial review amendment to its constitution. The people now had the right to vote to recall a judge's decisions, although they never utilized it. Times change, however. The Colorado Supreme Court declared the amendment unconstitutional in 1921, with no attempt to overturn the decision by a vote.

Coloradans, however, drew the line when Lindsey suggested the idea of "companionate marriage," a couple living together without the benefit of marriage to see whether they were compatible. This might be a possible way, it was suggested, to slow a climbing divorce rate. The idea proved too much for the residents, though, and Lindsey eventually left for California. Coloradans were also opposed to birth control, another hotly debated subject.

The Progressives crusaded against prostitution and for prohibition. Some Progressives worried about urban dance halls and movie theaters as threats to young people's morals and well-being. Young women who frequented such establishments particularly concerned them.

Once women gained the right to vote, the drives against "demon rum" and the white slave trade gained rapid momentum, although they ran up against those who wanted to retain these relics (now sometimes called sins) of another western age. An undercurrent of social control motivated the Progressives. They wanted to be sure that the "good" people, translated to mean folks like themselves, stayed in control or regained control politically, socially, morally, and economically.

An old friend or foe, depending on one's outlook, Washington, D.C., also impacted westerners, and sometimes in positive ways. Westerners applauded the Newlands Reclamation Act (1902), which helped states finance construction and maintenance of irrigation projects. Roosevelt's interest in conservation did not receive much applause in rural areas, but city dwellers in Denver, for instance, backed the idea and cheered the effort.

They might have cheered, but the capital city had its own troubles. Denver typified problems that very much aroused the Progressives, reflecting what was happening in some places back East. With nearly 80,000 new residents in the century's first decade, Denver was growing at a faster pace than any of its oldest residents could remember. And with that growth came associated problems—crime, slums, traffic congestion, corrupt politics, and the start of "white flight" to the prestigious residential areas located around the core city. It also gave birth to the rise of a big-city political machine and boss control.

Robert Speer became the man of the hour. A contemporary Dr. Jekyll and Mr. Hyde, he ran his city with a firm hand and yet looked ahead to a greater Denver. He wholeheartedly supported the City Beautiful movement, with its parks, tree-lined boulevards, and other amenities—all of which would improve the quality of life and help reduce the stress of living in twentieth-century, urbanized America.

Speer, like thousands of others suffering from tuberculosis, had arrived in Denver in 1878 hoping the "salubrious" climate would provide a cure. The sunshine, ozone, and dry, crisp Colorado air did for him what it did for many of the "one-lunged army," and he recovered his health. Ambitious, friendly, shrewd, and intelligent, Speer entered the booming real estate market.

Politics, however, proved his real love. Speer joined the Democratic Party—a real gamble in Republican-dominated Colorado—and climbed up the political ladder. Taking small positions, and then more important ones, he skillfully used a combination of patronage, city contracts, and Democratic clubs he organized to create the most powerful political machine ever seen in Denver and the Rocky Mountain region. On election day he marshaled his troops, and they voted—early and often. A master power broker, he had the rare talent of understanding and working with people from all levels of society.

By 1900, Speer was dealing with businessmen, underworld denizens, city employees (who found it wise to join and contribute to the Democratic clubs), and ordinary citizens with equal aplomb and friendliness. A friend of the poor and the working class, of blacks, Italians, Jews, and Germans, of native uptown whites, and of those crowded into the "bottoms," Speer supported everyone through jobs and welfare programs. As Denver historian Thomas Noel wrote, "Even without such shady underpinnings, Robert W. Speer was a crackerjack vote getter—a large, congenial, open-hearted man who seemed to be everyone's friend."³

A master power broker, he knew his city and its people better than did most of his contemporaries. Politics became his all-consuming job. His opponents had neither the time nor the interest to make their political crusades such a full-time endeavor. That proved their Achilles tendon.

Speer stayed in the background of the political scene until Denver gained home rule in 1902. At that same time, an amendment removed the capital city from Arapahoe County and created the city and county of Denver. The city also annexed several of its nearby neighbors as a step in realizing its ambition to acquire metropolitan status. That aggressiveness worried Denver's smaller neighbors; finally, seventy years later, Colorado voters curbed such annexation with an amendment to their constitution.

In 1904, voters approved a new city charter establishing a powerful mayor and a comparatively weak city council. This situation proved tailor-made for Speer, who had helped move it along, and he ran for mayor. Despite the opposition of every major newspaper, Speer won the first of a series of terms. His opponents claimed that at least 10,000 illegal votes had carried "Boss" Speer to victory, which was likely true. The well-organized Speer machine operated like clockwork in turning out the voters. His coalition effectively and efficiently directed Denver from 1904 until his death in May 1918, with one four-year exception, 1910 to 1914, when reformers gained control.

In complete control after 1904, Mayor Speer turned to changing his dusty, nearly treeless, somewhat drab community into a city beautiful. Despite having a splendid location, Denver had not capitalized on its attributes and suffered like many other large urban communities. Speer set out to change all that.

He succeeded in transforming Denver. Across from the state capitol he planned and constructed the new City and County Building, whose complex included a library, gardens, fountains, and an outdoor Greek theater. The Municipal Auditorium, the largest in America at the time after Madison Square Garden, was dedicated in 1908. The city installed and repaired sanitary and storm sewers and began cleaning sidewalks and streets.

Cherry Creek, once beautiful but now an eyesore, ran through the town. Speer had it cleaned up, lined with parks, and landscaped. He had the same idea for the South Platte River, but that dream took longer to achieve. Denver's tree-lined parkway system started during his era, and he inaugurated tree-planting programs. By 1918, Denver had given away over 110,000 trees to citizens who agreed to plant and care for them.

With a great deal of foresight, Speer inaugurated Denver's unique Mountain Parks system and started construction on a highway that ran to the top of the 14,000-foot Mount Evans. The mayor doubled the city's park space to over 1,000 acres, and he fervently believed parks were to play in, not just to view. Down came the "Keep off the Grass" signs, and in came the kids. The zoo in City Park became a model for zoological gardens, where animals roamed in natural habitats. A bathhouse and showers were installed in lower downtown so that slum dwellers, who lacked such amenities, could wash somewhere besides the river.

Robert and Kate Speer, childless themselves, focused on Denver's children. They had playgrounds built throughout the city. Combined with the parks, they gave kids the opportunity to enjoy themselves. Concerned about ruining the view of the mountains, Denver's greatest asset, Speer had telephone and telegraph lines buried and put a twelve-story building-height ordinance into effect. Not always did he succeed. His idea of trying to ban billboards, an excellent thought, failed to stem the tide of this plague.

In a January 1908 speech, Speer outlined his philosophy: "I believe city government should be progressive along conservative lines—push needed improvements and add the ornamental at the lowest possible cost. Refuse to be puritanical or used in spasms of reform, yet earnestly strive for betterment year by year along all moral lines."[4] He understood why men got drunk to escape their problems and why boys stole coal or men stole food for their starving families. He eased the heavy hand of the law in such cases.

All of this depicts the positive side of Speer's heritage, but there was another side as well. Boss Speer ran the Democratic Party in Colorado and often seemed to run Denver as his fiefdom. Speer-controlled police closed their eyes to violations of liquor, prostitution, and gambling ordinances. Officials were bribed to pad voting lists, classes were held to teach people how to vote early and often, and machine workers gained city jobs as in any other big-city political machine.

Likewise, the Speer machine gave rise to Progressive opposition, which came to a head during the state's most corrupt political season in 1904. What would have been humorous—the state having three governors in twenty-four hours—was hardly laughable when the corruption behind the debacle was unveiled.

Voting in mass, the Democratic Speer machines seemingly elected Alva Adams governor. The Republican legislature promptly investigated and threw out enough of Adams's votes to place the incumbent, the reactionary James Peabody, back in office. The Republicans were not free of corruption either; the so-called rotten boroughs in the coal camps padded their numbers. A compromise was reached, with Adams out and Peabody taking office, but it was quickly turned over to Jesse McDonald—all in one day. Colorado's image as a progressive state was dragged through the political mud.

These developments, combined with violent labor strikes, put Colorado in the national news—and not favorably. Meanwhile, Speer's opponent, Ben Lindsey, came to the forefront. He had gained his law degree and had begun working with juveniles as his lifelong crusade. Lindsey, as mentioned, became nationally known for his juvenile courts, which emphasized rehabilitation rather than punishment. Speer worked with Lindsey on his plans, but the latter still joined the opposition to the boss.

Hearings and testimony followed, outlining some of the mayor's "sins" and the problems with the 1904 election. Many others joined the anti-Speer crusade, including those who felt taxes were too high and that politicians were ruining Denver those who opposed sin, and those who believed that utilities received special treatment. This rather strange coterie of unhappy people and groups wanted to drive Speer out. Then they believed, with popular British poet Robert Browning, "God in his heaven, all's right with the world," or, at least, in Denver.

Speer did not run for office in 1912. The reformers lasted four years, beset by personal fallings-out, failure to develop attainable programs, saving the city less money than promised, and no longer having their single unifying issue—Speer. Speer easily won reelection in 1916 and continued his plans for Denver until his death in May 1918. Some of his programs lived on, to be finished by others, including the Denver Mountain Park system and the completion of the Civic Center in 1923.

Wyoming and Montana did not go through the same major Progressive upheaval as Colorado experienced. That is not to say that the years 1900 to 1916 failed to have an impact on the two states; however, except for Butte, they lacked the urban base of the Progressives. Company-controlled Butte was able to attract urbanites who picked up the Progressive banner, however.

Montana had some national political leaders, including Jeannette Rankin, Thomas Walsh, Burton Wheeler, and Joseph Dixon, who served on both state and national levels. For a western state with a small population, Montana wielded inordinate influence on the national scene through its senators.

On the local level, urban Montanans did the same things Denverites accomplished, but in a quieter way. They beautified their towns and cleaned up local government, along with adopting the city manager position and city commissions. At the state level, they tried to curb the power of large corporations—read: Anaconda Copper—without much success. The legislature did pass some mine safety measures and workers' compensation laws.

Montana gained more success curbing railroads, a longtime target of the Populists. The more radical Populists wanted the government to take

over the railroads; the more cautious Progressives favored state regulation. The 1907 legislature responded by creating the Montana Railroad
Commission, which, in 1913, became the Montana Public Service Commission. It had authority over electrical utilities and all public carriers.

Politically, Montanans gained the initiative, the referendum, direct pri-
maries, and direct election of senators. It became the first state to adopt, and
use, the Australian, or secret, ballot. "All power to the people" swept the day.
As in Colorado, the legislature passed pure food and drug legislation and
milk and meat inspection laws, and the state created a board of health.

Wyoming came to the Progressive scene later than the other two
states. The conservative Republican administrations early in the century
carried on much as they had for years. Not until the 1910 election and a
Democratic revival, headed by the able and lifelong Progressive (once
Republican) Joseph Carey, did reform hit the state.

The Democratic platform featured the initiative, referendum, recall,
and the secret ballot. It favored laws to curb lobbyists, to build good roads,
and to initiate the eight-hour workday for children and women. While
the Democrats called for conservation of natural resources, they wanted
the state, not the federal government, to handle the issue.[5]

What they called for and what they achieved were two different matters. A more conservative legislature balked. The direct primary was
approved, along with limiting campaign expenses, and the legislature
did submit to the people an initiative and referendum amendment. The
measure passed, but unfortunately it did not have a majority of all regis-
tered voters as the state required, so actually it lost.

Regardless of the state, the Progressives paid little attention to the
plight of the poor. Except in a few cities, the poor were not concentrated
enough to be noticed, and they wielded little political power — except perhaps in Denver in a negative way under the Speer machine. Poverty, to
some people's thinking, was almost un-American. Minorities also tended
to be ignored, except for the fact that they seemed to be undermining the
virtues and character of white Anglo-Saxon America. The middle-class
Progressives were generally more concerned about their own world than
about that which they did not know or perhaps even see.

Politics in the Rocky Mountain states ran from the well-oiled and well-
funded Speer machine to campaigning reminiscent of a free-wheeling
earlier age. Frank Mondell, a longtime Wyoming politician, described it

this way: "I enjoyed those campaign dances, though one had to be careful not to confine his attention to the younger and better dancers." Added
a newspaper man who traveled with him, "During the campaign in those
days there were always a great many 'doubtful' voters and it sometimes
required several quarts of liquor and an unlimited number of cigars to
convince them."[6]

Nationally, the federal government, with its land-leasing policies—
and the Roosevelt administration, with its conservation measures—had
infuriated rural westerners and a few town dwellers as well. In Wyoming
and Montana, and to a lesser degree in Colorado, controversy surrounded
public lands. Eighty percent of Wyoming, for example, was public land
at the turn of the century. Ranchers could not get enough land for their
needs under the law; therefore, a variety of schemes appeared and a great
deal of scrambling occurred—along with perjury—to gain acres they
needed for a sound, profitable ranch. Sheep men proved equally ada-
mant about gaining land, using public lands, and leasing. Both sheep
men and cattlemen could agree on one thing: neither the federal government nor easterners understood their needs and problems. The western
state governors' meeting in Salt Lake City, in April 1900, supported a
resolution opposing federal leasing. Washington did not listen.

The national conservation movement was another sore point, because
it threatened the use of public land. In the 1890s the federal government
began setting aside forest reserves, eventually called national forests. The
issue gained a full head of steam when that "bully" of a conservationist,
Theodore Roosevelt, assumed the White House. He did for conservation
what he had done for other reforms, but even more.

With his usual vigor, TR set about withdrawing land with the aid of
his chief forester, Gifford Pinchot—not a favorite among westerners—
and Frederick Newell, who helped establish the Reclamation Service.
By the time he raced a year into his "own term," as he described his 1904
election victory, Roosevelt had withdrawn fifteen million acres of timberland, created five national parks, authorized fifty-one wildlife refuges,
and set aside millions of acres to be studied for their potential mineral
and water power. Easterners and urbanites applauded; the "whirlwind in
a derby" had championed their cause.

Outraged westerners shuddered and pointed their fingers at the president, including many of those rural people who had supported TR.

Another issue did not impact them until efforts surfaced to restrict usage of the forestland. In 1906 the introduction of grazing fees made the "crime" worse. All three states objected to what had been considered the right of pioneers to use public land to build their prospects—simultaneously improving the prospects of the state and nation.

Roosevelt's insistence on strict and impartial enforcement of land, grazing, mining, and lumbering laws—though fair and lawful—upset his opponents even more. The federal government now went after miners, ranchers, timber companies, and others who violated the laws and plundered the West's natural resources. Uncle Sam eliminated illegal enclosures within the reserves and physically destroyed illegal fences when necessary. Pity the poor federal employees who tried to enforce these laws; they were harassed, threatened, and even shot at by irate Coloradans. Some started wearing guns in an effort to defend themselves.

Fraudulent acquisition of coal land in all three states, particularly Wyoming, also caught the president's attention. In 1906, legal proceedings were started against the Union Pacific Railroad, and other companies followed the UP into court. Then, by executive order, Roosevelt withdrew over 66 million acres of agricultural land to see if they had mineral potential. A favorite ploy, besides "dummy" land entries, was to take up coal land for "agricultural" purposes. At the least, such lands were tied up in litigation for a few years, leaving the claimants in limbo until a decision could be made.

Westerners took out their frustrations in meetings and rallies. Newspaper editors blasted forth, and letters to the editors proved pointed and none too polite.

When Congress—led by senators from all three states among others—objected and passed a bill in 1907 that required congressional approval before further withdrawals, TR outfoxed them. He and Pinchot worked far into several nights, setting aside 17 million more acres before Roosevelt signed the bill, which he knew would be passed over a veto. Stunned westerners shouted their disapproval in frustration.

They did not stand by silently. The Public Lands Convention in Denver in 1907 produced bitter debates, with almost all leaders from the Rocky Mountain states solidly opposed to the new federal policies. Western opponents relished the chance to express their views, but the matter ended there. No overall reversal of policies came about.

A White House conservation conference followed in May 1908 and gained the movement further attention. It led to broad support for conservation and showed states how to create their own conservation commissions.

Infuriated westerners wanted the land given to the states, which would then administer it. The love-hate relationship between those states and the federal government, which had percolated repeatedly during the previous century, grew hotter in the twentieth century. Furthermore, westerners did not like urban easterners, who, they felt, controlled Washington, telling them what to do in the West.

Coloradans, Montanans, and Wyomingites now fully realized the government's growing influence and involvement in their lives and workplace. That set the stage for two themes that wove through the twentieth century: they wanted Uncle Sam out of their lives, and out of their work.

Although the Progressive movement finally quieted as World War I started, it had changed Colorado, Wyoming, and Montana. Roosevelt's administration had regulated the railroads, passed the Pure Food and Drug Act, and busted the trusts (the popular name for big business), as TR liked to claim, with more enthusiasm than accuracy. He had pledged a "square deal" for labor and promoted conservation and national parks, perhaps his most enduring legacy.

He had made reform popular, called attention to problems (although some folks worried about too much muckraking), and left a stamp on his generation. Despite some vocal opposition to TR, the West had been the most progressive of any part of the country. It would now have to live with the aftermath.

The Old West and the New West came together as the twentieth century progressed. The yearning for a simpler, more black-and-white world captured Americans' attention. Perhaps this came about because industrialization, urbanization, a faster pace of living in a seemingly "smaller" world, and mounting paternalism by state and federal agencies made individualism passé and individual opportunity less attainable.

Americans looked back nostalgically to a golden age West that in many ways had never been, a frontier where the individual stood tall as the master of his or her fate. There, according to legend, freedom to act out one's destiny could be found. To realize this fabled place, Americans created a mythical time, a national Camelot. This fantasy time surfaced in a variety of ways—in literature, motion pictures, and local leaders realizing that they could publicize "legendary" events that would attract visitors.

When did Camelot occur? It appeared sometime between the Civil War and this new modern America. The popular dime novels, and the Buffalo Bill and other Wild West shows, had already fostered the idea of a mythic West in many Americans' imaginations. The new ease in reaching the West, thanks to the railroads, helped as well.

No one event or trend brought this about. Contributions came from many venues. When all was said and done, the whole proved greater than the sum of its parts. The cities and large towns provided fertile places for it to grow. With people crowded together, and the workaday world dominating, a prosaic rural America and the romantic West seemed far, far away and unattainable, yet magical.

The cities, for example, had the first motion-picture theaters. The early westerns, such as *The Great Train Robbery* (1903), and the other one- and two-reelers that soon galloped along, became the cornerstone of a new industry. Initially made in New Jersey and other eastern locations, they captivated audiences. When movies moved west to Hollywood and other parts of California, western locations became the norm.

The western movie created a mystic, imaginary, and idyllic West in a formula format. The beautiful setting, the good versus evil characters (the latter of whom always seemed to have the upper hand early on), a chase or two, a daring rescue by a "sure-shot" hero, and, finally, good triumphing over evil captivated audiences. By the time of World War I, the western had become a staple in the rapidly growing movie industry.

For those who liked to read but wanted something more than the dime novel, the answer came in 1902 with the publication of Owen Wister's *The Virginian*. The book was a sensation and went through sixteen printings in its first year. Wyoming and the West would never be the same again for easterners and others.

Wister had gone to Wyoming in the 1880s and fallen in love with the West. Despite graduating from Harvard, becoming a member of the bar, and attaining social prominence, Wister seemed to yearn for the freedom of the Old West. Unable to return to an earlier era, he created it in his novel. His readers thrilled to the story of the stoic, brave Virginian ("When you call me that, smile!"); the young, cultured easterner, Miss Molly Stark; and the evil villain, Trampas.

The cowboy hero, the easterner, the beautiful heroine, the gun-fight—all were given respectability by Wister. Wister, trying to regain his health, spent his first ranch summer in the region of Medicine Bow and Buffalo, Wyoming, in 1885. From those locations the Virginian eventually galloped forth. To readers, *The Virginian* epitomized the West they believed had once existed. In his book, Wister combined the mythic with the real. He understood this, even if his readers perchance did not. "But he, the horseman, the cowboy," Wister said, "will never come again. He rides in his historic yesterday. You will no more see him gallop out of the unchanging silence than you will see Columbus on the unchanging sea come sailing from Palos with his caravels."[7] His readers paid little heed to his admonitions. The book has been in print since the initial publication. It has been turned into a play and four motion pictures and inspired a television series. Wister wrote no more western novels, only articles, but nothing after has made such a lasting impact or shaped the western image quite as much as *The Virginian*.

Yet as Robert Athearn pointed out, "It may appear to some that he [Wister] had invented literary prospecting, when, in fact, he merely was among many—a very lucky one who frequented those diggings."[8] Before or at the same time as Wister, James Fenimore Cooper, Washington Irving, the dime novels, Mary Hallock Foote, Hamlin Garland, Zane Grey (whose 1912 *Riders of the Purple Sage* rivals *The Virginian* as a classic western), Willa Cather, and artist Frederic Remington had tapped this expanding bonanza. They all contributed to an image, to an imagination about a time and place.

In the century since *The Virginian* reached the reading public, the Rocky Mountain West has lived off the legend and the visitors' yearning for a chance to renew vicariously a connection with a vision that will not die. The West became the real America, the hope for the present and the future. The writings and movies—filled with individuals and dramatic action—promoted a West that seemed much more exciting than modern urban life. Even Wister's friend President Roosevelt wrote western history, and it, in a historic way, focused much of the drama and the action of the era.

The rodeo appeared in the Rocky Mountains, trying to capitalize on both the legend and the growing interest in trying to recapture the cowboy West. No community can solely claim to be its birthplace, but

Buffalo Bill's Wild West show took what became part of the rodeo idea (such as the wild-steer-riding exhibitions) on the road and gave it national and international popularity. As the role of the cowboy decreased on the range, the rodeo preserved some of his skills, starting as early as the 1880s.

Two of the most popular and long-lasting rodeos started at the turn of the century: Cheyenne's Frontier Days and Denver's National Western Stock Show. From the first 1897 show, Frontier Days promoted the western image. Besides a rodeo, the 1897 show reenacted a lynching, a pioneer wedding, and an attack on a wagon train. Newcomers could witness the heritage of the West in one sitting. As the new century progressed, Cheyenne became famous for its rodeo, the "granddaddy of them all," and continued its promotion of an older, earthier era.

Denver's initial 1898 show ended in a disastrous riot at the barbecue, with gate-crashers, fistfights, and food shortages, that soured community leaders on the whole idea. The first success came in 1906, with a show that brought in ranchers from Wyoming, Colorado, Montana, and the entire region. Following that success, community and ranching leaders worked to make the Stock Show bigger and better each year. They hoped to solidify Denver's role as the major livestock market in the West and even the nation and to introduce new ideas into the agriculture industry. Eventually, the show became a way to connect urbanites with ruralists and their world.

Easterners had many ways to see the "untamed" West of yore, to enjoy its striking natural beauty and its health-giving benefits. From national parks to dude ranches, the Rocky Mountain states lured visitors. Mining towns still existed, where one could sample the flavor and pleasures of an earlier day. Even if towns like Cripple Creek and Butte had become industrialized twentieth-century communities, they catered to a masculine world—just as Virginia City, Montana, South Pass, Wyoming, and Central City, Colorado, had done back in the 1860s.

The visitor could arrive in a train in speed and comfort (what would the real pioneers have thought?) and sample a few of the forbidden, or unusual, things that he or she might not have had access to back in the old hometown. Then off one went to tell the tale, which probably grew with time, about an Old West that still lived.

The larger towns offered a variety of attractions, from family-oriented parks, zoos, and museums to the red-light districts featuring entertainment for males. Denver, befitting the region's largest community, beckoned with a varied host of amenities. Cheyenne lagged behind Denver, and industrial Butte offered little for the family. Colorado Springs, a tourist-oriented community from its birth, could boast of having Pike's Peak and the Garden of the Gods at its doorstep. A wonderful climate, and sanitariums and mineral springs for the ill, added to the attraction of Colorado Springs, as did the fact, for some, that it was a "dry" community with none of the "devil's brew" sold there.

Those nineteenth-century cure-alls, mineral springs, found throughout the Rockies from Durango, Colorado, to a host of hot springs in Montana, continued to be popular. Small resorts, promoting the benefits of drinking or bathing in their "special" mineralized water, promised relief from almost all of mankind's known ailments.

Sanitariums were also hailed for their health benefits, although they tended to specialize in treating tuberculosis. For decades, Coloradans advertised that their dry climate would bring sufferers some relief. It might, if the illness was not too advanced. Some of the more bizarre ideas (like putting the patient in a corral filled with goats, whose odorous fragrance would apparently produce a cure) did little good. In 1910 the Chamber of Commerce in Thermopolis, Wyoming, covered all the bases, telling one and all that this was the place to come for "health and recreation." The pamphlet enthusiastically continued, "Nowhere on earth are climatic conditions more favorable for the cure of consumption than here."

Towns like Jackson, Wyoming, near national parks or other scenic or historic attractions, soon found tourist dollars sparking the local economy. Tourists' cash was needed, especially as some of the old economic pillars showed signs of weakening.

Dude ranches catered to those who preferred less urban western experiences. Some old-time ranchers, searching for needed extra income, also welcomed the dudes. Wyoming and Montana led the way. They provided vacations for the upper class, who could afford an extended trip and the expense of traveling west. Few others could afford the costs of journeying so far.

Starting in the late nineteenth century as basically an experiment, dude ranching gained popularity in the years before the outbreak of World War I. The ranches tended to be near another attraction, such as Yellowstone National Park. The largest in the region at the time was the ranch operated by Howard Eaton near Sheridan, Wyoming, which could accommodate 125 guests while continuing as an operating ranch. Up north only a few miles, the Buffalo Horn Creek Resort, near Gallatin, Montana, became the first to enter the business year-round.

Dude ranches offered a variety of experiences, from fishing and hunting to helping work the ranch to simply nothing more strenuous than relaxing and enjoying scenery and peace and quiet. This combination of rest and adventure held a growing appeal to those tired of the urban life and business pressures.

Tourism increased with the creation of three regional national parks by the time the National Park Service was established in 1916. The oldest national park, Yellowstone (1872), had slowly gained popularity, mostly as a result of railroad promotion. Both the Burlington and Union Pacific tried to entice visitors. Old Faithful Inn opened in 1903, providing better accommodations than the earlier tourist tents and scattered cabins. Tourists toured the park in green and yellow Yellowstone Concords and soon by automobile.

The newfangled, backfiring, noisy automobile, which frightened horses (involving possible lawsuits) and disturbed tourists, found itself banned in 1902. Concessionaires who had money invested in horses and rigs had protested, and so had some visitors. The roads were not ready, and the shocking 1912 estimate of $10,000 per mile to improve them caused further dismay among officials. While some cars may have sneaked in, at least around the edges, not until August 1915 were privately owned autos allowed into Yellowstone. By that time, concessionaires had joined the modern age as well.

Buffalo Bill led a parade of fifty cars out of Cody when the park opened to autos, heralding the new era. The Old West and the New West came together that day. With only one-way traffic and a variety of speed limits — 20 mph on the level, if no horse teams were in sight, to 8 mph on sharp curves — the Model T and its competitors legally chugged into the park.

Mesa Verde National Park joined Yellowstone as the result of a decade-long fight by a determined group of women, who organized themselves as the Colorado Cliff Dwellings Association. Worried that vandalism was destroying a cultural heritage, they hastened to save this ancient treasure. Their campaign succeeded in June 1906, when President Roosevelt signed the bill creating the park. That same month he also signed the Antiquities Act to protect other ancient sites.

Extremely isolated in the state's southwestern corner, Mesa Verde's popularity and attendance grew slowly. Not until 1916 did over a thousand visitors arrive in one year. By that time, and ahead of Yellowstone, the automobile was climbing the steep road into the park, also giving way to any horse or horse-drawn vehicle. The federal government carefully regulated speed limits, but scared visitors on the steep, narrow roads—often with a terrifying drop-off on the outside—did not push their luck.

The world's first cultural park focused attention on other similar, prehistoric sites. It generated new interest in archaeology and public interest in prehistoric peoples. Other national monuments followed in the Four Corners area and the Southwest. The women in the Mesa Verde project had accomplished all they had set out to do—and more. They could be justly proud of what they had set in motion.

Meanwhile, to the north, two strikingly beautiful areas were set aside. In northwestern Montana, along the Canadian border, Glacier National Park preserved a stunningly spectacular region. Isolated also, it had an advantage over Mesa Verde: the Great Northern Railroad's main track ran into the area starting in 1891.

A campaign to create a park was launched early in the twentieth century, aided by railroad lobbyists. The Great Northern saw tourist attractions and dollars right along its tracks and promoted them. In May 1910, Congress approved legislation for the park, and Montana now had its own park, along with the benefits of bordering Yellowstone.

Colorado gained a second national park with the creation of Rocky Mountain National Park in January 1915. Enos Mills, conservationist, author, and promoter of the idea, played the same role here as the women had at Mesa Verde and had to overcome opposition as well. Losses of private property, timber, and mining rights were raised as concerns but failed to carry the day. The park's timely creation came none too soon, with an estimated 56,000 people already visiting the region in 1914.

With the goals of protection and regulated use, the park established an office in Estes Park. With Denver, Cheyenne, and other urban centers nearby, it quickly surpassed Mesa Verde in attendance (120,000 visitors and nearly 20,000 cars in 1917) and popularity to emerge as one of Colorado's major tourist attractions. The park drew more people than

Yellowstone, Glacier, and Mesa Verde combined at the time. With easy access via Denver and its railroad connections for tourists from the East and the Midwest, Rocky Mountain National Park's visitation numbers continued to increase.

By mid-decade, the obvious need to create an agency to oversee the parks and national monuments—thirty-one by then—arrived. The creation of the National Park Service in August 1916 fulfilled that need and challenged the present and future to continue to preserve these national treasures. Congress mandated certain goals for the parks. For example, the Park Service was to "conserve the scenery, the natural and historic objects and the wildlife therein" and "provide for the enjoyment of the same in such manner and by such means as will leave them unimpaired for the enjoyment of future generations."[9] That huge task dominated the century's remaining decades, with mounting tension between use and preservation.

Meanwhile, other signs of an evolving West were emerging in the changing world of the Rockies. Would these events and trends chart the future, or would the three states generally cling to their past? That would tell the tale of the twentieth century.

Although few American youth were graduating from high school, more were achieving that goal than ever before, and the number going to college was increasing each year. Wyoming, Colorado, and Montana all had state universities. Colorado also had several colleges, including the world-famous School of Mines and Colorado College, with its grand view of Pike's Peak. A town was fortunate to acquire an educational institution, and legislatures doled them out carefully. Montana, for instance, located the state university in Missoula, the agricultural college in Bozeman, and the normal school in Dillon.

The University of Colorado, with its beautiful setting in Boulder and its growing numbers of undergraduate students, offered summer school, graduate and medical schools, and a school of law. It did not take long before athletics played a big role in campus life. College teams from Wyoming, Montana, and Colorado played each other, as well as teams from beyond the Rockies. Football gained in popularity, with alums and students taking pride in victory over a rival.

Some complained about frivolous sports siphoning time away from serious study; others thought college life corrupted students more than it educated them. Still others could see little need for much beyond the practical education gained in the school of hard knocks. Higher education despite such complaining pointed to the future for the region.

So did that new "boy on the block," the "aeroplane," more of a novelty at the time than something that had a serious impact on regional life. If a few issues could be worked out, such as airports, larger planes, mechanical and technological advances, more powerful engines, and a public willing to fly, the age-old Rocky Mountain problems of distance and time conceivably could finally be eased or overcome.

Most Rocky Mountain residents had never seen an airplane, let alone flown in one. Nor had they ridden in an automobile and grasped what cars meant for the West. They did appreciate the need for good roads, however. Traveling a few miles away from the urban centers, drivers found the quality of roads declined noticeably. For tourists, finding their way could be traumatic. Locals unaccustomed to motoring visitors sometimes unintentionally gave confusing directions to points they knew well, but that tourists did not. A state highway system, with good roads, road signs, and maps, remained in the future even as far as the twenty-first century in some locales.

With the coming of the gasoline buggy, the push for better roads gained momentum. Colorado and Wyoming both had local "good roads clubs," and the latter organized a voluntary highway association in 1912. Volunteers worked on roads—removing rocks, filling holes, and doing whatever else was needed. Convicts serving time sometimes worked off part of their sentences on roadwork.

Early on, Wyoming appreciated the coming importance of auto travel. The state, as the Union Pacific Railroad had shown, offered one of the shortest and quickest ways to cross the continent. A 1908 automobile race from New York to Paris proved the point as cars sputtered and bounced their way through the state in March where, only a few decades before, covered wagons had rolled. The national Lincoln Memorial Highway Association gave Wyoming a further boost by endorsing a route for the transcontinental highway along the Union Pacific line. Once again in the Rockies, the past met the future.

Major highway planning, cost, and connections proved too much for any one state to undertake. Thus, the federal government had to step in and provide the money. As in the previous century, Uncle Sam rode to the rescue, this time with the 1916 Federal Highways Act. Congress appropriated the money, but the states had to match it dollar for dollar; further, the federal government controlled expenditures. Dollar matching gave the Rockies a big boost, but the federal government intruded even more into westerners' lives.

Roads and reclamation projects hinted at future federal involvement in the Rockies. That long-recognized key to western settlement—water—attracted Washington's support. The Gunnison Project brought water to Colorado's Uncompahgre Valley on the Western Slope via a 5.8-mile tunnel. By 1910 water flowed through the project, but valley residents were plagued for years by cost overruns, fees, and overly enthusiastic expectations for lands unfit for irrigation. Wyoming attempted some state-funded projects, but eventually the Riverton Project, for example, looked to the federal government for help. Not all requests for assistance were approved, and the love-hate relationship with Washington entered a new area.

National parks, dude ranches, a spectacular variety of scenery, an invigorating climate, the Old West, government projects—the Rockies offered a tourist mecca. Tourism had already begun to be a factor as the century turned. Now, with the automobile and better roads, the Rockies were about to become one of the most popular American vacation spots. No longer would the beach, eastern foothills, or crowded amusement parks do. The open spaces and the mountains were the real thing.

At the same time, nostalgia about what had transpired in the pioneering days brought people west. They visited ghost towns and historic sites and Indian reservations, talked to old-timers, and tried to recapture a legendary America. They managed, along the way, to help craft the legend. Locals were not shy either; they added to the stories, which grew by the year. A speaker at the meeting of Wyoming's Natrona County Pioneer Association in November 1902 could hardly contain himself: "What sort of people will then inhabit this oasis in the Great American Desert? I will tell you. Women so surpassing fair that all the world pays homage. Men of vigorous strength, with an unheard of power for effective action, capable of solving the deepest riddles [of] the ages. Giants, physically, intellectually and morally."[10] Those "surpassing fair" women took on new roles in all three states. Besides voting and being involved in politics, they were involved in a variety of businesses. Actually, the Rocky Mountain states had always been more liberal than commonwealths back East when it came to women's roles. Particularly in the mining communities, jobs had opened early for women while men made money in the mines.

In the new century, a few women lawyers, doctors, school principals, newspaper reporters, college professors, barbers, dentists, cowgirls, and evangelists appeared. Women constituted the majority of public school teachers, telephone operators (their pleasant voices seemed more soothing), nurses, and typists (their dainty fingers supposedly better adapted for it). Businesswomen also ran a variety of Main Street businesses. Seldom did these advances for women shock Rocky Mountain residents, although the more conservative among them were appalled that women's sports had entered high school and college.

Seeing women riding bicycles, playing tennis, and getting involved in other activities beyond the home shocked others. They wondered if all these things undermined their traditional roles of wife and mother. Some men were not excited that women now "wore pants," and had moved into the men's world, so to speak.

The Rocky Mountain world had moved beyond its nineteenth-century roots in almost every area. As already discussed, a revolution came with the automobile and tourism. As roads improved and middle-class Americans found the tin lizzie affordable, they took to the road.

As the century advanced, the gap between urban and rural America continued to widen. Rural folks might bemoan the city's sinfulness, municipal corruption, slums, noise, crowds, smoke, and lack of open space; nonetheless, the advantages of urban life had been steadily eroding the attractions of rural life for several generations.

The urban West could continue to lay claim to better hospitals, schools, entertainment, cultural advantages, variety of jobs and businesses, and transportation. The latest modern conveniences and inventions, from telephones to electric lights, from indoor plumbing to a wide variety of other improvements, graced the homes of many a city dweller. As newspaperman and author Walter Lippmann would later say, "A great society is simply a big and complicated urban society."[11] The city had become the center of the universe, some declared.

No longer could the small farmer proudly proclaim himself the backbone of America; the new, hustling urbanite gained that honor. Amid all the commotion, America's rural roots were vanishing. Although perhaps less true in the Rocky Mountains than back East, the trend could none-theless be seen and felt on the prairies and in the mountains. Colorado, with its mining heritage, had been heavily urbanized from the start and continued to be so with Front Range cities—Denver, Pueblo, Colorado Springs, Fort Collins, and Boulder—coming to the forefront. Mining communities, such as Cripple Creek, Leadville, and Telluride, faded.

Change had taken place and would continue to take place. The foundation of the New West was already set in place. How it would play out depended on the players in each state and, to a degree, on forces acting from the outside. The Rockies no longer enjoyed an isolated existence.

Wyoming and Montana remained basically rural, with only Cheyenne, Laramie, Helena, and Butte as urban oases amid the ranches, farms, and villages that dotted the two states. Politically and economically, urban and rural folk watched each other warily. It was no longer an even contest, though; urbanites held the high cards, and with them the future rested.

CHAPTER 3

The Great War, the Great Reform, and the Great Pandemic

1914 to 1920

> The United States must be neutral in fact as well as in name during these days that are to try men's souls. We must be impartial in thought as well as in action.
> —President Woodrow Wilson, message to the Senate, August 19, 1914

PERHAPS THE VAST MAJORITY of Montanans, Coloradans, and Wyomingites supported President Woodrow Wilson's sentiment regarding a war. It seemed the last thing any of them wanted their country involved in. Nor were they out of step with their fellow citizens. European culture seemed decadent to many Americans, with the countries ruled by an elite class, and their ancestors had sailed to America to get away from such a life. Yet not everyone thought that way, even at the start of the war.

From their homes in Helena, Casper, Grand Junction, and places in between and beyond, they had watched as Europe tiptoed on the brink of war for years before it finally erupted in late July 1914. Before a fortnight had slipped by, the "Great War" had begun, a war unlike any Americans had ever seen. Most could not remember the Civil War and its brutality, and the few months of flag-waving in the war against Spain hardly prepared them for what they now read about and saw in their newspaper photographs.

All the major powers, with breathtaking speed, joined in combat, with only America remaining on the outside. Wilson promptly took a stand; on August 4 he announced that the United States would remain neutral and reemphasized that stand in the August 19 quote above. He reiterated that theme and took an even bolder step in the following May, saying that "there is such a thing as a man being too proud to fight." That proved too much for ex-president Theodore Roosevelt and others who thought

America should join with England against the barbaric Hun. TR had not trusted German intentions for a decade and now worked to arouse his fellow Americans east and west.

President Wilson, however, never retreated from his position in the early months of the conflict. As the year wound down, he told Congress that the European war was one "with which we have nothing to do, whose causes cannot touch us."[1] He expressed the hope of his fellow citizens, who felt immune and secure, thankful that their families had emigrated from the old country years or decades ago.

Unfortunately, that hope proved impossible to sustain. Many Rocky Mountain residents had come directly from their European mother country. Even if they had not, like many other Americans they had ties, no matter how tenuous, to somewhere else. For that reason, complete impartiality could never be achieved. An elusive goal at best, it became even more of an illusion as the war unfolded, especially for first- and even second-generation immigrants who had strong ties to friends and relatives across the sea.

Colorado, Wyoming, and Montana had many residents from both generations—some of whom lined up with the Allies (England, France, Russia, and others) and some of whom supported the Central Powers (Germany, Austria, and their allies). From the smelters of Colorado and the coalfields of Wyoming to the farms in eastern Montana, those with ties, no matter how tenuous, to somewhere else found it impossible to remain impartial. Even those who had thought they might be neutral found that increasingly difficult because of America's ties with England, a common heritage and language, and skillful British propaganda.

From the first months of the war stretching into the years that followed, Rocky Mountain farmers and ranchers benefited, as their crop and live-stock market prices rose to fill the needs of war-torn Europe, whose farmers were fighting over their farmland. Prairie farmers nestled in eastern parts of Montana and Colorado never had it so good, nor had Wyoming's few prairie homesteaders. Suddenly, the country and the West, which had been in a mini-slump economically, saw good days ahead. America became tragic Europe's breadbasket and meat market.

For Montana, the war provided an economic boost across the state. The rush to homestead rebounded after a slight dip. Farmers obtained better prices for wheat (up nearly a dollar per bushel, it topped two dollars by 1917) and other crops. Adding to the blessing, the rain cycle continued over the plains. Counting on continuing prosperity, homesteaders went further into debt, purchasing more uncultivated land and equipment. In such good times, loans became easier to get.

To make the situation even better, land values also marched upward. Homesteaders borrowed more money to buy more land; yet at the same time, equity in the land they owned increased. It now seemed that the forecasts for those with "get up and go" who came to Montana were true. Maybe rain did follow the plow.

These were optimistic, robust years for the honyockers isolated on the plains. In the chaos of the general excitement, however, the vast counties in eastern Montana were broken asunder. In 1910, nine counties were spread over the eastern 60 percent of Montana. The vast distances needed to travel to reach the county seat needed to be rectified. Over the next decade, the counties were divided and divided again, finally resulting in twenty-eight new counties plus the old ones. Sadly, land promoters, town movers and shakers, and politicians seeking offices often dominated the drive. It did not prove a rationally thought-out process.

However, the plow continued to break sod that had never been worked, in a land where old-timers knew wet cycles did not last for long. What the boosters and eternally optimistic settlers did not comprehend, or refused to face as a highly possible reality, was that farming on the Great Plains represented a gamble, even in the best of times. They had no experience with the vicissitudes of weather, in which hail could destroy a crop in minutes, or with a sudden insect invasion that would leave fields nearly barren. Wheat rust, a fungus, could quickly ruin a season's work.

Meanwhile, Montanans took a precedent-setting step; they elected a woman, Jeanette Rankin, to Congress. Born on a ranch near Missoula and educated at the University of Montana, the suffragist had built upon the grassroots organization she helped create during the suffrage movement to run for Congress in 1916 as a Progressive Republican. Campaigning on a platform that stressed national women's suffrage and child welfare, she won. As the first woman ever elected to Congress, Rankin became a momentary celebrity. It was a proud moment for Montana women; they led the nation.

Meanwhile, by 1917, despite the labor turmoil of recent years, Butte was also prospering. With the owners in control and high war demand for

copper, production and prosperity returned. On the surface all seemed
well. Underneath, trouble lurked; some of the miners digging deep in
the mines still had grievances.

Uncle Sam's involvement in the war had hardly begun when labor
tensions hit Montana. It started with a wildcat strike at a small mine in
June, followed by gatherings of the strikers that resulted in the organization of the Metal Mine Workers' Union. Although they disclaimed any
Industrial Workers of the World (IWW) connections, owners and the
press doubted that was true. Familiar demands appeared—higher wages,
better working conditions, an end to the "rustling" cards, and union recognition. In return, the miners pledged to avoid violence.

The wildcat strike ended with no resolution. Matters hardly had settled down when another strike was called at the end of the month; this
time 15,000 men went out.

Anaconda reacted quickly and typically, with detectives working as
spies and "goon squads" to harass strikers and protect property. Both sides
were ready for a final showdown.

To add to Butte's miseries, on June 8 a fire engulfed North Butte
Mining Company's Granite Mountain shaft. Over the next three days,
163 miners died in the smoke and fire—making it one of the worst hard-
rock mining disasters in American history. The blame, at least in part, lay
with the company's lax attitude toward safety, a not uncommon attitude
throughout the Rockies. Sadly, only a small amount of the money the
company publicly promised the bereaved families ever reached them.
Realizing that this disaster would strengthen the union movement, the
copper companies vigorously pushed their campaign against unionizing
rather than worrying about improving workers' conditions.

Just as the companies feared, a unionizing push happened. The IWW
spokesman—the impulsive, outspoken, and hard-hitting revolutionary
Frank Little—arrived on the scene on July 18. His goal was to draw the
local union into the IWW. Unfortunately, a series of stinging, radical
speeches by Little against the war had caused patriotism in Butte to reach
new heights, while Little and the IWW marched in the opposite direction. All this played into the companies' hands.

Considering what the town had been through over the past few years,
strong feelings on both sides, combined with wartime emotions, deto-
nated a predictable explosion. On August 18, masked vigilantes entered

the boardinghouse in which Little was staying, beat him, dragged him behind a car to the town's outskirts, and hanged him. They left behind the Montana vigilante symbol of the 1860s, "3-7-77." The murder remains unsolved. Little became a martyr for the cause, although that came too late to save Butte's unions. The IWW was about to be broken in Butte in a predictable scenario.

Federal troops had already arrived in Butte to maintain peace and order. The soldiers promptly began suppressing disorder. With public opinion rubbed raw and four-square against the "un-American" miners, the strike quickly lost momentum; by early fall, it had collapsed. The metal miners' union, along with the IWW, disappeared. IWW members either left or dropped their membership. The company and other owners held even firmer control over the district and had no intention of relinquishing it.

Jeanette Rankin tried to mediate the bitter dispute but met stiff resistance from the company. She called on the government to nationalize the mines, a move she said was essential to the war effort and that put her beyond the pale as far as Anaconda was concerned. Her efforts and those of others did no good. Super-patriotism, internal labor divisions, press attacks, and behind-the-scene manipulations by Anaconda caused the company to win out. The long struggle had reached a predictable end.

Another IWW strike, this one affecting not just Montana but the entire lumber industry throughout the Northwest, was called in April 1917 with some justification. Working conditions within the industry were abominable—workers had to cope with low pay, terrible living conditions, seemingly uncaring management, and dangers that rivaled coal mining.

Neither side appeared willing to compromise. Anaconda, which also owned timberland and lumber mills, absolutely refused to deal with any union. The press picked up on the Wobblies' antiwar position, and some editors hinted openly that German money and saboteurs stood behind the strike to hinder the war effort and hurt "our boys over there."

The end came in late August and early September 1917, when the federal government launched a series of raids on IWW headquarters and meeting halls throughout the West, seizing records and arresting Wobblies. The strike was broken and the IWW defeated. Courts eventually sentenced over one hundred union members to prison. Despite supporting some good causes, their radicalism and violence had turned the public against the union.

Wyoming farmers and ranchers benefited just as much from the rise of agricultural and livestock prices in the 1915–17 period as their northern neighbors did. Coal production also improved. Overall, the state seemed to be affected by the war only in a positive, profitable manner.

Colorado continued to prosper, particularly with its new cash crop of sugar beets. More acreage came under cultivation and, as discussed earlier, the crop emerged as a leading agricultural product prior to the country's entry into the war. The cool weather, high altitude, and irrigation combined to place Colorado in the nation's first rank. Like Montana, although to a smaller degree, Colorado observed a homestead rush on the eastern plains. The outbreak of hostilities elsewhere benefited the lagging Colorado agricultural economy as it did throughout the nation.

Coal mining prospered in both states, as industrial and transportation demands increased and miner-versus-company disputes decreased. Despite the highly publicized Ludlow Massacre, Colorado coal mining rebounded as wartime needs increased. Before U.S. entry into the war, steel mills at Pueblo prospered, as did molybdenum and tungsten mining. Gold and silver mining, understandably, continued to decline, particularly when the war's outbreak immediately checked all British-backed financing and expansion. Many English companies sold their American investments to bring back home funds desperately needed in the war effort.

Despite Wilson's admonitions, Rocky Mountain folk could not be neutral in thought and action. Popular sympathy from the outbreak ran heavily in favor of the Allies and against the Central powers. No amount of preaching by the president or anyone else was going to change that.

However, in all three states, as elsewhere, a large segment of Germans, Austrians, and other immigrants sought a new life in the New World. They believed the war was created by the English and feared what might happen if America should jump into the conflict. The Irish had traditionally disliked—*hated* might be a better word—England because of its policies toward Ireland. In Butte and other areas with large Irish contingents, some people openly displayed pro-German sentiments. The ruthless British suppression of the Irish Easter Rebellion in April 1916 further inflamed feelings among both the Irish-Americans and the general American public.

The tensions and emotions seen in the West reflected those of the East as well. Except in pockets heavily settled by German immigrants (particularly in the Midwest), public sentiment steadily swung toward England.

Because of such cross-tensions, Wilson's hope of neutrality, however impractical, seemed the best approach. Both sides quickly violated American neutrality over issues of contraband, goods that could be used in warfare. Germany was using a new weapon, the submarine, to challenge British control of the seas, and the Berlin government had no intention of requiring its U-boat commanders to observe conventional rules of warfare. The decision to wage unrestricted submarine warfare cost lives and property. England's policy was limited to stopping and searching ships for contraband and taking suspected cargoes and ships into port. As long as the price of wheat and other products stayed high and freighters could reach England and Europe, westerners were not unduly alarmed.

All this tension occurred far away from the Rockies, where people could read about the conflict while they busied themselves making profits during this unexpected boom. That changed on May 7, 1915, when a German submarine sank the British passenger liner *Lusitania*, killing more than 1,100 passengers and crew, including 128 Americans. Shocked and stunned, citizens throughout the country cried out for war. Following the sinking of the *Arabic* in August, the Germans agreed to a so-called pledge not to sink liners "without warning" and to provide safety to noncombatants.

Wilson tried to mediate the war while simultaneously launching a preparedness campaign. Opposition and apathy dogged his every step, but America and the Rocky Mountains were slowly moving toward a war footing. Propaganda, emotions, and Old World ties were taking their toll.

Against this background of growing tensions, the 1916 presidential election pitted President Wilson against the Republican challenger, former United State Supreme Court Justice Charles Evans Hughes. It turned out to be one of the closest elections in the twentieth century, with Wilson going to bed thinking he had lost. But the western states gave him a victory, including sixteen electoral college votes from the Rocky Mountain states, which continued the recent pattern of being in the Democratic column.

Back in 1900, Colorado and Montana had voted Democratic, and Wyoming Republican. Four years later they all voted Republican, but in 1908 Colorado retained its loyalty to William Jennings Bryan and the Democrats, while the other two states remained solidly Republican. Finally, in 1912, all three voted Democratic, as the Republican Party split into two factions—the regular party and the reformed-minded Bull Moose Progressives with TR as their standard-bearer.

Despite Wilson's best efforts, the international situation soon turned worse as 1917 began. Germany resumed unrestricted submarine warfare, gambling that it could win the war before America mobilized. Many ships stayed in harbor, the American economy wavered, and German subs were soon sinking American ships.

Matters turned even more tense for Rocky Mountain patriots and Americans in general when the British sent Washington the intercepted Zimmerman Telegram in February. The telegram promised that should war break out with the United States, Germany would give Mexico land it had lost in the American Southwest back in 1848, if it would join the Central Powers. Released to the press on March 1, the telegram stunned and infuriated easterners and westerners.

In such uneasy times, hardly a day passed without Rocky Mountain newspapers reporting new sensations. In February 1917 a revolution broke out in Russia with workers, housewives, and soldiers pitted against the autocratic regime of Tsar Nicholas II. Although Russia was a member of the Allied coalition, Rocky Mountain residents and Americans elsewhere applauded the creation of this new republic. It seemed much like their own revolution, but they soon came to realize that dark forces lurked in the background.

Meanwhile, Wilson called Congress into special session on March 20. On the evening of April 2, he went before a joint session, presenting his war message, declaring, "The world must be made safe for democracy." It would be a patriotic crusade to save America and the world.

Congress passed a joint resolution declaring war against Germany—ironically on Good Friday, April 6. One of the fifty House members voting against the war was Montana's pacifist Jeanette Rankin, casting her initial vote (joined by all but one of Colorado's representatives). From her Montana political days, she knew women faced different attitudes than their male opponents. Rankin had quickly learned that the same thing was true in national politics and brought more attention. Despite the fact that fifty-five male members of the House and Senate also voted no, many people viciously attacked Rankin, saying her vote proved that women did not have the constitution or the mental capacity for politics. The men escaped generally unscathed. The goal of equality still danced elusively ahead.

The vote cost Rankin politically. In 1918, the lifelong pacifist ran as an independent for a Senate seat and lost. The vast majority of Montanans disagreed with her position and felt she had embarrassed the state. The nervous state caught in labor troubles wanted to be sure patriotism ruled supreme. She would return, however, for another moment of fame.

When war broke out, Montana exploded into a frenzy. Historian K. Ross Toole described it this way: no "state in the Union engaged in quite the same orgy of book burning, inquisitions of suspected traitors, and general hysteria." Uproarious Montana was not acting alone; it stood in the vanguard. Toole commented on "America's loss of sense and judgments," a commentary on the complexity of the times.[2] It also showed the tension and fear that spread from west to east.

From Montana to Washington, D.C., and back to California, the country and its government raced to stamp out anything un-American. The federal government worked to unify the country and limit the influence of those opposed to the war—pro-Germans, anti-British, antiwar groups, socialists, pacifists, and anyone else who dared to take such a stand. As a result, Congress passed, and Wilson signed, a series of acts promoting national unity.

On April 17, 1917, the Committee on Public Information was created, headed by muckraking journalist George Creel from Denver. It disseminated information and propaganda to depict the war as a mighty crusade to save democracy and Christianity from militarism, ungodliness, and autocracy. It sold the war to America and created fear that translated into unreasoning hysteria against anyone opposed to the war.

The Espionage Act followed on June 15, leveling penalties of up to twenty years in prison and a $10,000 fine for persons who, among other things, obstructed recruiting, incited insubordination within the armed forces, or were found guilty of espionage. It gave the postmaster general sweeping authority to ban from the mails any written or printed matter that advocated treason or resistance to U.S. laws.

Two 1918 acts imposed more sweeping prohibitions against criticism and dissent. Before the federal government finished, it trampled free opinion and other constitutional liberties. Hysteria seemed to rule the day nationally and locally. Local communities, vigilante mobs, a state defense council, hysterical people, and judges and juries joined the parade. The Montana legislature passed a criminal syndicalism law, aimed at the IWW, that made it even easier for the state to restrict individual rights. The death knell for the IWW was ringing in the Rockies, and scrutiny of several other organizations mounted.

Frightened legislators passed a Montana sedition law that made it illegal to criticize the federal government, the armed forces, and the state government during wartime. Under its terms, forty-seven people went to prison. The legislature even passed a gun registration law, something previously unthinkable in the West.

Montana's state attorney general, Sam Ford, insisted that such broad powers granted to the defense council were unconstitutional. He was probably right, but the times did not support such rational logic.

What the legislature probably achieved, intentionally or not, was allowing Anaconda to finally demonize and destroy organized labor. Elsewhere, other smaller companies and individuals did not hesitate to follow the same logic down the same path.

In the midst of these sad and serious national attacks on the Bill of Rights, some absurd sidelights emphasized the stupidity. German-language courses, which zealous patriots claimed aroused base passions and undermined patriotism, disappeared throughout the country. So did "Hun" music and German conductors of orchestras. Some demanded German be spelled with a small "g." Montana even banned the use of the German language. Irrational and senseless as these actions were, they appeared truly rational in those times.

Then the patriotic censors discovered that German had infiltrated American English. As a result, out went German measles, hamburger, sauerkraut, and dachshunds. In came victory measles, liberty sausage, liberty cabbage, and victory dogs. Furthermore, energized patriots found that "subversive" libraries contained German books; out they went to community book burnings amid sighs of relief. One school even clipped German songs out of books and blotted German flags out of dictionaries.

Such asinine, ridiculous behavior masked more serious activities. With the Butte labor troubles fresh on everyone's mind and the IWW singled out as a subversive organization, members of the IWW still active in Montana faced physical danger. Liberty committees, "100 Per Cent American Clubs," and Patriot Leagues were organized in almost all the state's villages and towns (also in Wyoming's and Colorado's towns) to seek out German sympathizers and traitorous activities. Meanwhile, they served as the local arbiters of patriotism. Bullies took advantage of the situation to terrorize people. The Council of Defense urged all Montanans to watch their neighbors and report at once any "suspicious activity" or lack of enthusiasm for the war. The state council and its local county counterparts pressed Montanans to buy war stamps and bonds; only the unpatriotic, un-American, or treasonable would fail to purchase their share.

The vague definitions and concrete pressures opened the door to even more hysteria. German planes reportedly flew at random over Montana from a secret airfield supposedly in the Bitterroot Valley. United States district attorney Burton Wheeler received so many enemy airplane sightings that he could not track them down. Planes were seen around Helena, "always going south," followed by the rumor that they planned to bomb the capital city. The Helena *Independent* offered a $100 reward for anyone spotting a "huncraft" flying there. One crashed near Hamilton, the story went, and the sheriff who investigated returned looking "mysterious." Spies reportedly lurked in the mountains, with a wireless station to report on state and local activities.

The Wobblies, rumor had it, were secretly poisoning wells, cutting down crops, and organizing an army of 3,500 who stood ready to pounce on Montana at a moment's notice. Germany had sent "vast sums" of money to stir up trouble. German immigrants, no matter how hard they tried, found it impossible to demonstrate loyalty to the "red, white, and blue" self-appointed arbiters of patriotism. The Germans were not alone as suspects. Finns, Irish, Austrians—foreigners of any kind, and those with a foreign accent—came under suspicion. As Burton K. Wheeler later observed: "Just how and why the German High Command expected to launch an invasion of the United States through western Montana, 6000 miles from Berlin, never made the slightest bit of sense to me, but the reports generated by this kind of emotion could not always be brushed aside."[3]

As a result of all this commotion, the German-speaking Mennonites—already much suspected as neighbors—left eastern Montana for Canada, joined by other Germans and thousands of Scandinavian farmers. They had brought antiwar sentiments with them to the New World, something that worried the already wrought-up Montanans.

The flimsiest of evidence, much of it being hearsay, could place a person under suspicion. Hundreds of people were hauled before local and state defense councils for being "slackers," making seditious remarks, exhibiting a lack of patriotism, or spreading rank rumors. County and city jails were crowded with suspects. The press, in reporting and editorializing, literally tried and convicted. The concept of innocent before proven guilty died a quick death in the frenzied state.

All in all, the state of Montana and Montanans embarrassed themselves with their actions during the war. Nor were residents of Colorado and Wyoming exempt from engaging in such activities. They too were driven by fear and hysteria, thinking their actions aided the war effort. Tragically, the dark side of the human character too frequently took control.

Still, embarrassment about such actions came with hindsight to most. Caught up in the moment's fear and hysteria, they thought they were doing the best they could to protect their town, county, state, and nation while making the world safe. Fortunately, it all proved to be a temporary aberration, fueled by the frustration of labor troubles, the anticipation of war, and then the war itself.

Coloradans were somewhat more hesitant about going to war, as indicated by their legislators' votes. This may have reflected an older, anti-imperialistic, isolationist attitude, which flared after the Spanish-American War and during the later brutal suppression of the Filipino "insurrection."

When war came, though, they rallied to the cause, and locals busied themselves with patriotic sacrifice. They too worried about sabotage to tunnels, bridges, reservoirs, and industrial plants, but they never became as frenzied as Montanans. When the Colorado National Guard was federalized in August 1917, however, one of its initial assignments found troops guarding vital tunnels and reservoirs.

Colorado's railroad transportation, as in the other two states, was overburdened and often in poor repair when the war broke out. With little opposition, Coloradans accepted having the railroads placed under government control and operating as a unified system (December 1917). Old-time Populists, and other nineteenth-century reform groups, thought such an action was long overdue. The agency did succeed in eliminating part of the traffic congestion, moving supplies more efficiently, and actually modernizing some of the lines. The government might have run them, but the railroads remained under private ownership.

Coloradans burned books, harassed "enemies," and stopped playing and listening to German music. They purchased huge amounts of war bonds, exceeding their state quotas. City dwellers took up gardening, people saved a variety of things needed for the war effort, and the women canned fruits and vegetables. The younger generation helped with the war effort as well; in June 1918, 11,000 boys and girls from areas outside Denver were enrolled in agricultural and garden clubs under trained supervision.

Mining, as mentioned, also improved, with tungsten, molybdenum, and vanadium (needed as a steel alloy) enjoying price hikes and prosperous times. Coal production recovered from the earlier trying days and prospered once again. Precious-metal mining continued to languish.

Coloradans cheerfully participated in home-front campaigns for the "-less days"—meat, wheat, light, and sugar—when they used substitutes if possible. Councils of defense were formed, and Colorado women sent clothing and supplies to war-torn Europe and goods to the "Sammies" at the front while gathering gifts to send with the men on their way to training camps. They worked for the Red Cross and at home to do their part to win the war. Gov. Julius Gunter called a special session of the legislature, which promptly provided emergency appropriations for the war effort.

Farmers enjoyed the good times as well, particularly the sugar beet and wheat growers. They plowed up acreage in eastern Colorado that had never been turned and homesteaded farms abandoned when the boom had gone bust a generation before. Farmers and ranchers proudly pointed to their efforts in the "Great Crusade" and to saving starving Europe, thus helping to make the world "safe" for Christianity and democracy.

Of the three states, Wyoming had the fewest German residents. Without question, the state's sympathies rested with the Allies. Pacifists, as rare in the state as the endangered buffalo, found little support. All in all, Wyoming displayed the calmest prewar attitude in the Rocky Mountains.

Wyomingites, enjoying rising prosperity, did raise money for the starving Belgians and to support Red Cross relief funds, but generally they went about their usual business. The legislature, however, passed a 1917 resolution commending President Wilson for severing diplomatic relations with Germany.

When war was declared, patriotism exploded. Mass meetings, flag waving, and wartime resolutions supporting the president became the themes of the hour. Pictures of Uncle Sam, with finger pointed, urged men, "Enlist Today. Your Country Needs You!" They did enlist in large numbers, and the state's national guard, ordered into federal service, went to France in December 1917.

Ranchers and farmers patriotically stepped up their production to the absolute limit while enjoying high prices and previously rare prosperity. Wyoming's oil production soared, doubling in 1916–18, and wages rose across the state labor spectrum.

Like its neighbors, Wyoming became extremely patriotic, although anti-American sentiment had always been negligible in the state. Following Wilson's proclamation, German aliens had to register, yet none of the 1,500 arrests for espionage and sedition across the country occurred in the state. Emotions boiled against anyone who might be inferred to oppose the war. "Disloyal" persons were forced to kiss the flag, buy extra bonds, or be painted with a yellow stripe for opposing the war. Wyoming, too, burned German books, and the Powell school board asked a pacifist teacher to resign.

"Vigilance committees," formed to ensure patriotism, rode forth. Laramie and Cheyenne organized active "100 Per Cent American Clubs" to watch aliens, ferret out sedition and traitors, and promote patriotism in schools, homes, and businesses. People felt better if they were involved in winning the war, even on the home front.

Patriotic Wyomingites followed the recommendations for meatless and wheatless days, gave draftees hearty send-offs, and worked on the four bond drives. They oversubscribed to state bond quotas (all three states did) and contributed to various agencies to support the war. They attended war rallies and listened to four-minute speakers encourage war efforts. "Four-minute men" even appeared when movie reels were being changed in the "one-projector theaters," to fire up the patriotism of the audience with speeches.

Housewives knitted various items, prepared bandages, planted victory gardens, saved a variety of things to donate to the war effort, and tried new recipes that helped conserve food for the starving children of Belgium and the Sammies "over there." They collected books for the troops and sent "goodies" to wounded men in hospitals. Families went to patriotic band concerts, fireworks displays, and special church services. They read with interest news from the war front that reached even the smallest Wyoming weekly. Overall, Wyoming did its share, and more, to defeat the "Hun."

All three states participated in a crusade other than the "Great" one: that noble experiment, prohibition, which became a part of the patriotic fever. The battle against the "poison in the pot" had been around for generations, but the war gave it a spectacular boost to help defeat the German barbarians.

Prohibitionists pointed out that the grains saved by not making "demon rum" could feed "starving Belgians," a surefire appeal. Alcohol consumption further threatened wartime production and military efficiency—and were not the "Hun" Germans prominent in the brewing industry? They argued that prohibition would end crime, close the poorhouse, improve home life for many families, end the saloon menace to young and old, and provide a great American moral uplifting. States that remained "wet" might become dumping grounds for all the undesirables, criminals, drunkards, and shady characters from their dry neighbors.

In December 1917 Congress, responding to such patriotism and morality, adopted and sent to the states for ratification the Eighteenth Amendment, which prohibited the manufacture, sale, and transportation of alcoholic beverages. Thirteen months later, the necessary three-fourths of the states had ratified the amendment. Prohibition would become the law of the land on January 16, 1920. Meanwhile, the 1919 Volstead Act established a federal Prohibition Bureau to enforce the Eighteenth Amendment. Colorado had already gone dry (January 1, 1916), with bootlegging well under way and speakeasies, as they were later called, on the planning board. By the war's outbreak, Denver was well on its way to being a bootlegging center, and the criminal element had found a new money-making scheme. Montana voted on Prohibition that fall (1916) and approved it overwhelmingly. The state officially went dry in 1918. Wyoming held out for that western "right" of a drink even when the dry states implied the "wets" were unpatriotic, if not downright traitorous, for not supporting the war effort and feeding the Belgians and others. All the states around it had gone dry when, finally, in the fall of 1918, Wyoming voters, by a strong majority, approved Prohibition.

Some Wyomingites did not follow the trend without fussing and fuming. The day of reckoning came on July 1, 1919. The night before proved memorable, the day after traumatic. "The melancholy days have come. Cheyenne awoke this morning with a headache, a yearning thirst, a fuzzy taste in its mouth, and not a chance for a morning eye-opener."[4] Many, there and elsewhere, had stocked their cellars against the lean times. Bootlegging started almost immediately in Wyoming also.

The war brought on another reform: women's suffrage. The highly important involvement of women in home-front activities and within industry, where some took the place of men called into service, crumbled the last resistance. The Nineteenth Amendment was ratified and declared in effect in August 1920. The region between the Great Plains and the Pacific pioneered the effort. Wyoming's Territorial Legislature had led the way in granting women the right to vote in December 1869. Colorado men, in 1893, were the first in the nation to vote to grant suffrage rather than having it accomplished by legislative action. Montana trailed its two neighbors and most of the West when it finally approved suffrage in 1914. Vivacious, energetic Jeanette Rankin, as mentioned, helped direct the campaign. In a tight election, the women triumphed thanks in particular to the homestead counties.

Perhaps the newcomers more fully appreciated the efforts of their wives, sisters, daughters, and sweethearts in carving out homesteads on the virgin land. Also, Montana had a larger concentration of more traditional European stock in Butte and other Anaconda properties; in other states such groups had been hesitant to give women more power.

Overall, Montanans, Wyomingites, and Coloradans made positive contributions on the home front. They contributed their share on the war front as well. Young men marched off with flags waving, surrounded by good wishes and tears and carrying gifts of wristwatches, tobacco, and mementos. Most served in the army, fewer in the navy, and a smaller remnant joined the exciting new air force. Some, concerned about the war and its causes, had volunteered in the Canadian and British military even before America entered in the war.

Although Americans first entered the battle zone in October 1917, on the southern tip of the western front, their main combat came in 1918. Brutal, gas-clogged, around-the-clock trench warfare had been the norm since the early days of the war, back in 1914. Colorado contributed 43,000 troops to the armed forces over on the western front. Of those, 1,759 were wounded and slightly over 1,000 died in service; battle casualties totaled only 326, however. The flu and other illnesses took the rest of them.

Montana demonstrated its patriotism with over 40,000 troops in the military, almost 10 percent of its population, the highest percentage of any state. It also suffered a record number of casualties. Nine hundred twenty-nine Montanans died in May 1918 at the French village of Gesnes during the German spring offensive that drove to within fifty miles of Paris before being thrown back.

Wyoming sent approximately 12,000 men into the military, or about 6 percent of its population—slightly above the national average. Of those, about 12 percent were wounded, or were killed in combat, or died while in service.

All this effort helped turn the tide in Europe. The German summer offensive collapsed in July 1918, and the Allies launched theirs, driving the Central forces backward. Savage fighting continued, but by October the German lines had begun to crumble. With its allies already out of the war, the German High Command urged its government to initiate armistice talks. On the eleventh hour of the eleventh day of the eleventh month, the armistice took effect.

People celebrated, honking their car horns, yelling, and raising a general ruckus as they drove down main streets. Impromptu paraders marched wherever they wanted, and cheers echoed across the treetops and down rural roads. Whiskey flowed, even in states that were legally dry. Bands played "There'll Be a Hot Time in the Old Town Tonight," and celebrators set out to make those words come true.

Celebrating locals hung the German kaiser in effigy in many towns, and he became the target for gun toters racing by in their autos. Celebrations spilled into the streets, overwhelming those who went to church to give thanks quietly for the victory. The *Wyoming State Tribune* (November 11, 1918) momentarily lost hold of reality: "This is the greatest day in the history of Christendom since the Easter Morn on Calvary when Christ rose."

The Great War, the Great Crusade, the war to make the world safe for democracy had concluded. The Rocky Mountain heartland now faced a different world from that of 1914. Americans had learned to hate, and hate cannot simply be turned off by an armistice. The hatred lived on and colored nearly all of the next decade. It had infected the American psyche.

Subversives and other un-American types reportedly still stalked the land. Most Americans did not know a Bolshevik from a socialist or an anarchist, but that did not stop the patriots from "Red hunting" them. Bolsheviks seemed particularly dangerous. Those radicals and their "Red" army had overthrown the Russian republic and, under Lenin, traitorously signed a separate treaty with Germany in late 1917. Now they talked of a world revolution. All three states watched for "Reds" and the Bolshevist threat. So did the nation's attorney general, A. Mitchell Palmer, who tried to round them up and send them off on a "Soviet Ark." The fear did not match that of the war, but it did generate editorials and lead to troops being sent to occupy Butte, that center of radicalism.

The hatred was further fired by a series of strikes in 1919, one of the most active years in U.S. labor history. Steelworkers in Colorado and elsewhere walked off the job demanding shorter hours, better wages, and other benefits. Management crushed the strike with the aid of state and federal troops, a familiar pattern. Coal miners left their jobs and stayed on strike until they gained a wage increase in December 1919. The IWW was involved in strikes, too, some of which turned bloody; and the union, along with socialists who had opposed the war, found most of the country united against them.

As the war ended, something far more dangerous and deadly than battles and strikes stalked the Rockies and ran rampant throughout the world. The parades, speeches, celebrations, and joyfulness that celebrated November 11 paled and fell silent. The great flu epidemic fearfully turned panicked people's attention to a terrifying present and an unknown future. At least 25 to 30 million people died worldwide, perhaps as many as an appalling 60 million. The exact death toll will never be known. The pandemic became the twentieth century's worst scourge and one of the most devastating plagues in world history.

The flu started in October 1918 as the war wound down and continued well into December before it ebbed. It returned again in a milder form before disappearing. Of the three Rocky Mountain states, Colorado suffered the most. The plague seemed to affect the young and the healthy, and this virulent strain of a flu virus proved especially deadly at higher elevations. No one could count on being immune.

The Spanish influenza, as it was called, may have started in America among troops training in Kansas and then spread to Europe before being reintroduced to the United States as the troops returned. A shocking total of 7,783 Coloradans died within ten months—five times the number killed in combat from the entire Rocky Mountain region.

Terrified people watched as a person could seem to be perfectly well in the morning and be dead by day's end. No known cure existed. Some tried whiskey; others, homemade concoctions and folk remedies. They all failed. Isolating oneself did not work either, nor did taking patent medicines or swallowing pills. Wearing medical masks in public became popular, although with unknown effectiveness. Meetings were canceled, schools closed, travelers arriving in towns quarantined, flu patients isolated, entertainments stopped, and church services called off—anything that might stop the spread. Nothing appeared to work. Doctors died, nurses died or became too sick to help patients; volunteers took their places and the fight went on. Bodies crowded mortuaries, and grave diggers could not keep up with the demand.

As just one illustration of how bad the situation became, consider the mining town of Silverton, high up in the mountains in Colorado's San Juan County. The mining district, with its gold, silver, zinc, and lead production, had prospered for the past twenty years. Then disaster struck. Silverton lost slightly over 10 percent of its population of 1,500-plus. The *Silverton Weekly Miner* (November 1, 1918) ran the forbidding headline and story:

THE GRIM REAPER
Number of deaths to date totals up to 128.
Past week has been the blackest ever known.

Space and time will not permit us to give but very little notice of the many sad deaths that have occurred in this community since our last issue.

There has scarcely been a household that has not been touched by sickness or death of a loved one or a friend.

Three quarter-page columns grimly listed the names of those who had died. A lack of time and space prevented the paper from printing individual obituaries. A long, common grave in the Hillside Cemetery marked the flu victims' final resting place. The good times at Silverton came to an end with that epidemic; mining declined, population slipped, and memories of bygone days faded.

To gain a perspective with Silverton and Colorado, the reader must know that the flu struck Wyoming in October 1918 and ran into January 1919. The state recorded 780 deaths, 169 from the flu alone and the remainder from the combination of flu and pneumonia.

The pandemic eventually ran its course in Silverton, Cheyenne, Butte, and elsewhere but took a terrible toll. Aghast, people tried hard to forget its hellish horror, and many just blocked it out of their minds. Sixty years later, old-timers spoke about the scourge with sadness and dread. Only after the dawn of the twenty-first century did researchers isolate it as an avian flu, transmitted by birds, which eventually mutated and infected humans.

The war had passed into history, and Americans looked at their efforts with pride. Hatred still lingered, and so did Prohibition, although that noble experiment did not seem quite so noble now. Women had gained the right to vote, and the automobile made the public more mobile than ever before. Corporations and business reigned supreme, and labor unions labored under the labels of "un-American" and "radical."

The Rocky Mountain states had just emerged from a transitional generation, from pioneering ways to twentieth-century lifestyles and economics. A new and different West awaited them. Apart from a few exceptions, the Old West had slipped into legend, a legend the New West planned to mine and exploit.

A new decade loomed and Americans wanted, in a sense, to forget, to celebrate, and to have a good time. Most of them had had enough of sacrifice and crusades, of wars and fears, of exposés and reform, of optimists and nervous Nellies, of labor strikes and worry about big business. They wanted to return to "normalcy," as the soon-to-be Republican presidential candidate Warren G. Harding unforgettably described it. He would typify both the good and bad of what was coming.

Americans from all walks of life yearned for something different, exciting, new, maybe daring, and modern. Many of them would not achieve this, and others longed for an older, simpler America. The 1920s promised to be a fascinating decade.

CHAPTER 4

Decade of Contrasts and Controversy
The 1920s

Tough times don't last, but tough people do.
—An old western proverb

There is no credit to being a comedian, when you have the whole
Government working for you. All you have to do is report the facts.
I don't even have to exaggerate.
—Will Rogers

More men have been elected between sundown and sunup than ever
were elected between sunup and sundown.
—Will Rogers

THE WHOLE COUNTRY LAUGHED with humorist, entertainer, and writer
Will Rogers during the 1920s. Rocky Mountain residents in town and
on the farm particularly liked the cowboy and rancher's western slant.
They were not always in favor of or in step with the changing times that
impacted them in so many different ways. Before it was all over, they
would sometimes wonder what had happened and why.

The 1920s are often referred to as the Roaring Twenties. At first glance
the label seems to fit when one thinks of the icons of the decade: Babe
Ruth, the "Big Bull Market," that popular dance the Charleston, speakeasies, and bathtub gin. Reality, however, is seldom that simple. The
twenties might better be characterized by the way Charles Dickens
portrayed his Ghost of Christmas Past, who startled Scrooge when first
appearing at his bedside: "It was a strange figure—like a child: yet not so
like a child as like an old man. . . . Its hair, which hung about its neck and
down its back, was white as if with age; and yet the face had not a wrinkle
in it, and the tenderest bloom was on the skin."[1]

The twenties, like Scrooge's ghost, represented a series of contrasts,
even contradictions. In the West the times "roared" for some city residents,

but an undercurrent of tension and anxiety could be felt everywhere. New freedoms brought by the car, a relaxing of moral standards, and the flouting of Prohibition troubled many western old-timers and their contemporaries elsewhere. Times were rapidly changing, at a pace few Americans had experienced. The ongoing rural-urban tension heightened, and in both arenas people felt left out, dropping behind mainstream America. This created an insecurity that did not bode well for the new decade. Culturally, socially, educationally, and economically, lines were being drawn across the country. The Tennessee Scopes trial regarding evolution might as easily have occurred in any of the three heartland states.

While the decade could be fun, it could also be cruel and insensitive, as the rise of the Ku Klux Klan amply displayed. The decline of "old-time religion" disturbed many rural and urban Americans, as did "jazz" youngsters who flouted the standards of an earlier age. Yet this was also the age of the birth of modern advertising, which promised an answer for almost everything from bad breath to being a social failure. Perhaps in a subconscious way, if people thought the decade was a "roaring" one, then partaking in just a bit of it might make them feel better about themselves and their lives. The image then became a reality.

The Rocky Mountain West would never be the same again, as it continued to become more a part of the nation. The old rural West stood in stark contrast to the growing, vibrant urban West. As the decade marched along, Denver solidified its ever more dominant role within its Rocky Mountain "empire," as Denver newspapers and movers and shakers liked to call its economic hinterland. The regional giant had a population of 256,500 in 1920. Such a position aroused jealousy among some of its urban neighbors.

Most locals, however, seemed little concerned or excited about "empires" or hinterlands; they had more exciting things on their minds. Hollywood, clothing styles, jazz, the Lone Eagle (Charles Lindbergh), Sinclair Lewis, the new morals, football, and the Big Bull Market—Coloradans, Wyomingites, and Montanans had much to mull over and discuss. Before the decade ended, thanks to radio, they could hear events as they happened or soon thereafter. They could even see the well-known individuals and events, first on the silent screen and then in the talkies.

Politically, the Republicans reigned. Republican presidential candidates Warren Harding, Calvin Coolidge, and Herbert Hoover carried all three states, although Progressive candidate Robert LaFollette made inroads in eastern Montana in 1924. On the state and local levels, the story was slightly different, a familiar Rocky Mountain pattern.

Anaconda still held the trump card in Montana's politics. A variety of issues, such as mine taxation, would arouse the company and its legion of newspapers to support or attack a candidate. Conservatism, here and elsewhere, ruled the day. The state's progressivism disappeared with the defeat of Gov. Joseph Dixon in 1924, whom Anaconda viciously attacked during the campaign. It was also Dixon's misfortune to be in the governor's chair during a downturn in the economy. From mid-decade on, conservative Republicans controlled the state legislature with dominant majorities. The economy, not spending or reform, was the most important issue.

Voters in Montana did elect the popular Democratic governor John Erickson every time he ran during the decade, and he served in that office from 1925 to 1933. Although he was a party regular, "Honest John" fit in well with his conservative legislators. He did not fight Anaconda, he ran the government economically, and he reduced the state debt.

The picture that emerged at home did not match the senators Montanans sent to Washington. The voters seemed to have a schizoid personality when it came to politics. Throughout the decade, they elected and reelected Thomas J. Walsh and Burton K. Wheeler, both progressive Democrats. From such a conservative, Republican-dominated state, these two men became favorites of the liberal community.

Wheeler had been driven out of office (resigning as federal district attorney) by refusing to follow the lead of the wartime patriots and vocal conservatives and for refusing to prosecute "traitors" on flimsy evidence. During the emotionally charged late teens, such a stand gained few friends. Then, in 1920, Wheeler ran for governor, falling victim to one of the most lopsided defeats in the state's history. Anaconda would not let him denounce the copper octopus and get away with it. Undaunted, he rebounded with an amazing political resurrection and won a Senate seat in 1922.

Wheeler, who had a long and distinguished career (1923–47) in the Senate, loved politics and campaigning. A "rock-'em-sock-'em" campaigner, he emerged a progressive to the core; in fact, the young senator ran on the national Progressive ticket with LaFollette in 1924, a major reason that ticket did so well in parts of Montana.

In contrast, Walsh, first elected in 1912 as a Wilsonian Democrat, proved a more moderate progressive. Honest and dignified—and a tough lawyer—Walsh had been involved in Montana Democratic politics for nearly twenty years when he won his seat.

He had helped Wheeler become district attorney (the latter had resigned in part during the war rancor so as not to harm Walsh's reelection bid in 1918). A conservationist who emphasized local control, a friend of labor, a great legal mind, and an able but unexciting campaigner, Walsh served his state and nation well, as Wheeler did.

Numerous reasons have been advanced as to why Montana voters sent liberals to the United States Senate and conservatives to state offices. One reason is that conservatives wanted liberals out of Montana. Liberals argued that conservatives had more campaign funds and spent more money on state contests and that they worked harder on local and state issues and candidates. Conservative Anaconda and its newspapers certainly worried more about local issues than national ones. Voters selected individuals, not party or political labels—a Rocky Mountain pattern. All of this maintained a delicate political balance between liberal and conservative factions.

Wyoming followed the same conservative Republican path as Montana. Republican Francis E. Warren, whose political career stretched back to territorial days, served as United States senator throughout the decade. When he died in office in November 1929, he held the record for length of serving in that body—thirty-seven years. Highly regarded by his constituents, he scarcely needed to campaign. A great patronage dispenser, Warren provided a powerful voice for the state in Washington.

Warren's colleague in the Senate, Democrat John Kendrick, also served throughout the 1920s after being elected in 1916. A hard-driving, wealthy rancher, he, like Warren, furthered Wyoming's economic interests in the nation's capital. Kendrick (he was said to look like the "Virginian in the flesh") paid particular attention to cattle, sheep, sugar beet interests, and reclamation projects.

Republicans held on to the state's lone representative in the House. A total of three men served at different times during the decade. They did not wield the power of the two senators.

The congressional seniority system benefited all three states. Each had senators or representatives who served long terms, giving them power and prestige on the congressional floor and in committees beyond the political significance that those states warranted. They also had a strong say in national party politics.

One occupant of the governor's chair brought Wyoming national attention. The territory that had long ago first given women the right to vote now as a state had also elected the first woman governor, Democrat Nellie Tayloe Ross. Elected the same day as Texas's Miriam Ferguson, Ross assumed the position twenty days before Ferguson, and thus laid claim to being the first woman governor. Ross had won a special election in 1924 to fill her late husband's unexpired term.

Facing a Republican legislature, the inexperienced Ross experienced a difficult time in the governor's mansion. While sympathy, charity, and chivalry might have helped her win in 1924, as her opponents believed, they did not help in her failed campaign two years later, when Republicans regained the governorship. Ross went on to second the presidential nomination of Al Smith in 1928 and to campaign for Franklin Roosevelt in 1932; she also became the first female director of the United States Mint.

Meanwhile, Jackson, Wyoming, became the first community in the state to elect an all-female municipal council. Women also appeared in state legislatures and other elected offices. Wyoming once again became a pacesetter.

Of the three states, Colorado generally seemed to be the strongest Democratic bastion, although it was a token claim at best. The party won the two-year governorship four of five times during the 1920s; however, Republicans held both Senate seats for all but two of those years. The Democrats captured only one of the four House of Representative seats for the entire decade, and another for only one term.

The one exception to this Republican trend was Western Slope representative Edward Taylor, who won for the first time in 1908 and continued in office until 1941. He gained the seniority that served his state well. He was a strong representative for the western part of the state, which was the smallest in population, the largest district in size, and the weakest politically.

Conservatism dominated the Centennial State, and except for a governor or two, the politicians had little impact. Some grabbed headlines, as in the case of two who gained infamy by being associated with the Ku Klux Klan (KKK) along with a Denver mayor.

Colorado, Wyoming, and Montana clearly reflected the era's business-oriented conservatism. This was not a time for reform, new ideas, or challenges to the status quo. Americans wanted to relax and have fun, and they did not take up reform crusades or push for changes. Some of the hard-pressed farmers out in the hinterlands had no time to relax. Problems did exist in the Rockies, especially in the rural outback, and those affected wanted help, but most other Americans paid no heed. Farmers and farm problems were not in their sight.

Washington played its usual role in the region, despite the increased grumbling. Uncle Sam continued to build dams and underwrite reclamation projects, which most locals favored. However, each project had strings attached. Dreams and hopes often proved to be mostly mirage, not boom and profit. It seemed, however, that without federal help, the long-held hope of making the prairie bloom would die.

Federal projects took years to plan and build, and each state received its share of the money as the government doled it out. Montana's Sun River and Milk River projects, Wyoming's Riverton Project, and Colorado's Gunnison were either planned, built, or improved—some all three—during the century's first quarter.

These water projects never proved easy, as historian T. A. Larson wrote. Reclamation projects became "three-ring circuses"; with private, state, and federal interests facing each other, the main problems were how to reach the goal and at what cost, and who would pay.[2] Water lawyers were finding new interest in their profession, and as that western saying that bounced down the century advised, let your "sons and daughters grow up to be water lawyers."

Water lawyers and water experts found themselves in high demand in all three states. Rivers might head in the Rocky Mountains, but they flowed elsewhere. Who owned the right to that precious water? What was the best use for that valuable commodity? Those questions had been asked for years, and rural westerners understood that their livelihood depended on the answers. In western eyes, Washington had been both saint and sinner when it came to water.

The struggle had started in the previous century, with Colorado squaring off against its neighbor Kansas over Arkansas River water. Did not the rain fall on Colorado first and then flow into the Arkansas? Coloradans often felt they held first claim on streams whose headwaters fell on *their* mountains and plains and then into *their* streams—the North and South Platte, Colorado, Rio Grande, Arkansas, Republican, and San Juan, among others. Not so, argued their neighbors. The issue became a hot and desperate one when irrigation gained popularity.

Wyoming was in court at the same time, because Nebraska sued over North Platte River water. Montana dodged the issue for the moment. It all involved interstate water, and the fight had just begun. Much of the Rocky Mountain heartland's future development hung in the balance. Agriculture might have been predominant at the moment, but lurking right behind it were the needs of urbanization.

The first major fight, and the longest ongoing one, involved that mightiest of all rivers to come out of Colorado, the one that gave it its name, the Colorado, which drained around 244,000 square miles. The three lower basin states — California, Nevada, and Arizona — and the four upper basin states — Utah, Wyoming, New Mexico, and Colorado — all had a stake in what emerged as a battle royal. Water diversions were already producing threats of legal action.

Common problems of water needs and water resources brought the seven states to the conference table in 1919. The problem, however, proved too big to be resolved by the states. National interests were also involved, so the federal government stepped in to broker a settlement. The Colorado River Compact resulted.

Meeting in Santa Fe, New Mexico, in 1922, the participants hammered out a compromise. Negotiators assumed that the river's average flow totaled more than 20 million acre-feet. So they took 15 million of that amount and split it evenly between the two basins. From the remainder, Mexico would receive its share, to be settled by treaty later. The rest would be used to fulfill future needs. Arizona initially stubbornly refused to sign, worried about its share and the future, so Congress decided that six state ratifications proved enough. In 1929 it declared the compact in force, and the milestone compact took effect throughout the huge basin. Unfortunately, a flaw existed in the compact: no one knew exactly what the annual runoff might be. At least the states had made a start, though, and treaties, rather than legal fighting, carried the day.

Sometimes these agreements led to individual tragedies, as happened in southwestern Colorado. A rather small river, La Plata, became a bone of contention. Its headwaters were in the mountains of the same name, and it then flowed southward into New Mexico. By the end of the 1920s, Colorado and New Mexico had agreed to a division of the water in La Plata River. Based on the concept of prior appropriation — "first in time, first in right"—Colorado farmers along the river found that, with prior claims, New Mexico took their water. Once known as the dry side (the region southwest of Durango), farming had blossomed with La Plata water irrigation from the teens to the early 1920s. Now it withered. Farmers lost their water, and the promising village of Marvel lost its future.

On a larger scale, Wyoming and Colorado reached an agreement over the Laramie River, and Nebraska and Colorado agreed to divide the waters of the South Platte. Such agreements, however, would be severely tested as populations grew and economies changed. They, like the La Plata agreement, also curbed some of the hopes of upstream people.

Water disputes reflected both the present and the future in the Rocky Mountains. Some other events or groups of the 1920s reflected more localized, current concerns. Four of these in particular—the Ku Klux Klan, the Teapot Dome scandal, Prohibition, and the eastern plains homesteading fiasco—reveal much about the decade, its people, their expectations, and their attitudes.

The hatred engendered by the First World War could not be instantly turned off amid the joy and celebrations on Armistice Day. It continued, often manifested as generated bigotry, antiforeignism, and fear of the unknown. The "Red Scare" of 1919–20 reflected these factors; so did the attitude toward labor unions and strikes, and American rejection of the League of Nations.

The Ku Klux Klan, a classic group of fear and hate, reemerged at this time. The Klan first rode violently forth after the Civil War, opposed to Yankee reconstruction and wanting to intimidate the newly freed slaves. Eventually it was crushed as an organization by the federal government, but the bigotry that spawned it did not die. Revived in 1915, perhaps by the movie *The Birth of a Nation*, the Klan's membership increased after the war, eventually reaching an estimated peak of 5 million nationally in 1924. Its members were found among Main Street's "good people"—white Protestant middle-class storekeepers, farmers, laborers, churchgoers, and teachers, among others. They defended the traditional values of small-town Protestant America and at the same time preyed upon the insecurities and tensions rampant in the 1920s.

Although the KKK kept the uniforms and paraphernalia of the post—Civil War Klan, along with its intolerance and willingness to use violence, the new Klan was different in some respects. Its reach became national,

and its intolerance now included Catholics, Jews, Bolsheviks, those violating Prohibition, foreigners, and anyone or anything deemed un-American.
Its hates almost ran the gamut of modern bigotry, along with such interesting sidelights as attacking birth control and Darwinism. The changing
morals and standards of the twenties did not sit well with members either,
who fought to protect flag, women, and old-time Protestantism.

Active in all three states, the Klan had little success in two of them.
It was only marginally active in Montana and just slightly more so in
Wyoming. A few hooded members painted "KKK" here and there or held
a few secret meetings. Rumors floated about of Klan political involvement. That pretty much comprised its activities in those two states, but
not so their neighbor.

Colorado became the most Klan-dominated state in the West,
although Oregon can also make a strong bid for that dubious claim. The
KKK recruited members so rapidly that it grew into a dominant political
force, even briefly capturing the Republican Party. It backed and helped
elect Klan member Clarence Morley as governor and, at the very least,
shared common interests with one senator and Denver's mayor. Only
in Indiana did the Klan have more political influence than it enjoyed
in Colorado. Under the leadership of the charismatic Dr. John Galen
Locke, the Colorado KKK prospered.

Although the Klan became a statewide organization, its stronghold
rested in Denver among the dissatisfied and seemingly disenfranchised
who had been bypassed by prosperity. There and elsewhere, it burned
crosses, held parades, published newspapers, and occasionally threatened
those who did not appear 100 percent American. In Bayfield, in southwestern Colorado (for which records have survived), the Klan seemed
mostly to be one of the popular 1920s clubs rather than an outright racist
organization. No minorities threatened the small rural Bayfield; there
were only threats to old-time virtues from the surging urban lifestyle of
the roaring twenties.

The Klan proved to be a money-making organization. Good members needed to have all kinds of items in their possession, from rings to
hoods to books such as *Priest and Woman*, which the Klan piously
reported, "should not be allowed to fall into the hands of children." The
neighboring Klan in Durango published monthly the *Durango Klansman*,
which in its August 1925 issue warned, "The dances at near-by resorts are

objectionable because their tendency is to break down the American Sabbath, . . . and they are not conducive to the best and highest interest of our young people."

After trying and failing to attract Southern Utes on their nearby reservation into their Klavern, as local chapters were called, Bayfield turned its attention to the physical evils of the day. Bootlegging caught a major focus of members' attention, in between their meetings and social activities.

The Klan burned crosses, too, although Durango Catholics took care of that problem by planting dynamite on the Klan's favorite burning spot. It held parades, invited the public to picnics where members took off their hoods, conducted Klan rodeos, and did whatever it could to show its power and legitimacy. In the Klan's effort to reach out to the whole family, women and children's auxiliaries often participated with the men.

Within a year, Coloradans started to come to their senses, and the KKK began to fade, particularly after Locke resigned and a series of national scandals was exposed. Why the Klan had done so well in Colorado and not in Wyoming and Montana is an interesting question. One need look no further than John Locke to find a prime factor; the Colorado Klan benefited from a natural-born organizer, leader, and master of publicity. Another factor was the 1920s threat to those American virtues still held by small towns (like Bayfield) and rural Americans. In Colorado, more urbanized than the other two states, it was easier for rural folk to see, read about, and look askance at what they characterized as big-city sin.

In Denver, the KKK gave folks being pushed aside by the roaring twenties a chance to gain a feeling of importance and to have a voice in the rapidly changing world around them. Locke's use of ritual and the fact that he was the political force behind Governor Morley also helped the state Klan. The Klan flourished for a season but by 1927 had nearly disappeared, although the bigotry and hatred did not fade until the 1930s depression settled in. The KKK's involvement in Colorado left an ugly stain on the state's history.

Colorado was not alone among the heartland states to capture, for a moment, national notice. Neighboring Wyoming caught even more of the country's attention during the infamous Teapot Dome scandal. Wyoming prospered as the oil excitement of the 1910s became an oil boom in the 1920s, with production zooming to 44 million barrels in 1923. Some locals dreamed that the state might gather enough royalties that taxes would disappear, roads would be built, and an elaborate system of schools would be constructed. That wish was never realized.

Thirty miles or so north of Casper lay the Teapot Dome oil reserve, for years a reserve for naval oil. Set aside for national defense emergency, it was under the jurisdiction of the Navy Department. Secretary of the Interior Albert Fall, in 1921, convinced President Harding that the Teapot Dome should be under his department's control. A secret executive order transferred that control. Over the protests of naval officers, Secretary of the Navy Edwin Denby acquiesced.

Within a short time Harry Sinclair's Mammoth Oil Company secretly leased the field, which came in with a gusher—a well flowing briefly at 28,000 barrels a day. Protests soon appeared on the desk of Wyoming's senator John Kendrick, spurring him to look into the situation. Complaints arose about the absence of competitive bidding, the secret and strange activities that seemed to surround the deal, including Fall's sudden good fortune with improvements on his New Mexico ranch, and the threat to national security posed by losing oil reserves. As some facts emerged, Congress called for an investigation that Montana's Sen. Thomas Walsh agreed to chair. Hearings began in October 1923.

The hearings, under Walsh's able guidance, uncovered the sordid mess. Special prosecutors eventually took over the case. Found guilty of taking a bribe, Fall became the first cabinet member sentenced to jail; Sinclair soon joined him. Denby resigned, and the Supreme Court eventually invalidated the fraudulent leases.

Harding died before all the transgressions had been uncovered and publicly aired, but that did not save him or his administration's reputation. The Teapot Dome scandal added to the besmirched record of his corrupt administration. The bipartisan investigation's findings aroused near-universal revulsion. Unfortunately, the government never received its rightful share of revenue from the leases.

The scandal, however, managed in a small way to promote a stronger conservation program—and it did preserve the naval oil reserves. The disgusted American public, amid the exciting twenties, did not have time to consider seriously all of the implications of Teapot Dome, nor were many in a position to point fingers at their government.

Many Americans were having too much fun breaking the law themselves, even if not to the same magnitude. That "Noble Experiment,"

Prohibition, went into effect on January 16, 1920, after years of individual states going dry. The aforementioned Volstead Act (October 1919) defined intoxicating liquor as any beverage containing more than one-half of one percent alcohol, thus ending the chance to have a beer or a shot of whiskey at one's favorite saloon. That favorite saloon disappeared also. The newly formed Prohibition Bureau seemed ready to go to work, and the country was on alert.

After decades of struggle, the prohibitionists had reached their goal primarily because of fervent efforts during the Great War. After all those war years highlighting that grains were needed to feed the starving Belgians, that liquor was undermining troops' morale, and that money was being wasted in saloons at home when it could be better utilized in the war effort, the prohibition message finally took hold. Now the long-promised millennium had arrived. Among other things, crime would decrease and the poorhouses would disappear. Family abuse caused by drinking would become a relic of the past, and that dastardly institution—the saloon—would vanish from the American scene. No more would intoxicated people be driving automobiles and speeding through town and countryside. Only one of those points proved accurate—the old-time saloon was never resurrected.

One had only to look at Colorado or any other states that went dry prior to 1920 to see what would likely occur on the national level. Before the state prohibition date arrived, that dreadful January 1, 1916, people stored liquor supplies in their homes. Hometown bootleggers, with their assortment of wares, marketed "home brew" within weeks. What became known as speakeasies, along with suspicious ice-cream and soft-drink parlors (serving soda laced with booze), appeared almost as quickly. Pool halls stored liquor in their back rooms ready for customers.

Increasing numbers of the public patronized these institutions, thereby enjoying breaking the law. Some folks who had not patronized saloons seemed to get a thrill out of doing that. Before long, criminals had joined the profitable business. Now, in the 1920s, these activities had spread through all the Rocky Mountain states, as well as across the nation.

This blatant law-breaking, seemingly focused on sinful urban America, shocked rural Coloradans, Wyomingites, and Montanans and became one of the Klan's main rallying cries. Many already expected the worst from their city cousins, and this unlawfulness confirmed what they had feared.

Within months of prohibition, liquor agents and state, county, and city law officers were making raids and confiscating contraband. So were criminals, who in April 1920 stole a large supply of whiskey stored in a warehouse by two prominent Cheyenne attorneys. In December, federal agents arrested sixty-two people in Rock Springs and the surrounding area and seized 4,000 gallons of liquor. Protection money and bribes passed through many a hand. In clashes between bootleggers and officers, innocent citizens were caught in the crossfire and killed. Lawlessness hit cities and small towns.

Disillusionment quickly set in, and the enthusiasm for prohibition waned steadily. Some local law enforcement agencies soon gave up trying to enforce prohibition. In May 1930, for example, the Thermopolis and Rock Springs city governments were charged with violating the law. It appeared they used a system of fines as a form of "licensing." That same year the *Literary Digest* called Wyoming and Montana the wettest states in the region.

Montana worked hard to live up to that reputation. A former baseball player and now a sawdust evangelist, Billy Sunday, took a horrified look at Butte's empty bottles after one weekend and declared that they "would build a stairway from the top of its highest peak to the utmost depths of hell."[3] Sunday had a point: Butte reportedly led the nation in per capita consumption of illicit liquor. And Montana's long stretches of isolation proved ideal for local stills, producing for home markets and beyond.

Montana law enforcement agents confronted a special problem that neither of the other two states faced. Wet Canada sat right next door. High-speed cars raced to bring booze to Montana's cities and to arrange for distribution elsewhere. Rumrunners carried their goods down rural roads, where neighbors became used to nightly traffic. This risky, highly exciting business was curbed, if not eliminated, by federal agents by the mid-1920s.

There and elsewhere, it became fashionable to violate the Volstead Act, either openly or covertly. "Bathtub gin," home brew, the hip flask, and mixed drinking (women had not been invited into saloons, but they were to the speakeasies) became signs of the times. Montanans soon realized that the Great Experiment had failed. They repealed state prohibition in 1928 and waited for Washington to follow suit.

Designated the "Roaring Twenties," the "Lawless Twenties," and the "Era of Wonderful Nonsense" by writers and the public, the 1920s

witnessed the nearly complete failure of prohibition. Instead of the promised millennium, it produced contempt for the law, expensive drinks, health
problems developing from strange bootleg mixtures, corruption, crime,
and huge profits for criminals. No golden age accompanied prohibition.

The twenties also spelled the end of an American dream: homesteading. Not only did agriculture prices dip depressingly low, but
nature seemed to be conspiring against those struggling to turn prairie
land into farms. In fact, everything appeared to be working against the
homesteaders.

Still, the dream did not vanish easily, or the hopes disappear. In the
1910s and 1920s, the county-making mania continued to hit Montana and
to a lesser degree Wyoming. Nine new counties were added to the latter, as homesteaders moved into previously scantily occupied areas. This
expansion naturally created the need for county government, political
jobs, and a tax base to support the new status. That cost money, which
led to an increase in property taxes. All this could be sustained as long as
the boom continued.

During Montana's frenzy of county making, as mentioned, twenty-
eight new counties were created. Montana now had a total of fifty-six
counties. Some of the newcomers' futures rested solely on a land boom.

No sensible geographic boundaries generally delimitated these new
political entities. Yet all the county-splitting created jobs; helped sell
land, thereby generating profits for agents and salespeople; gave birth to
prairie-locked villages; caused real estate to boom in those small communities; and created an aura of permanence. To the visitor and newcomer,
it looked promising and a bit like home.

The agricultural boom that had accompanied the Great War ended
soon after it. Tragically, so did the wet cycle. Out on the plains of eastern
Montana, Wyoming, and Colorado, debt burdened the farmers, many of
whom had never farmed before. They had expected that the good times
would last long enough to allow them to get out of debt. If not, they
believed they could still continue on well into the future. The "Great
American Desert," it seemed, now stood on the threshold of becoming
America's Garden of Eden, just as boosters had promised.

Agricultural "experts" knew far too little about rainfall—and about
evaporation, climate, and proper agricultural methods on virgin land—to
give the farmers much assistance. Local and state governments were not

much help either. Few Americans seemed concerned about the tragedy unfolding, as the homestead dream died a painful, tragic, prairie death.

The exodus started as the war wound down. Drought (which appeared in some counties in 1917) and declining prices hinted at what would happen, and many left at the start of the 1920s, their hopes crushed. By that time, Montana's farm mortgage indebtedness topped $175 million, most of it on the almost 25 million acres homesteaded between 1909 and 1923.

Each year the situation seemed to get worse. The revival of European agriculture eliminated that market, and American farmers easily and quickly had a crop surplus. The result for Montana farmers was predictable. Land values went down, past what the eager honyockers had borrowed to secure it, but the mortgage payments still regularly came due. Hope faded as the hot summer winds withered their crops and crushed their spirits. The exodus picked up pace.

Then came the grasshoppers, wireworms, and cutworms, along with more hot, dry, windy weather and the traditional long, cold winters. The homesteaders left in droves, leaving behind wind-battered houses and outbuildings and shattered dreams. Some went back home, others drifted on to the new promised land—whatever appeared most encouraging. Well over 50 percent had departed by the early 1920s. Where now were those salespersons who once promised a new life on the prairies?

As grim as things became on the prairies, they were grimmer perhaps in those raw, desolate, isolated, jerry-built villages that once seemed destined for the status of being important communities. After all, were not these people the backbone of America, "upright" farmers and progressive rural townspeople, not those sinful denizens of western mining camps and cattle towns? Such righteousness could not save them from their fate.

The gray clouds of prairie dirt darkened the village folks' future as much as they did that of farmers on whom they relied. Building stopped, business declined, Main Street looked bleak, real estate lots went begging, and confidence waned. Residents and their counties found themselves overwhelmingly in debt for schools, libraries, highways, teachers' salaries, and county administrative costs. Banks, with a boom-and-growth mentality and enthusiasm, had early loaned money. Now that came back to haunt them. Over half of the state's commercial banks failed in the first half of the decade.

The state and counties did not have the resources to help the settlers through these lean times. Local charities, the Red Cross, and other agencies could not withstand the burgeoning demand for their limited resources. So the homesteaders found themselves on their own, with almost nothing working in their favor. They and the rest of their neighbors fled.

What had caused this disaster? Real estate boomers, railroads, local promotional organizations, and agricultural "experts" shared some of the blame. Ignorance of the land, lack of knowledge of weather patterns, limitations of growing seasons, and over-optimism about rainfall and local water conditions played a part. No substitute existed for rain, no matter what dry-land farming boosters promised. Too much hope, too many unknowns, and too little farming experience—particularly plains farming experience—spelled trouble.

The county-building mania did not help when the bust finally arrived. The explosion of new counties had a negative impact, particularly on Montana, once the homesteading craze ended. The problems were only magnified when the boom turned to bust. In debt and defeated, property owners increasingly failed to meet their taxes, leaving the counties no choice but to seize lands for tax delinquencies, thus "devouring their own property owners." The problems did not end there. "Today, the problems arising from reckless county-splitting are still very much with Montanans. Many rural counties have either lost or barely gained population since 1920, and they find themselves hard pressed to support their own local governments."[4]

As the homesteaders departed, they left behind a dry, dusty, wind-seared land that would take years to recover, and then not to its previous condition, when bountiful native grasses covered the rolling prairies. Besides abandoned farms that dotted the prairies, declining or abandoned villages stood as stark relics of dashed hopes. Out of them ran roads to nowhere, past only dreams. These communities and their farms never became as fascinating and alluring to visitors as those ghost towns and mines to the west in the mountains.

The communities that survived were little better off. Located in heavily debt-burdened counties, with a shriveling, if not disappearing, economic base, their futures appeared none too promising. The lucky ones had been named county seats—often the only thing that gave them even a semblance of life and hope. How quickly their prospects had vanished.

Schools, stores, and churches—built with great aspirations—sat nearly empty, epitaphs to the hopes of a vanished America. From Main Street front doors, the future looked equally bleak; and for the railroads, which had helped create the debacle, profits plummeted. County commissioners, confronted with what seemed to be unmanageable debts, laid off employees. No doubt some counties wished they had never been created as they desperately searched for answers.

Yet out of this failure for eastern Montana and Montanans, some good would eventually come. New, highly mechanized agricultural methods would emerge, along with new seeds and moisture-conserving practices, all allowing larger acreage per farm. When the world again turned to war and the wet cycle returned, Montana wheat growers would be ready.

Eastern Wyoming farmers suffered through the same saga of optimism and hope. The years 1920 and 1921 were huge years for filing homestead entries, with over 10,000 claims filed in each. Some ranchers even joined in the rush to file on homesteading land to "square up" their ranches.

The salesmen and the promoters pushed homesteading, and this time this state joined in the frenzy by creating a board of immigration. Veterans here, as elsewhere, received preference and could deduct up to two years of the three-year residency requirement for time served during the war. Wyoming set up a farm-loan board to provide low-cost loans. It mattered little in the long run. One unexpected and undesired result haunted the state for years. It eventually ended up gaining possession of farms and ranches as owners, unable to make payment or a living, simply left.

The drought continued, joined by an agricultural depression settling throughout the region and beyond. Adding to the woes, a section (640 acres) offered by the government at twenty-five cents per acre proved to be too small for a ranch and too large for a farm, without irrigation. Much of the land was impossible to irrigate, something the enthusiasts had promised would be overcome in no time. Land values collapsed, and eventually many of the homesteaders left. Unlike the situation in Montana, however, ranchers had used the homesteading act as a means to enlarge their holdings. They stayed, and ranching continued to dominate in Wyoming.

In Wyoming, farmers raised sugar beets in areas where water was abundantly available and soon had their own sugar-beet-producing plants. This was one of the few crops to be grown and processed within the state. For example, Wyoming saw the Holly Sugar Company founded to process the beets, and company factories eventually opened in Colorado, Montana, and California.

A similar story took place in Colorado when the postwar farming depression hit. Farmers' income fell and many left the drought-stricken eastern plains, although the excitement there had been more restrained than that to the north. Colorado had already gone through a failed excitement back in the 1870s and 1890s. Throughout the state, repayment of loans for irrigation projects declined, and some residents faced bankruptcy by the decade's end.

Specialization of crops provided some relief. As in Wyoming, sugar beets were particularly attractive, but potatoes, peaches, melons (particularly the famous Rocky Ford melons), and lettuce helped Colorado farmers in places where irrigation water flowed to fields.

Farmers in all three states found that even fashion was working against them, as well as a change in the American diet that seemed to conspire against the beleaguered prairie farmers. Americans shifted away from bread, meat, and potatoes and toward fruit, fish, and vegetables. Those mainstays of earlier days—fat and heavy foods—did not allow one to achieve the svelte figure so popular in the twenties. Meanwhile, growing numbers of Americans worked at white-collar jobs that did not demand high-calorie intakes, as farming and physical labor did, and their eating habits were also changing. City dwellers again impacted their country cousins.

Rural Coloradans, Wyomingites, and Montanans looked longingly at the prospering urban areas and wondered what had happened. Many migrated to the "sinful" cities, where plentiful jobs and more amenities welcomed newcomers, many more than they found in their own neighborhoods. Population and political power slowly eroded from rural counties.

The Ku Klux Klan, the Teapot Dome scandal, Prohibition, and the plight of the farmers provide insight into the era in the Rockies, as well as around the country. Speculation, intolerance, willingness to break the law, enjoying a good time, challenging agricultural times, and failure are factors that mark the 1920s. Americans were tired of prohibition, of reform, and of sacrifice and wanted to let their hair down and enjoy themselves. It had all happened before, most recently right after the Civil War.

The urbanites fretted little over the plight of the farmer. As long as their grocery stores and meat markets carried the products they wanted—

and at the lowest possible prices—they remained satisfied. For many of them, their rural roots were long forgotten. Indeed, a growing number had no rural roots at all, going back several generations.

For the urbanite, the city was where the action flashed in a variety of areas, mostly related to potential, profits, and pleasure. Denver stood out from all its neighbors but was in step with its contemporaries elsewhere. The 1920s have been referred to as the "business decade." As President Calvin Coolidge observed in a typically terse comment, "The chief business of the American people is business." So it seemed by the mid-twenties.

One trend that became obvious was the emergence of chain stores, from grocery through general stores. They threatened the "mom-and-pop stores" that had long graced Main Street and given life to their community. One such chain got its start in Kemmerer, Wyoming, when J. C. Penney opened a dry-goods store in 1902. He prospered, and from this store grew the J. C. Penney Company, which promoted "one price" and good merchandise. By 1920, 312 stores had opened and the company was expanding at the amazing rate of one new store every ten days.

The neighborhood mom-and-pop stores could not compete in variety or price with this franchised rival. A pattern started that would change the Main Street business community forever. Sale catalogs from Montgomery Ward and Sears Roebuck had cut into business for the past generation; now the rival was right next door, and more were coming.

The products offered for sale would have seemed unbelievable to the heartland's grandparents. Not only had refrigeration made items such as oranges and bananas available; these once-rare items were also fairly economical to buy at the store. From the radio to the phonograph, new gadgets tempted buyers. Electricity made the urban housewife's day much easier, with items like vacuum cleaners, clothes-washing machines, stoves, refrigerators, sewing machines, and primitive air conditioners. This was also true for the office and the store. It was not true, however, for the farm housewife or the crossroads store.

That wonder of the age, radio, changed American life in the 1920s in a variety of ways, including uniting it as never before. Farm families who were not too isolated and who had a battery-operated set enjoyed listening, but basically it was town and city dwellers who enjoyed radio the most. College football games, major-league baseball, opera, drama,

special events from all over the country, music programs, comedy shows—
the list stretched on and on. Never had people been so in touch with the
national and world situation. Now folks in the Rockies could hear news
stories almost as they happened, instead of a day or more later.

Hollywood, too, ventured into the Rockies via the motion picture
screen. For as little as a nickel, moviegoers could enjoy a short documen-
tary, a cartoon, news, and the main feature—and on Saturdays perhaps
a double feature. Then came the "talkie," and the viewers could hear
the latest songs and the story line, as well as see the action and the latest
Hollywood fashions. The movie "palaces" in the cities and the less prestigious theaters in small towns were also enticing on hot summer nights
with the newfangled air coolers many had installed. That Hollywood
staple, the western, gained the movies more fans and continued to do
much to shape the image of the Old West.

The radio, along with movies, broke down isolation and regionalism.
The latest trends, styles, gossip, advertisements, advice, and events came
into homes, or were seen and heard at the theater. Life in the Rocky
Mountain states would never be the same, although rural dwellers again
languished behind their urban cousins. Westerners were becoming more
like their eastern cousins in fashion, fads, and lifestyle.

Mining, like agriculture, suffered something of a decline in the 1920s.
Gold and silver mining became a mere shadow of its earlier prominence
as one of the region's economic pillars. Tungsten collapsed after the end
of the war in the face of a declining market. Chinese competition, offering a cheaper product, also undercut American miners. As the century
wore on, foreign competition became even stronger.

Oil shale briefly stirred investors' imaginations once again. Colorado
reportedly had a reserve of 20 trillion tons in 1918. Interest centered in
the Grand Junction region on the Western Slope. All that was needed
was to find a method to refine the shale profitably. Once again, golden
opportunity loomed in the West.

That small matter of refining problems did not hinder promoters or
investors. Within two years, more than 100 companies were offering stock
and pitching shale oil as the future now at hand. The potential uses were
limited only by the speaker's or the writer's imagination—gasoline, soaps,
fertilizers, sheep dip, paint, health products—the list seemed boundless.
Small portable refineries were set up on eastern city streets and set in

motion. The interested and the gullible watched as black "rocks" were placed in a heated retort and out oozed an oil-like substance. Captured by the ease of the process, money poured out of investors' pocketbooks only to evaporate just as easily. What they failed to grasp and certainly were not told was that it cost more to mine the ore and heat the process than the "oil" was worth.

By the mid-1920s, the oil shale boom had collapsed. The miracle product could not be profitably retorted; it was a fool's gold glittering just beyond reach. Also, as discussed earlier, the great 1920s oil boom in Texas and Oklahoma flooded the market at the same time, causing local oil shale prospects to fade. Northwestern Colorado returned to a more normal existence, and once-future millionaires could only look at their ornate stock certificates and remember their hopes.

Washington did not give up, however. The government built a pilot oil shale plant near Rulison, Colorado, and continued to test shale in a small way in the years ahead. Despite optimistic forecasts, nothing proved cost-efficient, and the plant closed during the Depression.

The mining industry meanwhile had been in a consolidation mode for a generation, much like the rest of the United States. Anaconda epitomized that trend, as it gloried in its heyday of power. Although the company never completely ran Montana politics, it continued to exercise significant power.

Farther south, Colorado saw a corporate giant emerge, the Climax Molybdenum Company. Just off Fremont Pass, a score or so miles from the once booming Leadville, sat Bartlett Mountain, full of molybdenum. Moly, not silver, primarily kept the old town alive. Alloyed with steel to produce hardness, toughness, and resistance to wear and corrosion, molybdenum was perfect for axles and springs in those increasingly popular automobiles.

Despite the fact that Climax's laborers had to work as high as 12,000 feet above sea level and endure long winters, production soared in the 1920s. Labor turnover proved more of a problem, even after the company built the town of Climax, which offered many modern conveniences, including a ski run. Overall, though, Leadville was restored almost to its glory days of the 1870s. The old silver queen had gained a second wind. That relic of Colorado's greatest silver boom was not yet dead, as moly miners enjoyed its urban life.

Colorado coal mining had its ups and downs, but overall, coal enjoyed a better-than-average decade. By 1929, coal producers could proudly proclaim that annual coal output exceeded any other mine product in volume and value. The growth of population and businesses produced an expanding market. Long scorned as second-class mining citizens, coal owners and miners could hold their heads high—although not for too many seasons.

Coal mining in Montana, which had started in the 1860s, never matched the production in the other Rocky Mountain states. The pattern, though, became the same, with railroads and Anaconda—which needed coal in its operations—dominating the industry. Two innovations caught on quickly in the state: open pit and strip mining, both of which worked well for low-grade deposits and cut labor costs. Mines near Colstrip gained the most from these changes, which augured well for the future.

Coal mining in Wyoming did not generally prosper, and its future seemed to be behind it. The mines owned by the railroads continued to operate, because they had a built-in market. Other companies, without such a benefit, found themselves losing out or closing. Competition from two other fossil fuels, natural gas and oil, cut into the markets that coal once dominated, as happened elsewhere in the country. Accidents did not stop, though. In 1923 and 1924, two major disasters killed a total of 138 men, most of them immigrants. Nothing had changed.

Life in the coal camps was also little changed. A Wyoming miner's wife described how she made ends meet during those years. "Us ladies, we were pretty adept. We made our own clothes, and people would use up everything that they had." They improvised in other ways as well to help out. "I know when the mines would be off for two or three months, we'd live out of the garden. We'd just do everything we could to save money."[5] In their own fashion, her neighbors and women in other camps made similar efforts to keep their families going.

In Wyoming, Montana, and Colorado, coal mining evolved with the new techniques and yet declined during the decade. How the industry would adjust to the new realities would dictate the future.

Notwithstanding the gloom and despair that hit much of the Rockies economy, one bright spot emerged: tourism. The American love affair with the car provided a tourist and monetary benefit. Vehicles that were comfortable and easier to operate, improved roads, increased leisure time, higher income for the middle class, and cheap gas, thanks to Texas and Oklahoma oil fields, led Americans to take to the highways in larger numbers every year.

Local communities raced to promote themselves as the gateway to wherever and whatever. This competition led to urban squabbles and jealousies reminiscent of earlier debates over mining, railroads, and business. Each claimed it had the best, the shortest, and most scenic route to Yellowstone, Glacier, Mesa Verde, the Custer Battlefield, or any other spot that would bring the tourists and their dollars to its town before they ventured on.

Roads had improved, but it took planning, time, and money to extend them far past the urban areas, especially when going to an isolated national park such as Glacier or Mesa Verde. With the "auto age" upon them, the three states needed even more funds to expand their roads. The presence of more roads would break down isolation, improve mobility, shorten transportation time, and allow rural people to escape their confinement to a small area. If they built the roads, tourists would come. Tourists represented the region's future economic windfall.

Rocky Mountain folks stood ready and willing to accommodate. Hotels, new motels, auto campgrounds, restaurants, and gas stations made travel easier, and promotional pamphlets guided tourists onward. Tourism was seasonal, starting in late spring and lasting until early fall and the approach of snow. Mountain roads in particular were closed in winter. The West had much to offer, including those ever-popular national parks. Wyoming gained a second national park in 1929, when land was set aside in the Grand Teton Mountains and a strip of it along the foothills in Jackson Hole. Backers wanted more of the valley, but they ran into a hail of opposition. Locals, mainly sportsmen, ranchers, sheep men, lumbermen, and dude ranchers, were unhappy about this federal intrusion into their region. Many could not, unfortunately, comprehend the economic benefits soon to reach their pocketbooks. They saw only meddling outsiders arriving. In spite of the opposition, the strikingly beautiful Grand Teton National Park opened at the end of the decade. Its supporters hoped for even more land.

An earlier attempt to create a major park had failed in the face of similar opposition. Even the Forest Service objected, because much of the park would be carved out of Grand Teton National Forest. None of the other Rocky Mountain parks had seen such bitter fighting, which went on for years.

Help was on the way, however. John D. Rockefeller Jr., who had earlier provided funds for Mesa Verde's museum and archaeological expeditions, was looking at the Teton area's potential and liked what he saw. The first Yellowstone superintendent and later director of the National Park Service, Horace Albright, introduced Rockefeller to the Tetons, and together they developed a plan that slowly unfolded.

Other parks were already showing the strain of increased visitations. From Mesa Verde to Glacier, cars and crowds hindered the experience of being surrounded by these wonders of nature and history. Yellowstone "bear jams," scenic lookout points, Rocky Mountain elk views, and popular attractions such as Old Faithful, the Cliff Palace at Mesa Verde, and view stops to observe Glacier's remarkable scenery found tourists crowding in their efforts to see and enjoy. With crowds came trash and litter that some thoughtless people left behind. Noise also polluted the once quiet, pristine sites. Some experienced old-timers wished for a return to the "good old days."

Tourism could not be stopped, however—not with national and local newspapers and magazines extolling the Rocky Mountains. In Wyoming, for example, promotions urged visitors to come, and towns set up municipal campgrounds for the increasing number of "automobilists." The better camps included electric lights, hot and cold water, stores, and other facilities to ease the travelers' stay and encourage them to linger longer.

Locals never missed a beat in promoting the western theme. Some towns even asked residents to wear western garb to provide flavor for tourists. Cheyenne continued to have the strongest attraction along these lines, its now-decades-old Frontier Days. Other towns tried various things, but rodeos and county fairs attracted mainly locals, not visitors.

The westerns were more popular than ever in local theaters. When sound arrived they became even more realistic, if not truthful. The West would be repeatedly won in such 1920s films as *The Frontiersman* (1927), *The Covered Wagon* (1923), and *The Iron Horse* (1924). Now outsiders could sample the "gunsmoke and gallop West" without leaving their hometowns or spending much money. Thanks to Zane Grey (at the height of his popularity, from 1917 to 1924, he always had a book on the list of top best sellers) and other writers, they did not even need to leave their living room to experience vicariously the mythical West. Pulp western magazines replaced the dime novel for the less literarily inclined. Magazines such as *Western Story* appeared on newsstands, and more general popular magazines like the *Saturday Evening Post* and *Collier's* featured western fiction.

Charles Russell, still in love with Montana as when he first arrived back in 1880, continued painting into the 1920s. His "power," one scholar noted, "and his enduring legacy to western art—was the ability to make his yearning universal."[6] By the time of his death (1926), he, along with Frederic Remington, had helped inspire a generation of other painters, including Edwin Deming, W.H.D. Koerner, Olaf Seltzer, and Jo De Yong. Russell's inspiration lived far beyond the 1920s, and it echoes down the century.

The movies, art, books, and magazines did much to fix the western myth in the public mind, both the larger-than-life people who populated fiction and film and the redeeming character of the land. As historian Robert Athearn pointed out, "it has been told badly, yet the story of the westering experience has still drawn packed houses for a long time. Whether we think of it as the West of the mind or as something geographical, it has been an enormous stage."[7]

For those who decided to venture west, they, like their predecessors, wanted to find the comforts of home, although not necessarily in hotels, where parking was generally a problem. "Cottage camps" became popular, catering to tourists who did not want to rough it by camping. The presence of these camps helped boost the region's economy. The Wyoming Highway Department estimated that visitors spent between 6 and 7 million dollars in 1926. Boosters did complain that the development of roads did not match the increasing needs. Others complained that a rival got better roads. Even with dollar matching, Wyoming struggled constantly throughout the decade to maintain, improve, and build those needed transportation arteries.

Urban jealousies and intercity rivalries continued to flare, as they had in the previous century. Rival Colorado communities remained chronically jealous of Denver. Pueblo, Colorado Springs, and Denver had their ongoing feuds, sometimes joined by Boulder and Fort Collins.

Eastern and Western Slope communities squared off against each other over a variety of issues. Casper challenged Cheyenne for the state capital location in 1923, and Cheyenne and Laramie continued to fend off rivals. Southern and eastern Montana felt ignored by Helena and the western part of the state.

An exciting development that promised to reduce some of the isolation and travel time that helped stimulate such rivalries soared on the horizon—the airplane. It took only a decade from barnstorming and the "air aces" of World War I to actual mail and passenger traffic. It took only a decade even to try night flying. On an experimental basis, for example, in February 1921 large bonfires placed every fifty miles guided planes between Chicago and Cheyenne. Although that did not prove practical, it represented a pioneering effort. Denver and Cheyenne both built good airports, and both expected to be a part of transcontinental air routes. Montana looked on longingly, as it had with the initial railroad construction.

Cheyenne again won the first round, with its airport completed first. Denver found itself standing on the outside, as had been the case with the transcontinental railroad. Denver soon forged ahead, however—and its Denver Municipal Airport (later Stapleton Field) retained its lead throughout the decade and beyond. Flights to other Colorado cities soon complemented those to Cheyenne. Passengers, mail, and freight now could arrive faster than ever before. Most people, though, stayed on the ground and in their automobiles.

Inventions, changing times, ever-changing fads, the new morality— the 1920s had them all. Something old also held its grip, however—what westerners called colonialism. Outside capital and control, the federal government, and exporting natural resources while purchasing more expensive finished products had long been a part of the western experience, as discussed earlier. The seventeenth-century western Virginian colonist understood that equally as well as the twentieth-century Wyoming "Virginian." Colonialism did not diminish during the decade. Westerners might find that situation unfair, but there seemed to be little they could do about it.

Two Americas lived side by side during the roaring twenties. Depressed rural Americans west and east were not prospering, and urbanites, who on the surface appeared to be doing so, still suffered from insecurities and tensions. The cultural, social, and economic imbalance between the two groups was becoming alarming, as was each group's insensitivity toward the other and its particular problems.

Urban Americans and some of their country cousins were buying more, enjoying a higher standard of living and a quality of life unimagined a generation ago. That is, they were doing so if they had the money. But if they did not have the cash, fear not, credit beckoned alluringly. For the first time in American history, credit buying—buying on time—became the acceptable way of not denying oneself any of the tempting pleasures available. For example, in 1929, Americans purchased about 60 percent of their cars on the installment plan, with homes and other "needed" items right behind.

Advertising, which came of age across the country in the 1920s, worked from a variety of angles to create atmosphere. It seemed almost unpatriotic to deny oneself the benefits of the new life, when buying products profited your country's economy at the same time.

Everything seemed well in America, except on the farms, and in some respects (at least for the first two-thirds of the decade), evidence appeared to support that contention. Americans were buying more, which meant that companies and industries in general prospered, jobs increased, and dividends kept coming. Automobile companies, with Chrysler, General Motors, and Ford leading the way, fared well, as did the new radio industry and a variety of businesses catering to modernizing the American home. The construction industry flourished as it built modern American homes.

Underneath this boom, however, lurked true inequities and a maladjusted economy. Too many ailing industries struggled along, including coal mining, hard-rock mining, agriculture, and the railroads. All of them had once been vital to the Rocky Mountain region, which appeared to suffer more than some of its neighbors. Unemployment stalked some counties while others, those with larger cities, prospered. Too few people controlled too much wealth, and too many rural people seemed to have been bypassed. Furthermore, America was purchasing more foreign goods than it sold, creating an unfavorable balance of trade.

The 1920s mania and the good times came together in the Big Bull Market, the runaway stock market of the last third of the decade. On the surface, it appeared so easy, even magical: buy stock low, and sell when the price appreciated to the level at which the purchaser was happy with the profit. Even if one did not have the money, brokers beckoned with the opportunity to buy on margin, put up a percentage of the purchase, and pay off the rest—plus interest—with those "sure" profits. "Everyone Ought to Be Rich" proclaimed an August 1929 article in the *Ladies' Home Journal.*

That sentiment echoed what President Herbert Hoover had pronounced back at his inauguration: "We in America today are nearer to the final triumph over poverty than ever before in the history of any land. The poorhouse is vanishing from among us." And President Hoover had a basis for such thinking. America had become the richest country in the world by 1929, with more wealth, a better lifestyle, and more real income than any other country. Employment appeared strong, the workforce gained a reputation for high-quality output, and advanced technology promised an even brighter future.

However, speculation spiraled to an all-time high, generating a furor to achieve the American dream where once hard work and a steady job had held sway. Highly speculative stock market ventures matched equally speculative ventures in real estate in apartments, hotels, and office buildings. The average American speculated, to some degree, when buying a home or a car, on the assumption that the good times would continue.

Everything seemed to be working in the summer of 1929. Some signs of approaching danger and warnings from more conservative financiers failed to arouse concern. Many Coloradans, Wyomingites, and Montanans continued to buy and to wait for the promised profits and an expected life of leisure without a worry for the future. The illusion of ever-rising stock prices had replaced historical reality.

Then, in September, the market began to sputter and shake, forcing large banks to try to stabilize the situation. Matters seemed to improve, but not for long. Americans did not realize it, but the Big Bull Market had peaked, and prices started to drift downward.

The stock market crash did not come until October 24, Black Thursday (as it was latter called), with panic selling and a collapse of confidence. Black Tuesday followed on October 29, when the bottom seemed to fall out. Before the market closed, a record of more than 16 million shares were traded at collapsing prices. Panic, then frantic selling, then agony seized Wall Street and spread throughout the country, eventually reaching the far corners of the Rocky Mountain heartland. Within a month, about half of the market price of stock (30 billion dollars) on the New York Stock Exchange had vanished. Buoyancy, self-confidence, and faith disappeared along with the stock value.

"The fundamental business of the country, that is, the production and distribution of commodities, is on a sound and prosperous basis," President Hoover had reassured Americans on October 25. It would take more than words to restore people's faith. Summer's euphoria became fall's gloom and despair.

The optimism, the swaggering confidence, that had characterized so much of the decade disappeared like a morning sunrise over the mountains. Now it seemed that all would share the sad plight of the farmer, rancher, coal miner, hard-rock miner, and small-town merchant—all of whom had suffered through a less-than-prosperous decade while watching the success of others pass them by.

The Great Depression had begun across the country and into the Rockies. Some communities postponed the day of reckoning, but eventually the collapse hit them all. A watershed time had come to Montana, Wyoming, and Colorado, bringing a new era.

The image of the 1920s faded into a bad memory, although time would eventually soften the reminiscences of those who had lived through them. As Frederick Lewis Allen wrote in *Only Yesterday:* "Those charming, crazy days when the radio was a thrilling novelty, and girls wore bobbed hair and knee-length skirts, and a transatlantic flyer became a god overnight, and common stocks were about to bring us all to a lavish Utopia. They would forget, perhaps, the frustrated hopes that followed the war, the aching disillusionment of the hard-boiled era, its oily scandals, its spiritual paralysis, the harshness of its gaiety; they would talk about the good days."[8]

It had been a fascinating decade of contrasts and contradictions, progress and poverty for the Rockies. In some respects Coloradans, Wyomingites, and Montanans had marched boldly into the future, and in other respects had hung on tenuously to a vanishing past. Modern America and old America clashed, and they changed as the decades slipped away into history.

CHAPTER 5

New Deal Days, New Deal Ways
The 1930s

Happy days are here again, the skies above are clear again: Let us
sing a song of cheer again, Happy days are here again!
—Jack Yellen, "Happy Days Are Here Again"

DESPITE THE CHEERY WORDS and bouncy tune, happy days failed to
brighten the 1930s for Colorado, Wyoming, Montana, and the rest of
the country. Durangoan Jim Sartoris captured the Depression's heartbreak in a story he told the author in the 1970s. Working for a New Deal
relief agency, he toured one of the most depressed regions in Colorado,
the San Luis Valley, famous for its cold weather. On an unusually cold,
brutal day, he came upon a shack where a family lived. The kids were
running around in ragged underwear while the small stove's weak fire
tried to provide a semblance of warmth. On top of the stove, in a pan, lay
a newborn baby wrapped in a thin blanket. They could not keep warm,
shivering in the frosty chill, and the family held few prospects for a better
today and tomorrow.

Heartbreaking as this story is, it was only one of thousands like it in
the Rocky Mountains. Dull statistics tell a tale of woe unequaled in
American history. Between 1929 and 1932, industrial production fell by 51
percent. The number of men estimated to be out of work in the winter
of 1932 and 1933, the Depression's worst, ranged from 13 to 17 percent.
Workers still employed had their hours cut, and some, with wage cuts,
received as little as five to ten cents an hour. Women earned even less.
Street beggars became commonplace. The 1932 hit song, "Brother, Can
You Spare a Dime?" illustrated an all-too-familiar occurrence.

One 1933 survey estimated 1.3 million homeless Americans, but
figures were imprecise. The number of business failures jumped from
24,000 in 1928 to 32,000 in 1932; 85,000 businesses eventually failed. No
one could be sure of any of these numbers; most likely, they were higher

as people wandering around were not counted, nor were many others who drifted out of sight.

Farm income, which had not been strong for a decade, collapsed even further in 1932, to $5.6 billion—less than half what it had been three years before. National income fell by over half during the same period. More than 1,300 banks failed in 1930, and during the next year over 2,000 collapsed; 300 banks closed in September alone. Depositors counted their blessings if they received even a small percentage of their savings; the unfortunate ones retrieved nothing from their accounts. In this time before federal bank insurance, a bank failure could wipe out more than just institutions. Panicked Americans hid their money in mattresses and hoarded gold.

With federal and state funds exhausted, local Rocky Mountain communities, and those everywhere else, found themselves the only group to care for the destitute and homeless. The burden fell on families, relatives, local relief agencies, and a few private charities. Hungry people scavenged in dumps for morsels. A roundup of "Hoover Hogs" (jackrabbits) provided the participants with meat. Meanwhile, farmers raised surplus crops for which they could not receive a price to compensate them for their work.

Credit, so popular in the 1920s, virtually dried up. Foreclosures and evictions tragically became common. Even for those who avoided that fate, foreclosure threatened farmers, businessmen, and everyone else, and even hung over local governments. Teachers received promissory notes instead of checks, and charities and relief agencies ran out of funds to help those in need. Hoovervilles, where the homeless lived in shacks constructed of whatever material they could scavenge, appeared outside of towns and cities.

Men walked around with their pants pockets pulled out as a sign of poverty—"Hoover flags," they called them. Newspapers, used to keep people warm while sleeping outside in parks and other places, became "Hoover blankets." President Hoover emerged as the scapegoat for the country's woes, along with his Republican Party.

Tired of the homeless and tramps coming through their towns, police harassed them and pushed them on their way. Some communities would provide them with a meal or, as a common saying went, "one night in the jail, breakfast, and on your way."

By 1932 a growing despondency, even a desperation, had overtaken many Americans. Each month it seemed only to get worse and more discouraging. People lacked food and clothing, beyond what they had on their backs. Women and children were even worse off than men. Faith in government and other institutions plummeted, and politicians joined the crowded group of those out of favor.

The Rocky Mountain states were not magically immune to any of this. In fact, nature dealt eastern Colorado and other portions of the Great Plains a further blow: the Dust Bowl. For years, Americans—unknowingly, uncaringly, or greedily—had abused the environment. In the mountains, timber had been cut down recklessly, the land and water polluted by mining, and streams despoiled by towns; on the prairies, soil had been ill used and abused. The heritage of a century of despoliation had come home to roost.

Colorado suffered the most of the three states, because it was on the western end of the Dust Bowl's center. Nonetheless, eastern Montana and Wyoming were not immune from the "dirty thirties." Americans had deliberately set about dominating and exploiting this land and now they were paying the consequences. The biblical "they have sown the wind, and they shall reap the whirlwind" came to pass. Drought with intense heat combined with poor farming methods, overgrazing, and a never-dying wind to create havoc during most of the 1930s. An average of fifty dust storms a year hit the region between 1932 and 1939.

How bad was it? Dust from a Montana and Wyoming storm on May 9, 1935, riding on high air currents, reached Chicago by the end of the day. It arrived in Buffalo, New York, a day later and darkened the skies of Boston and New York the following day. Before the storm blew itself out, ships three hundred miles out to sea found dust on their decks. Old-timers called them "black blizzards."

For millions of years the plains had been beautiful grasslands; then farmers—with their disk plows, gasoline-engine-powered tractors, harvester-thresher combines, and other equipment—changed all that and enormously increased productivity. The pioneering "never-say-die" spirit and the drive for profit had produced an environmental impact of alarming proportions. When the inevitable dry cycle arrived, those pioneers found themselves in no promised land.

Roads closed, cattle suffocated in the fields, people died of "dust pneumonia," and streetlights barely penetrated the darkness at high noon.

Carcasses of jackrabbits, small birds, and field mice lay strewn along roadsides after severe "dusters." Dust coated river surfaces, and fish died.

Fine dirt drifted in through windows and door cracks, piled into dunes on city streets and farmyards, and covered everything. People shoveled dirt from their front yards and swept bushel-basketfuls of the fine particles that coated everything in their homes. Dust and grit became a constant part of diets and breathing. Even wet rags hanging over windows did little good; the dust drifted everywhere.

Gloom and depression affected everyone, and for some it proved too much. Giving up, they committed suicide.

Schools closed during the worst of the storms. Farming stopped, and business in already hard-pressed farm communities withered further. The exodus that had started in the 1920s continued. A dispatch to the *Washington Post* (April 15, 1935) summarized the situation: "Three little words achingly familiar on a Western farmer's tongue, rule of life in the dust of the continent—if it rains."

"If it rains." For seemingly a lifetime it did not. A 1930s poignant expression voiced it all: "dried out, dusted out, driven out."

Farmers and ranchers already faced a dismal future, as did their neighbors in small towns, when the stock market collapsed during bleak October 1929. With no savings, little income, and marginal prospects, they seemingly hit the bottom of the economic valley.

Conditions in mining were no better. In Butte, copper prices fell, production dropped, and smelters closed. At the start of the decade nearly 23 percent of Montana households received relief. Out on the plains, Glasgow cut its bare-bones school budget by another $12,000 and eliminated its night police force. Dude ranches were swamped with cancellations. Newspaper editors accepted produce or other goods in payment for subscriptions. Doctors, dentists, teachers, and others did the same thing in lieu of payment. Deer and elk hunting increased so drastically that some Montanans thought a "save the deer" campaign was in order.

Wyoming also suffered, although frugal living had emerged long ago as a way of life for many people by the time of depression. Surveys revealed thousands of undernourished and inadequately clothed children. County poor and pauper funds quickly were overdrawn.

Fewer tourists arrived and those who did spent less and stayed for a shorter time; the same occurred in Colorado. Wyoming's revenue dropped, and the state government was unable to offer much help to the needy. Self-reliance became the word of the day. Even so, by 1933, one out of every five people in the state was receiving relief in some form or another.

Like the other two states, Colorado witnessed an upswing in tenancy in rural areas. By 1939 the figure had reached 39 percent, and many of the tenants ("suitcase" farmers) stayed only long enough to try a crop or two before leaving. They cared little for the land, or the farm, or the future — just about getting their profits and getting out.

An estimated 56 percent of the mountain states' mortgaged debt had reportedly become delinquent by the start of 1933, a figure higher than the national average. Colorado faced a serious problem. This debt was not just marginal, resulting from questionable investments by the borrower; it represented "good" debt, debt of solid citizens, who had once owned farms, ranches, businesses, and homes and gathered in steady incomes to make their payments.

These desperate times accelerated the rush to urban areas where work might be more abundant. The newcomers did not receive a royal welcome, however, from the overburdened communities. Sustained for a time by soup kitchens and bread lines, they searched for work. It was not to be had, or, if found, it proved marginal at best. In many ways, the Depression's desperation and fury became even more visible in the cities as hope faded for the desperate.

Facts, statistics, and explanations mask the real tragedy of those years, which focused on the impact on people. What did the Depression mean and do to them? Several quotes illustrate what these days meant to people (interviewed by the author) who lived in southern and southwestern Colorado during the Depression.[1]

> I just got out of school, couldn't find work, decided to go back to the mines [coal], and Dad said, "No you don't want to go back to the mines." And I said, "I gotta go. I have nothing to do. I can't find anything." You couldn't beg, borrow, or steal a job.
>
> —Jim Sartoris

We managed to stay off the bread line, but it was hard times for a lot of people. We didn't suffer, a lot of people did. But that stands out in my memory as being a hard time.

—Mrs. Ed. McDaniel

I remember trading a box of shotgun shells for a turkey. And we had our friends over, somebody bought potatoes, somebody brought a salad, and we all ate. Oh yes, [times were] very, very hard.

—Lester Gardenswartz

We had a family across the street that had a little boy about the same age as my oldest son. This little boy would come over and have lunch quite often. One day he began to cry, and Jack said to him "Why are you eating so fast? You shouldn't eat that way." He said, "Well, if you hadn't had anything but squash to eat all winter, you'd eat fast too."

—Ethel Nelson

We fortunately had a home. We lost it. We couldn't make the taxes. [Bills piled up.] We couldn't keep up with the taxes, so we just walked out, didn't get a dime out of it.

—Bessie Finegan

Times were hard. People would come to the house to ask for food, they would work it off. One man painted our bathroom, he was a nice-looking man. [My husband] wanted to give him a job, he said no, he was single and others needed it worse than he did.

—Edna Goodman

A woman remembered that as a little girl, after being "especially" good for a whole week, she asked her mother for a nickel for an ice cream cone when they came to town from the farm to trade. Her mother started to cry and said they could not afford it—no nickel could be spared.

No depression in people's memory had hit the entire country as hard as that of the 1930s. Some Coloradans and maybe a few Montanans might have argued that the silver crash and 1890s depression had been as bad or worse; however, this one affected everybody in some way.

The federal government response to previous depressions had always focused on staying solvent and letting the business community, and the nation at large, pull the country out of hard times. The magnitude of the 1930s crisis made such a plan impossible to achieve. One of the prophets of the 1920s prosperity, President Hoover, might preach about rugged individualism and give optimistic forecasts that "recovery" lurked just around the corner, but nothing did any good and recovery proved mighty evasive.

Newspaperwoman and writer Lorena Hickok came west in the summer of 1934 and sent reports to her boss, Harry Hopkins, who was in charge of the Civil Works Administration. A few excerpts depict the complexity and trauma of the day. When she visited Pueblo, Colorado, on June 24, she commented on the Colorado Fuel and Iron Company's decision to hire a few men and let the rest go on relief: "But what are you going to do? Let the families go hungry? And suppose, unable to live on what they are earning, they all quit and come on relief?" On June 25 she discussed another problem: "Apparently, even the irrigated area is going dry this summer! Very little snow in the mountains." Continuing on, she discussed the effort to help the coal miners whom the New Deal was trying to turn into prospectors. "They give them the rudiments of mineral mining, grubstake them, and let them go out into the hills prospecting for gold. They've had pretty good success with it, too." Nor was it just the coal miners and the steel workers; others were wandering about. "This transient thing is funny. Men, unable to get work in California and en route to the Kansas wheat fields, actually meet in Denver with men unable to get work in the Kansas wheat fields and on their way to California!" In Wyoming Hickok saw further problems and misplaced hope in a September 9 report. "They tell me they built airports in places in Wyoming where there isn't a Chinaman's chance of a plane landing once a year." Then she found some satisfied Wyoming cattlemen, one of whom stated, "Many of us are desperate, I think we'd just pack up and move out and leave our stock to starve if the government hadn't stepped in. This gives us new hope, to try again."[2]

Montana's situation proved no better. Cattleman Maynard Smith summarized his situation in this fashion. "We were trailing from ranch right to the packer, and those big old grass-fat steers brought three cents a pound! That was in 1933, the depths of the depression." Farther out on the High Plains, Gerald Hughes described the homesteaders' disaster: "You'll find old plows still layin' in the fields where the homesteaders walked away and left 'em." He aptly described the death of the nineteenth-century

American agricultural dream: "People thought you could just stick a plow in the ground and grow a crop."[3]

Understandably but unfairly in many ways, President Hoover received blame for much that happened after October 1929. He did not sit idly by, despite what critics claimed. He acted more aggressively and boldly to stem the collapse than any president before him. Initially, the president hoped voluntary cooperation of state and local governments, businesses, and individuals would stop the slide. Voluntary organizations would offer help to the destitute as long as food, supplies, and money remained. When these hopes failed, he took action. What worried Hoover and others who shared his belief was the concern that federal relief, the "dole," would undermine personal initiative and self-reliance.

His administration increased public works programs and created agencies such as the Reconstruction Finance Corporation, which loaned money to rescue banks, but it all came about too little and too late. Critics complained that when help arrived, it went to the country's largest banks and did nothing for unemployed workers and needy families. As a result, by 1932 the country faced the worst economic crisis in its history.

The year 1932 dawned and with it a presidential election. The Democrats nominated New York's activist, jaunty, debonair governor Franklin Delano Roosevelt (FDR), and a cheerless Republican convention nominated the hard-luck Hoover for a second term. The public knew Hoover, a sacrificial lamb on which to heap the country's woes. Somehow his warning that "grass will grow in the streets of a hundred cities" with a Democratic victory did not stir their souls. Instead, hitchhikers displayed signs that proclaimed, "If you don't give me a ride, I'll vote for Hoover," and the president found himself greeted in his home state of Iowa with the slogan "In Hoover we trusted, now we are busted."

Most voters did not know the newcomer Roosevelt. His intelligence and toughness they would learn, and his supreme speaking voice, a decided plus over the radio, they would quickly hear. To overcome concerns about his health, he responded with a 13,000-mile whirlwind campaign. Americans applauded when he said before his nomination, "The country needs and, unless I mistake its temper, the country demands bold, persistent experimentation. It is common sense to take a method and try it. If it fails, admit it frankly and try another. But above all, try something."[4]

That sentiment exemplified the charismatic Roosevelt to the core. He had no clear plan for what he would actually do if elected, but in accepting the nomination he stated, "I pledge you, I pledge myself to a new deal for the American people." Thus did a poker term come to define an American epic.

Although Rocky Mountain folk did not know Roosevelt either, they listened with great interest. Well, two out three did. Wyoming residents clung to Hoover's philosophy longer than those in the other two states and the rest of the country. Rugged individualism and self-help still had a home in those plains and mountains. Of all the forty-eight states, only Wyoming rejected the Reconstruction Finance Corporation's offer of loans for emergency relief. Editors and politicians might take pride in that stance, but it did not help solve anything.

Montanans, as rugged and individualistic as anyone, listened with more sympathy. Coloradans listened too, and in the end all three states voted for Roosevelt, as did thirty-nine other states. Democrats also sat in the governor's chair in the three Rocky Mountain States. More Democrats were in the U.S. Congress and state legislatures than ever before as well. It had been a Rockies Democratic uprising unseen since the silver and Populist upheaval in 1896.

Western politicians in both parties had endorsed FDR. He now wanted to repay them and to assist the stricken area, which he had seen firsthand while traveling during the campaign.

March 4, 1933, fell on a Saturday, and as the country and the Rocky Mountains awaited Roosevelt's inauguration, the national situation seemed bleaker than ever. Agricultural prices had sunk further, more businesses and banks were closing or teetering on the brink, some local governments had defaulted on debts while others hung on precariously, and relief burdens had become unbearable for towns, counties, and states. The country's economy and financial structure lay in shambles.

"The only thing we have to fear is fear itself," FDR boldly reminded Americans during his inaugural address. They expectantly awaited what might be coming next, and the sooner the better.

The New Deal barged through the nation's door with its three "Rs"— relief, recovery, and reform. The Rocky Mountain states had never seen its like before, and neither had the rest of the country. Whether one approved or disapproved of the plan, everyone was swept along.

Democratic Colorado governor Edwin Johnson ardently did not approve. As a conservative, he distrusted FDR and passionately disliked the New Deal, even went so far as to denounce it, an unusual step during these years. Federal relief programs, in his estimation, were a waste of time and interfered with local and state affairs. Only when it became obvious that Colorado would be left out of the recovery programs was he dragged reluctantly into accepting funds, and with them more government control and mandates. His attitudes did not change when Coloradans elected him to the Senate in 1936, where he would be a critic of Roosevelt and big government throughout the next two decades.

Big Ed Johnson also gained notoriety when he declared martial law and called the National Guard to the New Mexico border in 1936 to repel the invasion of "aliens, indigent persons or invaders." The "bum blockade" reflected his passionate states'-rights attitude. Colorado jobs were for Coloradans, he solemnly intoned. Amid strong protests and laughter, Big Ed finally backed down.

The three states would never be the same again as Washington vigorously moved west. Uncle Sam, who had always been a player, if not always welcomed, in the West, now played an even larger role than Washington's critics had feared it would be allowed to do. The remnants of the Populist party cheered.

The New Deal started during what became known as the 100 Days, the first months of FDR's administration. The key was the president himself. Roosevelt oozed confidence during his campaign and right into the White House. The country needed to hear and feel that confidence.

These unhappy times call for the building of plans . . . that build from the bottom up and not from the top down, that put their faith once more in the forgotten man at the bottom of the economic pyramid.
—From a radio address on April 7, 1932

We are moving forward to greater freedom, to greater security for the average man than he has ever known before in the history of America.
—From a Fireside Chat on September 30, 1934

What he meant quickly became apparent, because he knew that "the millions who are in want will not stand by silently forever while the things to satisfy their needs are within easy reach."

The day after his inauguration the president closed every bank—a bank holiday—in the country, and called a special session of Congress. He had an Emergency Banking Act ready when the members came into session on March 9. Congress energized itself as never before, and bills were passed in days, not weeks or months—including, among others, the Beer Act (legalizing beer and wine hopefully improved people's spirits), bills creating the Civilian Conservation Corps and the Federal Emergency Relief Administration, the Home Owners Refinancing Act, and the Agricultural Adjustment Act. An amazed public looked on with approval.

The Beer Act paved the way to repeal the infamous Eighteenth Amendment, with the Twenty-first Amendment ratified in December 1933. Some folks never forgave "that man" for his betrayal in bringing back "demon rum." The FDR haters carried their feelings on for years, and some even went so far as to never want that man's dime, with his image on it, in their pocket or purse.

Much to the dismay of many supporters, the great experiment in prohibition had failed miserably in the Rockies and elsewhere. It simply proved too hard to legislate people's morals, or to stop them from having a drink. Alas, that old western saloon never rebounded except as a tourist attraction. The past slipped away as the New Deal and the New West took over.

No doubt, most people felt relieved that the liquor experiment had ended. Nonetheless, a few were negatively affected. Hard-rock and coal miners and others had supplemented their generally meager incomes during the Depression by operating stills, which were, after all, easy to hide in old mines. Also, the liquor traffic had provided a little income for hard-pressed farmers who raised the grain the bootleggers purchased.

Meanwhile, Roosevelt, a charming extrovert and master of the radio, launched the first (Tuesday, March 14) of what became known as "Fireside Chats." He seemed to be speaking to each Coloradan, Montanan, and Wyomingite individually as he explained what was occurring with their banks and why.

The first thing FDR promised was that their banks would be reopened as soon as bank examiners found it sound to do so. Seventy percent had already opened by the time of his address. Amazingly, money came out of the mattresses, or wherever it was hidden, and the next day deposits exceeded withdrawals. Confidence in the banks returned to the Rockies. Some banks, however, never reopened, and depositors received only a percentage, if anything, of their deposited money.

With the matter of beer and the banks taken care of, the New Deal turned to other matters. For the Rocky Mountains, the Civil Works Administration (CWA), Works Progress Administration (WPA), and Public Works Administration (PWA) proved particularly valuable. The first provided help during the desperate winter of 1933–34, and the second built, renovated, or improved public buildings, streets, and parks and employed artists, musicians, writers, and others on countless projects to quickly get people working again. The much slower, carefully planned, and more expensive, PWA projects also included federal buildings, improvement of harbors, municipal waterworks, electric light systems, schoolhouses, and naval and coast guard ships. If these programs sometimes worked at cross-purposes, or on similar types of projects, that illustrated one of the contradictions of Roosevelt and the New Deal.

What did the New Deal do specifically for the Rocky Mountain West? The Farm Credit Administration extended low-interest loans to farmers and ranchers to help them to avoid mortgage foreclosures. The agency loaned some $78 million in Montana, for instance, during the first four years of its existence.

The Taylor Grazing Act (1934), named for its premier advocate, Colorado representative Edward Taylor, further brought Washington into westerners' lives. Along with the Taylor Grazing Act came an executive order (November 1934) that virtually ended homesteading, except on reclamation projects.

Together, the first comprehensive legislation to regulate grazing on public lands and the government's withdrawal of unreserved public lands from homestead entry until their usefulness as rangelands might be determined ended a freewheeling western epic. Dating back to the Civil War, the homestead epic had offered everyone the opportunity to be part of the American dream. No longer would public land be open for use by all comers; now its use would be restricted and managed.

The Grazing Act allowed organized groups of stockmen to lease federal lands cooperatively (under a renewable permit system limiting the number of livestock that were grazing), thus gaining reliable pasturage at a low cost. The cattlemen would also not have to worry about problems of ownership. However, the act created another federal agency that bedeviled conservatives — the Division of Grazing, under the Department of the Interior.

Colorado, for example, was divided into six "grazing districts." Licenses would have to be secured and fees paid to run cattle or sheep on public lands. The federal government hoped this arrangement would satisfy both groups (who in some areas still clung to old antagonisms toward each other) and at the same time prevent overgrazing and promote needed conservation of the land.

Some opposition appeared in all three states. The Wyoming Stock Growers Association, for example, passed a resolution against the plan. Its members bitterly attacked this "iniquitous measure" and the idea of Washington bureaucrats taking more control. Montana, though, went along with the idea and had created grazing districts even before the Taylor Act passed.

The act did help promote conservation. Many ranchers worked diligently to restore the prairie from the damage the land had suffered as a result of inexperienced homesteaders farming it. The range, they hoped, would rebound eventually.

A conservationist at heart, with a genuine regard for regional developments, Roosevelt traveled widely in the West during the 1930s. In a January 1935 message to Congress, he presented the crux of his concern. "Men and Nature must walk hand in hand. The throwing out of balance of the resources of nature throws out of balance the lives of men." To him, the use of natural resources was not singularly exclusive. It had to be combined, "something that is interwoven with industry, labor, finance, taxation, agriculture, homes, recreation, [and] good citizenship."[5]

The government also tried to encourage farmers to take better care of their land. Washington paid them to reduce acreage or to plant soil-conserving crops, both of which brought the benefit of restoring the land. Slowly, the idea of conservation gained a hold in the West, particularly as the dust blew and drought seared the land.

The New Deal eagerly tackled the Dust Bowl, with its storms and drought. Washington created the Resettlement Administration, which offered aid to destitute farm families hard hit by the Dust Bowl. That stopgap measure was followed by one of a more lasting nature, one of FDR's favorite ideas involving trees. Roosevelt, who understood the value of systematic tree planting to help prevent soil erosion, issued an executive order (1934) that earmarked $15 million to construct a shelter belt, in a gigantic, 100-mile-wide strip from Texas to the Canadian border. It would serve as a barrier against wind, snow, and dust and would also hold moisture in the soil.

Critics decried the idea as another boondoggle. Bernard DeVoto snorted sarcastically, "God couldn't grow trees in this country but Congress would." Stubbornly and determinedly, under the guidance of the Forest Service Civilian Conservation Corps staff (popularly nicknamed Roosevelt's "Tree Army") and others, trees were planted. All told, they planted more then 200 million trees. The "forests" stretched across the plains over 18,000 miles by 1942, when the project was turned over to the Soil Conservation Service, itself a New Deal innovation.

The federal government also took it upon itself to prevent soil erosion. Washington promoted contour plowing, crop rotation, and other agricultural methods and, as discussed, regulated grazing on public lands. Together, the various programs all helped bring the land, people, and environment back into more of a balance.

Dams, to store water, prevent flooding, and provide other benefits, also caught the attention of the New Dealers. The most famous and successful project, the Tennessee Valley Authority, gave birth to a similar idea for the Missouri River basin. Although Roosevelt, in 1937, urged Congress to approve the plan, it never did see the light of day, as opposition to New Deal programs mounted steadily, if somewhat hysterically, among conservatives. The region and the river's needs, however, did lead to a spectacular project on the upper Missouri River in eastern Montana—the Fort Peck Dam.

The project displayed the scope and magnitude of the New Deal. The idea was not new. Discussions about storing water and improving downstream navigation had occurred during the previous decade. Now the Army Corps of Engineers took over the planning for a dam to be located some twenty miles from the nearest community, Glasgow.

Early on, the corps planned the village of Fort Peck with barracks for workers, bathhouses, schools, mess halls, dormitories for single women, homes for families, a business district, and recreational facilities. The first families moved in during September 1934, followed by thousands desperately hoping to find work in this lonely spot of eastern Montana.

There were arrivals like Seth Woodruff, who brought his bride to faraway Montana from Vicksburg, Mississippi. He would be one of the many engineers on the project; his twin daughters would be born there, and this New Deal project gave them their start in life. That symbolized the heart of what Roosevelt hoped would happen. The New Deal would positively affect individuals, communities, states, and the nation.

The town of Fort Peck would not be alone. Wheeler, New Deal, Delano Heights, and Park Grove temporarily blossomed nearby. These shantytowns provided services—saloons, brothels, gambling parlors—the government would not allow in Fort Peck, as well as other businesses such as laundries and barbershops.

At peak employment, 11,000 or so workers labored under often less than ideal conditions; some even called them deplorable. With temperatures ranging from a summertime 100 degrees to minus fifty in winter, life was seldom dull. The immense earthen dam, at the time the largest earthen dam in the world, ran nearly four miles in length and stood 250 feet high. A lake 16 miles wide and 189 miles long stretched out behind it.

Finished in October 1940, the dam had already gained a measure of fame when a photograph of its spillway graced the cover of *Life* magazine's first issue, in November 1936. The project also included construction of a power plant, begun in 1939, that four years later started generating electricity. Meantime, as 1940 ebbed, the residents left for other work or to join the military.

FDR visited the Fort Peck Dam twice during construction; the place was "dressed up" when he toured. On his way there for a 1934 visit, he saw a sign that stated, "You gave us beer, now give us water." With his usual sense of humor, Roosevelt quipped, "Well, the beer part was easy."[6] "Our Dam," as Montanans called it with pride, provided recreation, water storage, and flood control. It also eliminated wild water fluctuations downstream. The Missouri River, once nicknamed the "Harlot" because it changed its bed so often, would be more contained, benefiting downriver states.

The Fort Peck Dam, and those similar to it built throughout the West in the 1930s, stood as symbols of hope and progress. Critics railed about the expense, need, and "communistic" tendencies, which these projects engendered in their minds, but there would be no turning back.

Colorado gained an equally spectacular, gigantic development with what became known as the Colorado–Big Thompson Project. For several generations visionary Coloradans had dreamed of taking water from the water-rich Western Slope, beyond the Rockies, through a transmontane diversion and moving it to the northeastern part of the state—a rich farmland handicapped by too little water. Money problems and lack of technological skills to tunnel under the Rockies had stymied such plans, and when it had been discussed in the 1920s, the state did not have the resources.

Now, in the 1930s, the New Deal rode to the rescue, although not without numerous local concerns and objections. Western Slope residents protested loud and long about not wanting to lose their water; predictions appeared that farmers on the Eastern Slope could never repay their debt, and it was feared that the project would irrevocably mar nature's beauty. Critics also thought the project represented another boondoggle, a favorite anti–New Deal criticism. Proponents argued that electricity generated by the dams would help offset the cost, that the electric power would be used all over the state, and that the project would create jobs and help Colorado in the future. The Reclamation Bureau promised to clear all debris and maintain water at its usual levels.

Northeastern Colorado, which stood to benefit greatly from this project—initially the most of any region—appeared particularly hard-hit by the long-lasting drought. As one person commented, with everyone broke, "They don't even bother to have tax sales. The land isn't worth it."[7]

The most serious obstacle of the plan, however, came with the Eastern Slope–Western Slope split in the congressional delegation. The latter, as part of the bargain for its giving up water, wanted dams and reservoirs; the former hesitated to pay for them and add to the project's cost. Fortunately, the two factions neared a compromise, and just in time. Other states, particularly Oklahoma, complained that Colorado had already received far more than its fair share of reclamation funds. Eastern Slope leaders finally agreed to the plan, and in 1937 the bill passed Congress with President Roosevelt signing it on December 28.

The gigantic project, the largest construction project undertaken by the Reclamation Bureau to date, would take nearly nine years to complete, with time off for World War II. The Western Slope gained two dams and reservoirs plus recreational areas, and the Eastern Slope now had its water. The water was pumped to Grand Lake, then through a thirteen-mile tunnel under the Continental Divide, and eventually through a power plant. Finally, it reached the Big Thompson River and the plains and farmers' fields and city homes. Ultimately, four more power plants were constructed to complete the project. The Colorado–Big Thompson Project triggered the first major twentieth-century east-west Colorado fight. Traditionally, Eastern Slopers, those who lived along the Rockies from Fort Collins to Pueblo, had tended to flex their population and political muscles and pay little attention to the cries of the politically impotent and smaller-in-number Western Slopers. It proved to be only the beginning of an ongoing and often heated water war. Similar controversies would flare elsewhere in the Rockies in the years to follow.

In Wyoming, the PWA had a plan to make the North Platte River yield more irrigation water and power for the eastern part of the state. This, too, had been discussed the decade before, but the plan ran into the same types of problems the Colorado–Big Thompson Project had. Some Wyomingites were just as leery of Uncle Sam and of their neighbors. Two dams would provide power and storage, but they also sparked debates in both Nebraska and Colorado. Even some other Wyoming water users joined in the fray for fear of losing water rights. The Kendrick Project, as it would be named, was stopped, then restarted in 1935. The number of acres planned for irrigation, meantime, was sliced nearly in half, to 35,000 acres.

The conflicts over water on this overappropriated river were not resolved until after the war. No solution was found, and, unlike the project on the Colorado River, the case finally ended in the United States Supreme Court. The Court's decision limited Colorado and Wyoming as to how much water they could divert or store. The project, unfortunately, never met its boosters' expectations and proved less than a success economically. Only 20,000 or so acres were irrigated by the 1960s, and the crops produced barely seemed enough to justify the expense, hard work, and fuss.

Most New Deal programs proved neither as spectacular nor as controversial as these. The Colorado Historical Society, for instance, found itself a Depression victim. It was short of funds and facing a state legislature considering abolishing it as a financial measure, to help a depleted Colorado budget. It survived, thanks to a variety of help from the New Deal, from grants to establishing new programs. With the Civil Works Administration, followed by the Works Progress Administration, federal funds rode to the rescue starting in 1933–1934. With plenty of skilled workers and professionals looking for work, it was easy to undertake a multitude of projects. The PWA funded an intriguing selection. Interviewing pioneers, indexing collections, cataloging photographs, copying manuscripts, and similar projects were all programs the society accomplished or at least started.

The Works Progress Administration provided further money for continuing projects already started and adding others, some very ambitious. Perhaps no single facet of the New Deal impacted people of the Rocky Mountain region as much as the WPA. Designed to both create jobs and make worthwhile public improvements, its scope touched nearly everyone. White-collar, blue-collar, skilled, semiskilled, unskilled, and professional people worked for the WPA. New high school auditoriums, gyms, libraries, stadiums, bandshells, bridges, playgrounds, and parks, to name just a few, resulted from the program.

For example, as part of the writers' project of the WPA, the guidebooks *Colorado: A Guide to the Highest State*; *Wyoming: A Guide to Its History, Highways, and People*; and *Copper Camp* (Butte) were published, as well as numerous other state histories. Perhaps one of the most popular projects, the highly praised Colorado history dioramas, became part of the historical society's museum exhibits.

Several Civilian Conservation Corps boys, guided by rangers and others, produced dioramas at Mesa Verde that have been a well-liked feature of the park's museum ever since. These illustrate only a tiny sampling of the scope of projects the region's national parks gained from a variety of New Deal programs.

Roosevelt's favorite projects were the CCC, national parks, and conservation. With all three, he sought to preserve and restore the nation's land and heritage. Not only did the New Deal work with parks, it also established conservation refuges. The government, for example, withdrew land near Jackson Hole, Wyoming, from grazing permits and set it aside for winter range for elk. Montana profited too, securing more federal wildlife refuge ranges than any other western state but one.

Montana, meanwhile, gained in another way as well. Glacier National Park, like Mesa Verde, was too isolated for most 1930s cost-conscious tourists. It received a boost, however, when an agreement between Canada and the United States established the Waterton-Glacier International Peace Park. The two parks sit side by side on the border, adding a further reason to visit Glacier.

Wyoming benefited also. During the early 1930s, the Jackson Hole plans of Horace Albright and John D. Rockefeller Jr. started to gain momentum. By 1933, Rockefeller had purchased 33,000 acres in the northern part of Jackson Hole. He did it secretly, through his Snake River Land Company. Locals ferreted out the plan, however, and objections quickly surfaced about dictatorial, wealthy "easterners" taking advantage of westerners and locking up natural resources, thus depriving locals of developing and utilizing them. This heated fight took over a decade to resolve. An old battle, it touched the fears of westerners at every point from withdrawing land to favoring animals over people and easterners forcing their will on westerners.

Rocky Mountain National Park, meanwhile, faced two problems involving animals. One involved the poaching of deer, a not uncommon problem in the desperate Depression years. The other problem was the overpopulation of elk and deer, which finally led to culling some of the herds, over animal lovers' protests.

Interestingly, Rocky Mountain National Park had a continued stream of tourists during the Depression, unlike Mesa Verde and some other parks. Perchance, it offered a day or two of easy escape from the hard times for nearby folk, particularly those from Denver and its neighbors. A trip to Mesa Verde would take more time and money for most people than one to Rocky Mountain National Park.

Like the other parks, Rocky Mountain had a contingent of Civilian Conservation Corps youth. The first CCC group arrived in May 1933, to be greeted by a howling blizzard and short supplies. In the years that followed, they did what their counterparts did elsewhere and made a positive impact on the park. They cut and removed beetle-infested trees, built and improved trails, restored land, improved campgrounds, and performed scores of other jobs.

As in much of the American West, the most popular New Deal program among most Wyomingites, Coloradans, and Montanans was the CCC.

It had received broad, bipartisan support when enacted, something the agency never lost throughout the decade. With young people stagnating, bewildered, and even angry over their Depression-locked lives, something desperately needed to be done. For Roosevelt and many others, the Civilian Conservation Corps provided an excellent way to get youths out of unemployment, and into a healthful, beneficial environment. Mostly men served in the CCC, but a few women joined as well elsewhere in the country.

Wyoming had nineteen camps, and the young people, as elsewhere, did everything from eliminating rodents to building trails. They worked in Yellowstone and Grand Teton, and the state benefited in a variety of ways before the program ended in 1942.

Wyoming presented an unusual, perhaps unique, challenge to the CCCers. In the Gillette area a number of coal mines caught on fire. The CCC tackled seventeen smoldering mines, putting seven fires out and getting the remainder under control by the late 1930s. They sealed mines, covering them with sand and shale; or, if nothing else worked, they dug out the burning material. All told, this proved some of the most dangerous work the CCC did.

The CCC was popular not only in the Rocky Mountains; it seemed to have universal appeal. The *Chicago Tribune*, January 16, 1935, never to be confused with a charter member of the FDR fan club, had this to say: "The CCC is one of the best projects of the administration and the great majority of its recruits, we believe, appreciate its opportunities and are being benefited."

Some CCC enrollees at Mesa Verde National Park reminisced about their experiences years later. What they had to say would likely represent all those who went through the camps. They catch the flavor and spirit of both an era and the Civilian Conservation Corps, and they explain its significance to individuals as well as its larger impact.[8]

Jim Holsten's experiences were familiar to others of his generation. "I was in trouble in school when I quit and went in. It gave me something to do and I settled down. There was a lot of hard work but it was fun. I got out to go back to school [and] I graduated." Commenting about his daily routine he went on to say. "Oh, we had sometimes at noon—spaghetti, chicken, whatever the mess sergeant made up [for] the menu—salads, cakes, bread, desserts. Sick call every morning. Our hours were from 8 to 4:30. Barrack three was all Spanish."

"I drove a dump truck hauling dirt into the headquarters' loop and was supervised by park employees," remembers Herman Wagner. "I carried trash, tree limbs away from the side of the road so that tourists couldn't see it. The CCC cleared the brush away from under the power line. For a short time I helped with the porcupine elimination crew. Lots of trees were damaged by the porcupines."

Joe Espinoza worked three year through 1937. "I worked on the trees and landscaping. I worked on trails down to Spruce Tree House. In the winter we used to take down the dead trees. When we went to supper we had to wear a tie. If we did not have a tie, they would not feed us."

Durangoan Coyne Thompson used his CCC money to go on to college. For him, his experience had been "a growing-up education. By the time you left, you were able to cope with the world at large." Satisfied his experience was good for him, Thompson went on to say, "there wasn't any doubt about that. And one thing about it was that everybody was in the same financial predicament and you didn't feel embarrassed, because there wasn't anybody who was any other way."

The government authorized one fascinating segment of the CCC, the Indian Division. It came into existence a few months after the initial organization of recruits in 1933. The Indian Division was for males only, married or not, and the camps (single and mixed family camps) were located on reservations. Enrollees were not required to live in camps and could commute from their homes, if feasible, while in remote camps, families might accompany the men. The goal was to have them work under Native American bosses and supervisors—qualified tribal members, it was hoped—whenever possible.

The western reservations featured some of the worst poverty in the country. To make matters worse, many of the men tragically lacked the skills to move beyond that poverty and alleviate their individual and tribal despair. They were locked in a despondency and a dependent lifestyle that often created a gloomy outlook for the future.

The program contained the same general CCC goals of learning marketable skills and improving the work ethic. It also hoped to improve tribal resources on the reservations and to improve both future reservation economic possibilities and individual job skills. Still, the program never intended to make the enrollees walk the white man's road. The program encouraged them to retain their traditions and cultural heritage, and they received leave to pursue traditional and tribal activities.

Nearly 15,000 people lived on the seven Montana reservations, many in nearly abject poverty. Their superintendents served as relief administrators, assisted by social workers and Native American aides. Relief came on the basis of individual or family needs, not to the tribe in general, as had been the common practice prior to the New Deal.

The Indian Division undertook both temporary and long-term work projects. The projects were launched after selecting Indian men and giving them leadership instruction in the winter of 1934. Before the CCC ended, nearly 77,000 Native Americans found employment within the Indian Division through the popular CCC programs.

These CCCers worked on projects similar to those throughout the CCC, for example, clearing trees, fighting fires, constructing lookout towers, and building roads. On Montana's Flathead Reservation, the Jocko Camp became a home away from home for many. A priest visited every week, and a school was built for the children, who put on a popular Christmas pageant.

To keep people and parents informed, the camp published a monthly newspaper edited by the students, which included such homey items as this, from a student reporter, in the February 2, 1935, edition: "A porch has been added to the north door of the school house. We appreciate this very much, because it does away with a great deal of mud and water, which formerly accumulated at this entrance." Perhaps more exciting to the teenagers: "The usual weekly dance was held Friday and was well attended."[9] Besides dances, basketball, hiking, and ping-pong, a variety of family activities helped pass the time.

The long-range impact on the men involved in the Indian Division varied. Those who took the training program seriously improved their lives; however, many returned to idleness and poverty once the program ended. When World War II started, the skills acquired through the CCC did open war-industry jobs for them. For the Flathead reservation, in general, the program provided temporary work and income and put food on the table, helping residents get through the Depression's worst days. Some recreational sites, such as those constructed at Flathead Lake — one of Montana's most beautiful lakes — aided tourism. The long-term effects, however, proved more individual than tribal.

Far to the south at Ignacio, Colorado, the Southern Utes benefited from the CCC as well, including having dorms built at their school. The Utes, too, worked on a variety of projects, some of them "make-work" and others of a permanent nature. Unlike the Flatheads, the Ute reservation included a tri-ethnic mix of whites, Hispanics, and Utes—all of whom benefited from the CCC efforts.

The New Deal impacted tribes in other ways. John Collier, commissioner of Indian Affairs, decided that the best way to help the tribes was to restore tribal rights and practices. This policy included stopping the sale of Indian lands and ending attempts to try to have them walk the white man's trail. He sought to put boarding schools out of business and to establish day schools near the students' homes. Collier insisted that all agency officials respect tribal customs. Under his guidance, the United States Health Service paid increasing attention to reservation problems. New Deal agencies aided immensely in achieving these goals.

Federal legislation also made other gains possible. The Johnson-O'Malley Act (April 1934) called for the cooperation of federal, state, and local governments in providing Indians with the same services available to everyone else, including education, health, relief, and welfare. A second act in June stopped the individual allotment program, set in motion more benefits for the tribes, and gave preference to Native American candidates within the Indian Service. These milestone enactments helped turn the corner in the development of Indian rights and their twentieth-century history.

The New Deal and the CCC also proved a turning point for Indian women. For example, they were given the right to vote in tribal elections and to hold office under the 1934 Indian Reorganization Act. Trained for other occupations and professions, such as nursing, teaching, and secretarial work, women found jobs in the CCC and the WPA projects.

By 1941, this multiple approach had revived tribal authority, which consequently played an increasingly important role on the reservations. In general, reservation leadership became more integrated in relation to federal and state governments. However, these leaders and their fellow tribal members still faced a long struggle before some of the goals of the New Deal would finally be realized.

Nearly as popular as the CCC, except perhaps with electric and power companies, was the Rural Electrification Administration (REA). Because companies weighed construction costs against fewer customers out in the country, rural Americans saw electric lines fall short of reaching them. Without electricity, they were left out of much of modern America. Only 10 percent of American farms, for example, had electricity the year after the REA was authorized in 1935.

The REA lent money to cooperatives to generate and distribute electricity to isolated rural areas not served by private utilities. Jobs opened up, out went the crews, and in came the electric lines. Out went kerosene lamps and in came the improved safety, brightness, and ease of electric lights. Young children were thunderstruck when they turned on a switch in their farmhouses and a light popped on—no more "Don't touch the kerosene lamp!" Looking down with equal amazement from Mesa Verde, park employees watched the advance of electricity across the Montezuma Valley at night as the lights twinkled from farm to ranch and marched steadily across the valley over a period of months.

Two things happened as a result of the REA. First and foremost, rural Americans finally came into the twentieth century and improved their quality of life in many ways. Second, rather interestingly, private companies suddenly discovered a new market into which to stretch their lines.

Rural Rocky Mountaineers finally had electricity. Radios, electric lights, milking machines, washing machines, electric ranges, and various other home and farm electric-powered equipment eased life in the rural West. An illustration of what this meant: 527 Wyoming ranches and farms had electricity in 1935; the REA increased that number to 3,300 by 1939. In the same period the number in Montana jumped from 2,768 to 6,000. In both states, and in Colorado, that represented only the beginning. Rural electrical cooperatives joined the REA in providing electricity to nearly every farm and ranch over the next generation. Soon, "lights twinkled," as one person described it, in the once-dark rural homes and farms.

Some simple things that city folk took for granted, now their country cousins gained. Electric water pumps provided running water in homes for kitchens and the addition of real bathrooms. The radio brought news, current crop prices, soap operas, sporting events, weather reports, and popular comedy shows to brighten the days of farmers, ranchers, and their families. With the radio and the telephone (mostly multicustomer party

lines, on which nosey neighbors could listen in to conversations!), isolation disappeared and the modern world emerged. Life on the farm would
never be the same again.

Wyoming received help from the New Deal despite the criticism
some locals heaped upon the "socialism" that was ruining the character
of America. WPA projects improved schools and built playgrounds and
athletic facilities in coal camps, also providing jobs for the out-of-work
miners. The Public Works Administration built post offices, the University
of Wyoming's student union, and thirty-three schools across the state.
Highway construction boomed, and the National Youth Administration
offered jobs to high school and college students aged sixteen to twenty-
four, as it did throughout the region, at thirty cents per hour.

The state also received two reclamation projects besides Kendrick
and had another approved just before the war began. Wyoming felt it
deserved help because its oil reserves pumped a large amount of money
into the reclamation fund.

Colleges received money from various New Deal programs. They,
in turn, provided jobs for students to help cover necessary expenses. For
example, at Fort Lewis Junior College near Durango, Colorado, students
milked cows, shoveled sidewalks, worked in the cafeteria, and filled various other jobs that benefited both them and the institution. The New
Deal's variety and sweep of programs was truly amazing.

The depressed mining industry was not left out of the New Deal's
cornucopia of blessings. Western silver interests had been fighting for
federal support since the 1870s, only to face continual disappointment.
Both the demand and the price had been shrinking (down to twenty-
five cents an ounce by 1933), and what mines remained were struggling.
Montana, Colorado, and other silver-producing states wanted federal
help. It sounded like the generation before the emotional 1890s.

During the 1932 campaign, Roosevelt had promised to do something
for silver. The silver bloc did, in fact, gain more than it had for years.
With the International Silver Agreement in December 1933, the United
States and other countries pledged to buy silver at sixty-four cents per
ounce. While it did not produce all the desired or expected results, the
higher price helped those mines still operating and stimulated some
prospecting. Miners, shippers, and silver mining communities received a
measure of prosperity thanks to Washington.

Gold mining also received a boost in a similar manner when the United States went off the gold standard in January 1934. Initially, in March 1933, the federal government had prohibited banks domestically from paying out gold in exchange for gold certificates. Then the government nationalized gold, and Americans could no longer own it except in rare coins. Gold coinage stopped, and all gold coins had to be turned in for dollars. All this occurred because the government was about to raise the price of gold to thirty-five dollars an ounce from its previous price of just over twenty dollars.

Financial wizards generally found all this most fascinating; Rocky Mountain prospectors and miners did not worry themselves about fine points. Gold mining revived, and so did prospecting. If a prospector could find even a small portion of an ounce of gold per day, that exceeded the typical Depression day's income. A problem emerged, however; few retained either the skills needed for prospecting or the knowledge of where best to look. The New Deal sponsored, and some states actually conducted, classes to teach neophytes the rudiments—what to look for and how to pan. The jackass prospector of the nineteenth century would have laughed!

What, then, can be said about the New Deal and the Rockies as the decade came to a close? There were those who cried dictatorship and socialism. Some, according to Lorena Hickok in a September 9 letter to Harry Hopkins, were not unhappy about the latter possibility: "I have some more rather interesting dope. I still get more and more, that impression that they [people] are expecting a big change in our whole economic system." What did they see coming? "Socialism, many of them say—and that the President couldn't stop it if he tried."

Socialism did not occur, but big change did. The New Deal had lifted the Rocky Mountain states out of the Depression and started them on the road to a more prudent use of their resources. Conservation, public power, directed natural resources development, improved transportation systems, recreational expansion, and a better standard of living for all were part of the legacy that lived beyond the 1930s.

The New Deal helped stabilize and broaden the Rockies' economic base and break the region's major dependence on extraction industries that supplied raw materials. As such, it laid the basis for the Rocky Mountain states to take off in the following years in the areas of economy, population, standard of living, and job variety. Eventually, a greater mea-sure of equality with other parts of the country would be achieved.

Indeed, the New Deal produced a more profound impact on the West than it did on any other region of the United States. Westerners received more money from Uncle Sam for work relief, loans, and welfare than people in any other section of the country. They also benefited from coherent planning that transformed agriculture, water, conservation, and Indian policies. Beguilingly, and of long-range significance, the federal government's growing involvement in the Rockies proved the "main agent of the liberation from dependence on eastern capital," as historian Richard White has forcefully argued.

With this liberation came an expanded role for Washington in the entire region that soon became an integral part of western life. Many, if not most, westerners realized that problems could not be solved simply though state and regional action alone; the federal government needed to be a partner. Federal rules, plans, and regulations did not always sit well with individualistic westerners of all political and economic persuasions, but there would be no turning back. The old love-hate relationship with Washington, which received sharper focus and continued criticism, did not vanish as the years passed. Deep in the westerners' psyche individual-ism had long held sway. That independent-minded, rugged individualism needed to be maintained in many people's minds to preserve their West. This had been the Old West of both fact and fiction for both westerners and many others, a cherished image. Nevertheless, the birth of the new Rocky Mountain West loomed close at hand.

The Rocky Mountain States
A *Photographic Essay*

The popular image of Colorado, Montana, and Wyoming involves mountains—mountains for vacations, for skiing, for water, for natural resources, for second homes, and a variety of other "fors." But these three states have more plains than mountains, as well as a dash of plateaus and deserts. Nor were they, in the twentieth century, a romanticized frontier, except perhaps in the tourists' eyes. Instead, in many ways they—particularly Colorado—represented a land in transformation. They did not march to the same drummer, nor did they grow at the same pace. Yet what each did was to leave behind a photographic record of yesterday. Thus the reader may drop back into a distant and a not-so-distant past.

Mesa Verde represented the long story of human history in the region. It also became the first national park set aside to honor people and was eventually designated as the initial World Cultural Park.

Ouray, Colorado, represented both the past and the future, when William Henry Jackson took this photograph around 1900. Mining gave it birth, but tourism, thanks to the scenery and hot springs, gave it life.

The railroad opened the Rockies in a variety of ways, from ease of transportation to tourism and urbanization. A train pauses briefly at the railroad stop of Jennings, Montana, at the century's turn.

The rural school, whether one room or several, brought education to generations of Rocky Mountain children. "Reading, writing, and arithmetic" were the staples. Now the Rockies are one of the most highly educated sections of the country.

An early-twentieth-century farmer in Big Horn County, Wyoming, had high hopes, but reality soon set in, with low farm prices and worries about drought.

Out on the eastern plains, homesteaders tried to capture their part of the American dream. In the first twenty years of the century, they built their homes and towns and planted their crops. Then drought, low farm prices, and isolation killed the dream.

From Colorado through Wyoming and into Montana, the cowboy rode
to work—and eventually galloped into one of the West's premier legends.
As the song "The Old Chisholm Trail" had it, he was up in the morning
before daylight, and before he slept the moon shined bright.

Oil stirred men's souls and was another
natural resource that the Rockies contained in
abundance through the century. This mobile
drilling rig mounted on wagon wheels traveled
around Wyoming in the World War I era.

The nineteenth-century folk song "The Bold Miner" clearly described the coal miner's life: "He's sweating and toiling his every day round. He strains and he pines his poor life away." Coal, though, was essential in the rise of modern America, and plenty of it rested in the Rockies.

Yellowstone National Park, the nation's first, gained popularity throughout the century. The train initially eased its isolation; then the automobile arrived, and tourism became an economic pillar here and throughout the Rockies.

Agriculture was seeking a cash crop and found it with sugar beets. The Holly Sugar Corporation's factories started in Colorado, spread to Wyoming, and eventually moved into Montana and west to California. This plant was located in Sheridan, Wyoming.

Westerners were never shy about staging a parade, a celebration, or a
day honoring their past, however recent that past might have been. Miles
City, Montana, celebrated July 4, 1935, with a parade and fireworks.

The past was also "honored" in the ghost towns that dotted the mountains and were even more prolific out on the plains. South Pass, Wyoming, never had been much of a mining district but had become a tourist attraction by the 1930s.

The traumatic 1930s were a watershed for the region and the country. In rode Franklin Roosevelt and his New Deal. Nothing, among the sweeping programs that changed the country forever was more popular than the Civilian Conservation Corps. Here, a CCC crew is relaxing after a day's work.

High View Showing New Town-Site Fort Peck Mont.

The New Deal had great plans for the Missouri River Basin, but cost, political opposition, and the worsening international situation ended most of them. Not so Montana's Fort Peck Dam and the town it created.

Full of Victorian houses and buildings, Georgetown, Colorado, awaited a second boom in the 1950s. It was coming with skiing, new residents, and tourism. The completion of Interstate 70 and the Eisenhower Tunnel boomed the state and town.

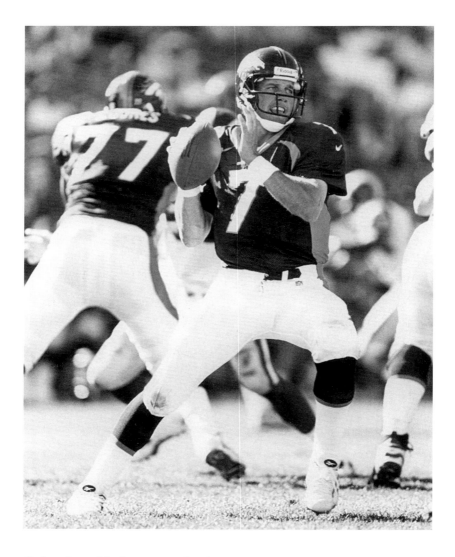

Colorado grabbed a monopoly of major league sports in the Rockies.
No athlete has been more popular than the Denver Broncos' quarterback
John Elway, who led his team to two Super Bowl victories.

Not gold and silver but uranium, coal, and copper sparked twentieth-century mining. Nothing proved larger, nor longer lasting, than the Anaconda Copper operations in Butte, Montana. The Berkeley pit was one of the world's largest copper mines.

The West is dotted with abandoned hopes and failed dreams. This ranch was located north of Cheyenne and could just as well have been in eastern Colorado or Montana, or in the mountains.

The Old West lives on in the ever popular rodeo. From this small one in
Encampment, Wyoming, to the "granddaddy of them all," Cheyenne
Frontier Days, tourists and locals flock to watch the fun.

The Rockies have much to save environmentally, and much to lose if a vigilant watch is not maintained. Its national parks provide regional crown jewels. A mountain goat looks over tranquil Hidden Lake in Glacier National Park.

The plains are being abandoned, and the mountains overcrowded.
With the surrounding land often controlled by the Bureau of Land
Management or the Forest Service, towns like beautifully situated
Durango, Colorado, find the price of land and homes skyrocketing.
Indeed, the average salaried individual cannot afford to live in communi-
ties like Aspen, Telluride, Vail, and others scattered among the Rockies.

CHAPTER 6

World War II and the New West
1940 to 1945

> Yesterday, December 7, 1941—a date which will live in infamy—the
> United States of America was suddenly and deliberately attacked by
> the naval and air forces of the Empire of Japan.
> —President Franklin D. Roosevelt, December 8, 1941,
> address to Congress

STUNNED WESTERNERS could not believe what had happened. Anger
soon replaced disbelief for the vast majority. Revenge was on their minds,
as well fear of the unknown future, as they turned off their radios that
bleak December day. Pearl Harbor unified American opinion as nothing
else could have. Although that Sunday morning raid damaged American
naval power, it also greatly stimulated and strengthened the nation's
determination to carry through a grim, now necessary, task of entering
and winning a war. It did not take years to build up an excited "Over
There" spirit of the earlier World War conflict, no longer called the
Great War, to permeate America. The country instead instantly gained a
determined, unwavering resolve to successfully carry the conflict through
to victory.

Concern, sometimes near panic, quickly grew about saboteurs and
spies. Aspen, Colorado, blamed the Japanese for shooting out its streetlights a week after Pearl Harbor. Probably local boys with BB guns were
to blame. Montanans worried about sabotage in the copper mines, and
Wyomingites were concerned about the railroads. The *Glenwood Post*
(October 22, 1942) warned its readers that great damage could be done by
"pyromaniacs" in the tinder-dry forests. With manpower short because of
the war, firefighters were scarce.

Fears aside, once again America marched off to war, a war that would
complete the transformation of Wyoming, Colorado, and Montana that

the New Deal had started. For the Rocky Mountain states and western-ers in general, World War II was a turning point in their history. When the country emerged from the conflict in the late summer of 1945, a new Rocky Mountain region confidently faced the future. After those water-shed years, there would be no turning back.

As the United States entered the war, though, the Rocky Mountain states' economies were less than booming, although they were doing better than during the depths of the Depression. The region's manu-facturing contributions to the country's economy were negligible. Many westerners also felt discriminated against by easterners, particularly in the realms of manufacturing, railroads, and financial institutions. They remained country cousins socially and culturally, at least in easterners' opinions. However, change was coming.

Agriculture and mining regained their status as economic pillars to supply wartime needs. The pattern continued of shipping out raw mate-rials to be processed in the East, which were then sent back as manu-factured goods. The West's colonial status had yet to be discarded; nev-ertheless, for the time being that worry did not arouse discussion. A war needed to be won.

Long before Pearl Harbor, the farsighted had seen a war coming, if still somewhat low on the horizon. The rise of militaristic Germany and expansionist Japan in the 1930s constituted serious warnings, and even Italy's misadventures in aggression should have raised concern. Hitler's attack on Poland in September 1939, soon joined by the Soviet Union in dividing that unfortunate country, destroyed illusions about Germany, Stalin's communism, and the general European state of affairs. Japan, in need of oil and other supplies, started making demands in the Pacific area and was already fighting a several-year-old war in China. Within months, these events drastically changed the economic and world situation.

The Rocky Mountain West had its share of vocal isolationists, from its leaders to the press to the general public. To them 1917 had been a mis-take, with lives sacrificed to benefit munitions manufacturers and others who profited monetarily from this tragedy. They fervently believed this new war was not the business of the United States, and noisily objected when Congress appropriated money for national defense. They blamed President Roosevelt for this "internationalism," much as many had opposed the "socialist" New Deal once the dark days of 1933–34 faded into history.

By the end of 1940 the defense budget topped $10 billion, and the spending jump-started the national economy as nothing had done in several decades, even as far west as the Rockies. When Congress passed America's first peacetime Selective Service Act in September 1940, young men became liable for the draft. American neutrality ended in 1941 months before Pearl Harbor, with "lend-lease" to aid the hard-pressed English under heavy attack by the Luftwaffe. Then American naval ships hunted German submarines in the Atlantic.

Montana gained unfavorable publicity when its extreme isolationist senior senator Burton Wheeler prominently led the fight against Roosevelt's policies for breaking American neutrality. With words that came back to haunt, Wheeler branded lend-lease as an attempt to "plow under every fourth American boy" like Roosevelt's farm policies did corn and hogs in the previous decade. Then, ironically, pacifist Jeannette Rankin, back in the House of Representatives for a second term, cast the lone vote against American entry into the war, noting, "This time I stand alone." In 1917, she recalled, fifty members of Congress had voted against the war. Actions and comments such as those led to bitter name calling, including "political Fuzzy-Wuzzy" and "Japanette."[1]

All this faded as young men began to volunteer or were drafted into the armed forces. Young women would eventually volunteer as well, in the WAC (Women's Army Corps) and WAVES (Navy), for instance, as the war was about to generate a revolution in the role of women in America. Although barred from combat, women were not necessarily protected from danger. Captured in the Philippines and as nurses accompanying troops in combat in Europe and elsewhere, women came under fire and suffered in prisoner-of-war camps. Equality had not arrived; their pay averaged less than soldiers' typical pay.

Before the war concluded, women would perform in virtually every capacity once reserved for men, from the popular "Rosie the Riveter" image to leadership in various fields. According to government posters, "Rosie" was "making history working for victory," but so were all women—from the assembly line to farm tractors to offices, both civilian and military. They had done some of these jobs before during wartime as far back as the Civil War, but this time many women seemed less inclined simply to return to roles and occupations laid out for them in peacetime. The issues of equal status in pay and position would echo down the rest of the century.

Meanwhile on the home front, western families awaited the dreaded telegrams conveying the news of loved ones missing or killed in action. Letters from the wounded raised fears and hopes simultaneously. Young western men fought everywhere. They died at Pearl Harbor, patrolled for German submarines in the North Atlantic, crippled the Japanese war effort throughout the Pacific with their submarines, and flew bombing raids over Europe. They fought Japanese planes at the Battle of Midway and sank four carriers, ending the threat to Hawaii and the West Coast.

They landed at Normandy, freed Paris, and charged up Mount Suribachi on Iwo Jima. They suffered from Japanese kamikaze suicide attacks in the Pacific and in prisoner-of-war camps in Germany and throughout the Japanese empire. They turned back the Germans in the Battle of the Bulge, liberated Berlin, and fought a bitter winter campaign in Italy. In the heat, humidity, and jungles of Guadalcanal and scores of lesser-known islands, they faced an enemy that did not surrender. Eventually, they enjoyed V-E Day and V-J Day, and the survivors returned home.

The cold statistics tell what happened to those who went to war. The War Department listed 1,553 Montanans missing or dead, whereas Wyoming lost 1,095, and Colorado nearly 2,700 out of 138,832 men and women in the state who enlisted or were drafted. When it was finally over, they had changed the world and found life changed in the old hometown when they returned after the war.

For its impact on the postwar West, one group in particular stands out—the Tenth Mountain Division. This was the elite ski corps that trained in the Colorado mountains at Camp Hale, between Leadville and Aspen, in 1942 and 1943. The beautiful mountains and their snow conditions stuck with them throughout the years that followed. When the men finally arrived in Europe, they were thrown into the bitter, brutally fought Italian campaign and became a highly decorated unit. After the war, many of these veterans returned and became the backbone of several major Colorado ski resorts, as the sport escalated in popularity as never seen in earlier years throughout the Rockies and surrounding mountain states.

At home, the past, present, and future mixed as never before. Not everyone advanced or prospered equally. Financial attractions beckoned some to leave and others to the region.

Montana lost population to the higher wages and job diversity that could be found in Seattle and the shipyards and industries of the West Coast. War industries tended to cluster around urban centers, leaving rural states like Montana and Wyoming at a disadvantage. By the end of 1943, an estimated 88,000 left Montana. Ex-Montanans held picnics in their new homes and reminisced about their days in the "Treasure State." Wyoming lost population also, although a much smaller number than its northern neighbor.

Civil defense became a paramount concern as people read about and watched how German air raids destroyed European and English cities. The movie news brought the war right to their hometowns. State, county, and community civil defense councils had quickly organized even before Pearl Harbor. In Wyoming, a ten-point program was launched after the attack, including registering folks who wished to volunteer for civil defense training, air-raid warning systems, and local medical services. Meanwhile, Uncle Sam reminded everyone to keep calm.

Some Wyomingites thought they saw Japanese paper balloons carrying bombs, which they believed were sent off to start forest fires or to land in communities and create trouble there. They were right. Launched on the high prevailing westerly winds, the balloons were intended by the Japanese high command to do damage and frighten Americans. A few actually reached Wyoming and caused small fires. A couple of curious people managed to kill themselves when they found unexploded bombs and tampered with these strange things until they exploded.

Wyoming went through statewide blackout tests (1942 and 1943), during which lights were supposed to be turned off at a given signal and not turned back on until the all-clear signal sounded. Volunteer air-raid wardens marched around checking to see that all was dark. If someone forgot to turn off an overlooked basement light, there would be a forceful knock on their door, followed by a stern lecture about giving enemy planes an advantage. Just how the planes would manage to arrive safely over the Rockies while bypassing more strategic targets was seemingly not important.

Initially, there had been some fear about the air raids, but that soon faded. Indeed, it seems that in Wyoming and the other two states, few people except air-raid wardens took these defense drills too seriously. That was understandable, considering how far the three states were from either coast.

Rationing hit every home and town, although farmers and ranchers found it less burdensome than others did, because of their gardens and cattle. Victory gardens became part of the win-the-war effort. Farmers and ranchers could slaughter their own animals, although not for sale or gifts unless they collected ration stamps from the recipient.

The Office of Price Administration (OPA) soon affected everyone's lives through price controls and rationing. Created in January 1942, by April it had fixed prices based on their highest levels in March. By October nearly everything Americans used, wore, and ate came under the OPA. Tires, gas, typewriters, sugar, coffee, meat, and other products eventually joined the rationed list. Gas rationing started at four gallons per week, which was later cut to three gallons, and eventually two gallons in March 1944. That constituted a particular hardship on the ranchers and farmers living on the plains of eastern Wyoming. President Roosevelt also appealed to motorists to reduce speeds to thirty-five miles per hour to conserve badly needed rubber. With long distances to cover, eastern Wyoming, Montana, and Colorado drivers had a hard time honoring that 1942 appeal. Ration books were issued at the local ration board, where some people declined to give their ages as required and simply marked "over twenty-one," despite having seen many winters pass by since their birth. Other grumbling surfaced, but Americans in general pulled together to get through the challenging times.

Few black-market activities occurred in Wyoming, although locals knew who was supplementing rationed supplies illegally. Colorado, with more people, had more folks involved in black-market activities. OPA rules were not always popular in the Rockies and elsewhere. While the need for price controls and rationing was understood, enforcement caused resentment among some westerners and others. Nevertheless, controls did work to provide food and other essential items for military needs and tried to keep inflation down.

Wyoming's home-front record was particularly good in preventing large-scale the black-market activities that hit the larger states across the country. Conversely, the state's OPA officials showed little enthusiasm for cracking down on violators, something people in stricter states would not have appreciated.

Wyoming, Montana, and Colorado schoolchildren vigilantly carried money to school to buy war bond stamps, carefully placing them in stamp books. When the books became full, they received a $25 or $50 war bond. Their parents also purchased bonds, and their mothers took Red Cross courses, becoming involved in a variety of projects, from visiting military hospitals to being nurse's aides to making surgical dressings.

Children and their parents participated in scrap drives throughout the war. School classes gathered papers and scrap to be taken to a deposit point. Mothers saved cooking fat and worn-out stockings, and families donated radios, small arms, old jewelry, and a host of other things that aided the war effort. In January 1943, Wyoming women proudly pointed to the fact that they led the nation, on a per capita basis, in the salvage of fats.

Schoolchildren throughout the Rockies practiced air raids during class time, marching carefully to a predesignated spot to await the all-clear signal, then trooping back to class. Youngsters studied shapes of planes so they could identify enemy aircraft, and they participated in practice air raids at night by helping darken their homes and awaiting the all-clear signal, usually the town fire siren. They also joined in gardening to supplement the family menu. These activities all brought the war close to home for young and old.

Everyone enjoyed going to the movies for relaxation and a dose of patriotism. A staple feature was the war movie, in which viewers could cheer John Wayne and other all-American Hollywood heroes as they defeated the Germans and Japanese time after time. The popularity of action-filled westerns also gave audiences a chance to see what Hollywood thought the frontier was like and reinforced a legend for this generation. Saturday matinees with Tom Mix, Roy Rogers, and Ken Maynard planted the idea in youngsters, many of whom carried it right into adulthood. Perhaps even more popular were the radio shows, with such stars as the Lone Ranger and Gene Autry, which allowed the young or old listener to imagine a wild West, sometimes with programs several times a week.

Rationing, air raids, war news, casualty lists, shortages, long working hours, and all the other wartime activities caused tension and stress. Although some thought any type of gaiety was unpatriotic and unfaithful to the men and women in service, President Roosevelt and others realized that without some relaxation, the stress would become too great. In early 1942 FDR encouraged Americans to find as much time as possible for leisure and rest. A Wyoming editor recommended soon after Pearl Harbor that his readers, "above all keep busy. Read. Sleep. Attend the movies, especially comedies and musicals, and engage in sports."[2]

Not everything during the war effort proved that noble and uplifting. The treatment of Japanese residents living on the West Coast left a black mark against the government and many other Americans. Because of fears over security, combined with racism, Japanese were rounded up and moved inland, with Wyoming and Colorado each gaining a "relocation" camp out of a total of ten nationwide. More than a few people in each state protested that "traitors" would be coming.

Colorado governor Ralph Carr had to defend his position when he welcomed these unfortunate people. Despite heated criticism, much to Carr's credit he told Coloradans that the Japanese Americans had the same rights as all other Americans. A voice crying in the wilderness, Carr would later be honored for his stand, but not before he lost a Senate race to Ed Johnson, who played on the anti-Japanese sentiment.

Wyoming's internment camp at Heart Mountain, between Cody and Powell, opened in 1942, with people relocated from California, Oregon, and Washington. It did not close until November 1945, more than two months after the war's end.

When the first group arrived, in August 1942, the shock must have been disheartening. At 8,000 feet on windswept, barren, desolate land, the Wyoming site did not resemble the land or the climate these people had recently enjoyed on the West Coast. Nor had they experienced anything like Wyoming's very cold winters and hot summers. With a population of nearly 11,000 at its peak, the Heart Mountain Relocation Center emerged temporarily as Wyoming's third largest city. Here, and at Amache in Colorado, the center was divided into barracks with family-sized apartments. Community mess halls, baths and toilets, and recreational facilities gave it a semblance of home — except for the guardhouses and barbed wire enclosing the camp.

Two-thirds of the Japanese at Heart Mountain were American citizens, but Wyoming did not greet them as it did other visitors. Alarmists and racists concluded that a "Jap is a Jap," whether in cold Wyoming or in the vicious Pacific battle theater. The situation became a hot political issue in 1943, when the *Denver Post* charged, in a series of articles, that the government was "pampering" the residents, who were hoarding scarce food. Highly exaggerated and even untruthful, the articles stirred up more anti-Japanese feeling in both states.

Colorado's camp, Amache, sat on the desolate southeastern plains near the small community of Granada. Not quite as bad a site as Heart Mountain, it still offered few advantages, except, from Washington's view, isolation. The first Japanese Americans arrived in August 1942, and the camp eventually reached a peak population of 7,500—at least nearly 70 percent of whom were U.S. citizens.

Colorado reacted to these newcomers much as Wyoming did. Store windows in nearby Lamar soon had window signs stating "No Japs Wanted." They quickly disappeared when it was pointed out that the new neighbors equaled business and that they would go elsewhere if they were not welcomed. Some towns, like Durango and Glenwood Springs, in fact had lobbied to gain the camp because of the money it meant to the towns' hard-pressed economies.

In both camps the Japanese made the prairie blossom, raised their own food and other crops, opened schools, and created a community out of a tragic situation. Showing their patriotism, they joined in the war effort by making K rations for the troops, and over nine hundred of their young men from Heart Mountain alone volunteered for military service. Serving in the European theater, they became the most highly decorated units in the war. Wyoming people gradually mellowed toward their Japanese neighbors, as did others when their war record became known.

Colorado hostility and bigotry did not die even when the young Japanese American men joined the military. Out of the more than six hundred from Amache who served in the military, forty-five were killed in action. Even this did not matter to some Coloradans. Observed the still hostile *Denver Post* in an editorial, "The Japs in this country are the same breed of rats that American boys are trying to exterminate in the Pacific."[3]

Despite such rhetoric and racism, the Japanese Americans never posed a threat to America's war effort or to Americans in general. Eventually, the bitterness faded even in so tragic an episode as the treatment of these citizens, but that does not negate the lessons to be learned from it. The Heart Mountain, Wyoming Foundation is seeking to preserve the site and to educate people about what happened there. In June 2005 the foundation staff and former inmates gathered to inaugurate an interpretive trail with stations explaining the camp's history. Colorado has yet to commemorate Amache in a similar fashion.

In the *Denver Post*, June 26, 2005, Alan Kumamoto recalled his days at Heart Mountain and summarized what the experience meant to a two-year-old boy who had lived in Los Angeles's Little Tokyo: "I don't remember a lot about Santa Anita, but I do remember the train ride between Santa Anita and Heart Mountain, to the extent that I was miserable and people told me I was crying the whole time." His family left on the last train from Heart Mountain, and even with the war over they were not allowed to return to the West Coast. They went to live in Chicago. Others went elsewhere, with some moving to Denver. In fact, the 1960 census found about 4,400 Japanese living in Colorado, the sixth-highest total in the nation.

Heart Mountain and Amache are sad exceptions to what happened in the Rockies overall. While the wartime boom impacted the regional community, truly Denverites of 1939 would hardly have recognized their old hometown in late 1945, or, at the very least, they would have been stunned by what had transpired. The war sired the modern city, which in turn galvanized the surrounding suburbs, and the heart of Colorado's Front Range was born.

Denver had needed only to be energized. Its advantages—besides its position as the Rockies' business, social, economic, transportation, and banking center—included clean, dry air, mountain views, an energizing climate, parks, and civic pride. Now came the time for the realization of dreams.

Denver's population grew from 322,412 in 1940 to 415,786 (an increase of almost 780 per month) ten years later, and the suburban counties' population jumped by a third, to over 600,000. The *Denver Post*'s motto, " 'Tis a privilege to live in Colorado," hit the tone for the day.

The 1950 census of Denver and its three neighboring counties clearly showed what the long-range postwar impact of the metropolitan area would be. Denver, Adams, Arapahoe, and Jefferson counties represented 78 percent of the state's population increase since 1940 and, significantly, 42.5 percent of the total population.

The role of the federal government had increased with the New Deal; however, what happened in the 1940s clearly surpassed what had occurred earlier. The federal government employed about 6,500 nonmilitary personel in Denver as the decade opened, a figure that had exploded to almost 17,000 by war's end. Add to that their families, and a key to the growth emerged. They worked at a medical supply depot, Lowry Air Base, Buckley Naval Air Station, Fitzsimons Army Hospital, the Army Air Corps Technical School, and elsewhere.

The Denver Ordnance Plant, operated by the Remington Arms Company, built a complete plant in 1941, which at its peak employed 20,000 people and became one of the largest arms plants in the nation. The Rocky Mountain Arsenal employed 15,000 and produced chemical warfare weapons. The dreams of those who envisioned Colorado as an industrial and military center seemed to be realized. Even the Emily Griffith Opportunity School, long famous for its adult education classes and for giving youngsters a second chance at education, trained students seven days a week, twenty-four hours a day, in special war production programs.

While there was nothing unusual in manufacturing armaments, one might think the phrase "ships built in Denver" would be an oxymoron, but it happened. Submarine chasers were fabricated in Denver. They then traveled by train to San Francisco's Mare Island Naval Yard, where workers assembled them. Over sixty eventually took to the sea, a Denver-built navy in World War II.

Bustling Denver awoke from its Depression nap to find thousands of young men and women passing through the city on their way to military bases or overseas. Given a welcome by Red Cross workers and the USO at a Servicemen's Center and the railroad depot, many liked what they saw and experienced and planned to return after the war. So did some of those who spent time at various Denver hospitals recuperating from their war wounds.

During the 1930s, Denver's Chamber of Commerce had launched a promotional campaign with the slogan that it wanted to make Denver the "Little Capital of the United States." World War II made it a "second capital." Denver offered the perfect solution to the search for a safe place for federal offices, should Washington, D.C., be attacked. Some, eventually, did come to Colorado to find offices and work in the Federal Center, located on the site of the old Remington Arms plant. Further, a series of scientific-research/military installations spread out from Denver north and south along the Front Range.

Denver had become prosperous and had a diverse economic base. Little home construction had taken place during the war, however, and homes and apartments remained at a premium, if found at all. Newcomers, including a few minorities, had moved into town, creating a housing crunch; conversely, they brought with them varied cultures and approaches to issues. Denver's future was set in place as the war drew to an end and peace drew near.

Denver did not enjoy all of Colorado's blessings, however. Colorado Springs gained what eventually became Fort Carson; during the war it became the state's largest military base. The town grew as fast as Denver, and its military establishment provided the base for Colorado Springs' great growth in the next decade. Peterson Air Field near Colorado Springs trained air force personnel, as did the Pueblo Army Air Base and the La Junta Army Air Field. Several Front Range universities and colleges, including the University of Colorado and Colorado A&M, trained military personnel and conducted officers' training schools.

On the other hand, the neighboring state of Wyoming would have loved more military bases and war-related contracts. The selection of a site involved many factors, including available space, water supply, climate, ease of transportation, and expense. Considering its isolation, small population, and lack of political clout, the state did as well as could have been expected. It gained an expansion of Cheyenne's Fort Francis E. Warren, a prisoner-of-war camp at Douglas, and a new army air base at Casper.

World War II stimulated Montana's lumber production and coal mining and its oil production. Butte revived its old-time spirit as copper was needed throughout the war industries. As was pointed out in *Montana: A History of Two Centuries*, "Compared to many other western states, however, Montana's wartime growth seems less than impressive."[4]

The war jump-started the long-depressed mining industry. Initially, the industry faced more regulation than ever before. Wartime concerns and needs involved completing multiple forms and complying with new regulations. Grumbling was still heard within the industry, but the wartime needs generally muffled it. With miners leaving for higher-paying jobs, gold mining was already suffering in Colorado, Montana, and elsewhere when the government issued Gold Limitation Order L-280. It closed all nonessential mineral mines by stopping access to replacement parts and materials, to available miners, and to equipment needed in mines producing metals more critical to the war, such as copper, lead, and zinc. Gold and silver now became byproducts from base metal mines.

That was just the start of government involvement in mining, a trend that the industry had feared for years. In miners' opinion, the New Deal "monster" seemed to have gone berserk. The War Manpower Commission had, among its policies, granted occupational deferment to nonferrous miners and prohibited miners from changing jobs without government approval. A miner could move, but he automatically lost his draft deferment by doing so. The agency paid the transportation costs of moving miners to essential mines, built homes, and offered increased pay to those who migrated to states that had shortages of skilled miners.

The government-created Metals Reserve Company (1940) purchased critical metal and minerals, set ceiling prices, and paid premiums for production in excess of fixed quotas. It became the principal agent in purchasing metals. Under the Defense Highway Act (1941), Uncle Sam built, maintained, and improved roads to raw material sources. The Strategic Materials Act (1942) provided for the study of essential mineral deposits, and field offices in the Rockies quickly found themselves swamped with requests to examine promising mines and properties. The old-time prospector would have gaped in amazement at all this.

Finally, the government sponsored scientific research on a variety of topics, some of which—such as the atomic bomb—directly affected the Rocky Mountains. Washington emerged virtually as a silent partner in mining and milling. The agencies and policies affected the three states in a multitude of ways, especially Colorado.

During the war, the world entered the atomic era. FDR was warned in 1941 that the Germans had accomplished nuclear fission, which could eventually lead the way to an "extremely powerful bomb." Out of this concern eventually grew the Manhattan Project to develop the atomic bomb.

Attention turned to Wyoming, and Colorado, and several other western states that had proven reserves of pitchblende and carnotite ores needed to produce the vital uranium. Colorado, in fact, contained the largest known sources of uranium and vanadium ores in the country. During the war, the most accessible and important deposits were found in southwestern Colorado and the neighboring Four Corners region.

A $600,000 road-building program was instituted to make the deposits more available. It provided jobs and made local roads better than they had ever been. Prospecting and mining started with a rush, and during the war, Colorado produced most of the vanadium found in the United States.

Under government scrutiny and tight regulation, the United States Vanadium Corporation reopened the old gold and silver smelter in Durango and operated a second smelter under an army contract. The old mill processed vanadium, a key ingredient for producing a rust-resistant, stronger grade of steel. At the new plant all activities remained top secret.

The federal government improved roads to allow trucks to carry ore from the Four Corners area to Durango. The government made no effort, however, to improve the Rio Grande Southern narrow-gauge tracks to haul ore; the more versatile trucks captured the business. In fact, some engines and cars were shipped to Alaska to use on a railroad there for military purposes. The days of commercial railroading in southwestern Colorado were numbered.

No one knew what was being processed at the new plant; it was a "military secret," a local newspaper confessed. It remained a secret because the vanadium, pitchblende, and carnotite being milled contained both uranium and vanadium. The government did not want to let enemy spies find out what the plant was processing and strove to keep it secret. The fifty men working at the mill were sworn to secrecy; they may not have even grasped the significance of their efforts. Such secrecy created a lively topic of conversation in Durango, however.

Everything became abundantly clear in August 1945, when two atomic bombs dropped on Japan killed hundreds of thousands of people and quickly ended the war. Uranium from the Durango mill had also been used for the bomb tested earlier at White Sands, New Mexico, and in the construction of the two atomic bombs actually used in warfare.

Durango and the rest of the world were shocked and horrified by the magnitude of this new weapon. Uncontrollably and without a say, the world had been blasted into the atomic era in the name of winning the war.

In this new era, Washington controlled everything from prospecting to mining to the mills. The government set the rules, established the prices, provided the only market, and told miners where ore must be taken. All this hinted of what loomed ahead on the horizon.

More prosaic but nonetheless essential to victory was the production of base metals and fuels. Butte was revived and Anaconda Copper prospered as it had not for over a decade. Montana mines produced the manganese, lead, zinc, and chrome needed in the war effort. Wyoming, Colorado, and Montana coal production soared to heights that had not been seen since the Great War and its immediate aftermath. Colorado chipped in with increased lead and zinc production, and the Climax Molybdenum Company went to war with a vengeance. It had been the world's largest producer since 1924 and would continue to be so until the postwar years. Indeed, Colorado produced almost all the world's molybdenum supply during the war.

With the Metals Reserve Corporation providing subsidies, exploration surged in the Rockies. A rare, unexpected chrome deposit, for example, was discovered in Montana. By the end of the war, the region's total mineral potential was better understood.

Railroads, except the lonely Rio Grande Southern, joined in the profit parade, enjoying a prosperity they had not known for decades. Wartime demand found them carrying a tremendous volume of passengers and freight. The Union Pacific in Wyoming, the state's largest industrial enterprise and strategically located as a main east–west line, matched the war's needs—shipping supplies, equipment, and troops across the country. Long, double-headed (two engines) trains ran across the lines, giving little boys a chance to practice their math by counting how many cars the engines pulled and then comparing totals with their friends. Smaller lines like the Denver & Rio Grande (D&RG), particularly with coal and war-related freight shipments, also prospered to a lesser degree in all three states.

The D&RG, benefiting from the new rails and new, more powerful engines, went to war. Local and transcontinental traffic increased, and so did income. By 1945, the railroad had exceeded all previous income levels, with operating revenues nearing $75 million—an amazing rebirth for a line that had been struggling for decades.

Perhaps nothing was needed more than increased oil production. Each state's production rose and deeper wells revived several older fields in Wyoming. Northwestern Colorado's isolated Rangely Field, long known for its potential, at last jumped to the forefront, and a new era opened. Montana's oil production hit a new high, reaching 8.5 million barrels by 1945. All told, the Rocky Mountains made major mineral contributions to the war effort and enjoyed another boom. Again, optimists thought the good days would now, finally, last forever.

Another important element in winning the war was increased agricultural production, not only for the United States but also to serve their allies' needs. Again, as in 1917–18, America became Europe's breadbasket and meat market. Slogans such as "Food will win the war and write the peace" encouraged farmers and ranchers to go the extra mile.

Wyoming's cattle industry flourished for the first time in decades. With rationing in full stride, most of the cattle went to feed troops throughout the world. Farmers also enjoyed the boom, even when faced with rising expenses; winter wheat, oats, potatoes, and other crops all showed increased production. The higher prices consumers paid for beef and produce gladdened many hearts, especially since winning the war and making profits went hand in hand. Cattlemen, however, found that they faced price ceilings on cattle sold, keeping them from realizing greater profits. For them, like the farmers, production costs also went up.

The farming areas of Montana, Wyoming, and Colorado providentially benefited from another rain cycle just as the wartime demands and prices hit full stride. Montana had not seen so much rain in years; 1943 proved a record year in all respects. Those who had hung on during the lean years now earned their reward in the fat ones. Both farms and ranches were growing in size and adopting mechanization. The owners also watched their land increasing in value.

Shortages of hired men hurt both farmers and ranchers. High-school students, "city slickers," older men, and nearly anyone else who could be found and appeared able to work, took to the fields at harvest time. Women joined in the harvesting, and if prisoners of war or a Japanese relocation camp were nearby, some of them went to work in the fields. If they could be found, seasonal workers also came west from the southern border states.

The Rocky Mountain states emerged from the war more mature than when they entered it five years earlier. Colorado, and to a lesser degree the other two states, hovered on the threshold of a boom that would last for forty years. Coloradans marched confidently into the future. Except for tourism potential, there was no looking back to a wistful past.

Denver could now truly lay claim to being the "Queen of the Mountains and Plains," as its boosters had so long ago proclaimed. Around the core city suburbs grew and boomed, matching and perhaps surpassing the dreams of their founders a few generations or years back. Those servicemen and servicewomen who had been stationed there or passed through were about to return to settle down in Colorado. With plentiful jobs in a growing economy, beautiful scenery, and a delightful climate, the city had much to offer.

The war had greatly stimulated urban growth, and that trend, obviously gaining momentum, dominated Colorado. Even though Denver did not immediately face the multitude of problems Phoenix or San Diego did, as 1945 became history some were lurking about town— growth, city services, strained budgets, rising crime, transportation crises, social problems, slums, school needs, potential urban flight, and minority expectations.

Nonetheless, that lay in the future; for now, new job opportunities exploded, with both skilled and unskilled jobs beckoning along Colorado's Front Range from Fort Collins to Pueblo. The economy that emerged from the war, as mentioned, was more diversified than at any time in U.S. history. Gone were the days when mining and agriculture were the major players in the Colorado economy. Not everyone in the state marched to the same economic beat, however; sections of the Great Plains and western Colorado faced a potentially bleak future. The flight from rural to urban Colorado continued without much realization on the part of urban folk of the plight of their country cousins.

Unlike in the booming Southwest and California, however, no great inrush of minorities arrived in Denver, although Denver's black community continued to be by far the region's largest. Their young men had served with distinction in the military in spite of facing the same discrimination every black serviceman experienced. The Rocky Mountain states had never attracted many blacks. Now the booming factories on the West Coast proved more attractive to migrating blacks. They found a small number of jobs opening for them in Colorado's war-related industries, but few other opportunities were available. Their homes and social life concentrated around what was called the Five Points neighborhood near downtown Denver. Prewar attitudes toward minorities relaxed somewhat, but blacks were still often the last hired.

Young men of Colorado's Southern Utes and Ute Mountain Utes joined the military and served in both the European and Pacific war fronts with honor. In Ignacio and Towaoc they joined the home-front effort buying war bonds, raising victory gardens, and so forth. Some left their homes and migrated into more booming communities and defense industries on the West Coast. Others became seasonal farm laborers and migrated to wherever jobs could be found. The same was true for Hispanics, although they proved more willing to migrate to the big cities from the southwestern part of Colorado. Denver gained a significant number of them. But rank discrimination affected Spanish Americans as well. When workers were needed to build Camp Hale, the Hispanics were the only ones not provided with barracks and mess halls. They had to live twenty miles away in other towns and drive to work through the mountains and mountain passes in winter and in summer.

Montana and Wyoming had even fewer minorities than Colorado, except for Indians on the reservations. These Native Americans also served in the military, and some reservation residents did move to cities that had jobs in the war industries, particularly in the Northwest and California. In Montana, blacks were scattered about in some of the larger towns, and they were involved on both the home and military fronts. They, too, were lured to higher-paying jobs elsewhere. Wyoming had the fewest minorities of the Rocky Mountain states. Unfortunately, a few people in all three states still looked with disapproval on Indians, Hispanics, and blacks, who seemed to be moving into what they considered the "white world." There was none of the violence, however, that became associated with the racial troubles in California.

The war opened doors and mobility for minorities, but lower-paying jobs continued to be the norm. Job mobility remained limited. The region's racial characteristics, though, were changing, albeit much more slowly than in Sunbelt and West Coast states.

Meanwhile, World War II continued to impact the Rocky Mountain heartland in a variety of ways. Of the three states, Montana's wartime growth appeared the least impressive. It secured two air bases, one later named Malmstrom Air Force Base, near Great Falls, and another at Glasgow. The former served basically as a staging point for lend-lease flights to Russia via Alaska. Helena gained a War Dog Training Center to prepare sled dogs and men to help pilots downed in the Arctic, and Canadian special service forces trained with their American counterparts. The University of Montana and Montana State College provided facilities for training young men for the air force and Army Specialty Training. The war's impact on Montana, though, simply did not compare with what had happened in Colorado—an inequity that would help shape Montana's development in the postwar years.

Montanans wholeheartedly supported the war effort on all fronts, without the panic of World War I. They oversubscribed their war bond quotas, suffered though rationing, and even agreed, without too much grumbling, to cancel state high school sports championship playoffs because of wartime necessities. A sacrifice to the program for conserving gas, electricity, and other vital items to help the war effort, this action further brought the war home to the youngsters and their fans.

A few elements of the legendary Old West regained momentum during the war. Gambling and prostitution flourished near military bases, as well as in rural areas such as Miles City, Montana, and Silverton, Colorado. The ever-popular bars and other forms of "recreation" also remained available to help people alleviate wartime worries and stress.

The war impacted all three states, but the figures clearly show the emergence of Colorado's dominance. The value of manufactured products doubled in Montana and tripled in Colorado, but the total value of those for Montana and Wyoming combined still represented less than half that of the latter. War-related military and industrial projects had greatly benefited all three states, although, as discussed, especially Colorado.

Federal jobs in Colorado had jumped by over 20,000 since the late 1930s, and now neared 30,000 total jobs. Wyoming and Montana together gained a total of 3,000 federal jobs during that period, for a combined total slightly less than half that of their neighbor. While personal income went up in all three states, Coloradans gained the most.

The two census years that bracketed this era, 1940 and 1950, illustrate what transpired. Colorado's population jumped from 1.1 million to 1.3 million, while Montana and Wyoming lost residents. The loss was not a large number, but in the grow-or-die West, worrisome. Montana's population dropped by 58,000 to 501,024 (which, if you recall, actually represented a small postwar increase over the 1930s), and Wyoming dropped to 290,529 (a decrease of slightly over 200 residents).[5]

Urban areas, as explained, experienced the most expansion. War-related industries were clustered around urban centers like Denver and

Colorado Springs, and that spurred growth, which in turn encouraged others to come. This left Wyoming and Montana out in the cold. The future of all three states could be glimpsed as the war wound down.

Another trend was becoming obvious as well, at least in Denver and several larger communities: the downtown areas showed signs of deteriorating, while outlying areas prospered, a not unfamiliar twentieth-century urban phenomenon. White, middle-class westerners moved to the suburbs, leaving behind potential poverty and a less well-educated and skilled population. This increasing trend, which had started several generations back, was later described as "white flight."

In summary, 1940s Montana, Wyoming, and Colorado all witnessed an economic boom unmatched previously in the century. Agriculture had entailed surpluses and low prices before the war. During the war, with military and foreign-aid requirements and increased public buying power, shortages replaced surpluses, and better prices prevailed.

Mining prospered as well. New industries were started and old ones were busier than usual, particularly in Colorado. Still, the war-stimulated boom for these traditional standbys needed to carry over into peacetime. Throughout the past century, it had not done so. Some residents left all three states for better-paying jobs elsewhere, but some newcomers had come to stay, and after passing through, others promised to come back. They arrived on a firm economic base for expansion into the future.

With the rest of the West, the Rockies stood on the threshold of emerging as an economic pacesetter and a major influence on the federal government. War mobilization had speeded along what had started slowly by 1940. The region was becoming increasingly diversified and self-sufficient.

People who had been in the background for years, facing economic and social discrimination—Hispanics, Native Americans, and African Americans—were learning that the war and the New Deal offered them new opportunities. They would begin to play a new role in the postwar years.

The New Deal had not ended the Depression but had stabilized the Rocky Mountain states, and the prosperous war years brought them out of the hard times. Everyone was touched in one way or another by the changes and this new world. The memory of those days would linger among folks who lived through them, while the younger generation saw only the best of times here and now. This, in turn, would soon lead to generational stress.

Optimism fueled discussions of the future, as the Rockies faced the postwar years. In Colorado, the base had been established for an ever-thriving boom the likes of which the state had never experienced; in the other two states, formerly sleepy towns had taken on a new life. So many exciting things seemed on the verge of happening that even pessimists grudgingly felt a bubbling exhilaration. A transformation had occurred in the past fifteen years, and the future glittered with promise.

All that lay in the future on the evening of August 14, 1945. Americans turned to celebrate the end of World War II when the news that Japan had surrendered spread across the land as they listened to their radios or their excited neighbors telling them the news. Westerners remembered vividly that evening; they paraded, cheered, partied, gave thanks, and listened to patriotic music. One young girl in Durango, Colorado, was in the midst of a slumber party with her friends when her father offered to take them downtown to see the celebration. So off they drove, dressed in their pajamas, and they were especially excited because he let them stand on the car's running board until a policeman told them to go home for being "improperly" dressed. The past and the future caught up with the girls that evening. By the time the officially designated VJ Day, September 2, 1945, arrived, the celebrations local and regional were generally over, and the Rocky Mountain states had turned to peacetime.

The *Casper Tribune-Herald* on July 20, 1945, placed the future in perspective. The same could have been said by any Colorado or Montana editor.

> Here lies Wyoming, in the heart of America. Over enough coal to run the world a thousand years, atop vast reservoirs of oil, limitless mountains of metal, great expanses of virgin soil, vigorous climate full of health—a sleeping giant. Something is bound to happen. Hang on to your shares of Wyoming, unlimited!

Indeed, also hang on to your shares of Colorado and Montana unlimited! Every old-time booster must have cheered, and their contemporary counterparts, alive and well, looked forward with an eagerness not seen in two decades.

The no longer isolated and insulated Rocky Mountain states stood on the threshold of something they had only dreamed about. In the words of President Franklin Roosevelt (who did not live to see the end of the war, having died on April 13, 1945), who clearly comprehended what had occurred and what was coming, "We have learned that we cannot live alone, at peace; that our own well-being is dependent on the well-being of other nations, far away. . . . We have learned to be citizens of the world, members of the human community."[6]

CHAPTER 7

Water, Fuels, and Tourism
1945 through the 1950s

> When Kansas and Colorado have a quarrel over the water in the
> Arkansas River they don't call out the National Guard in each state
> and go to war over it. They bring a suit in the Supreme Court of the
> United States and abide by the decision.
> —Harry S. Truman, April 1945

PRESIDENT TRUMAN TOLD HIS LISTENERS, in this Kansas City speech, that
the same thing could happen internationally through the new United
Nations. Unintentionally, he touched upon two themes that would
impact Montana, Wyoming, and Colorado for the rest of the decade—
water and the international scene.

World War II brought America foursquare into world affairs, despite
some grumbling by a segment of the American public. The Rocky
Mountain states were no longer isolated and insular; ready or not, the
world came crashing into them in a variety of ways.

During the fifteen years after the end of the war, the West and the
whole country prospered as seldom before. The country entered several
decades of sustained economic growth, the longest such period in its
history. Prosperity became the norm for many Americans, who found
themselves enjoying middle-class status. By 1960, almost 60 percent of
all U.S. families had reached that rank. About the same percentage now
owned their homes as incomes rose; that combined with savings accumulated during the war allowed for an economic freedom previously
known only by a few.

Technology transformed the workplace and the home, producing
a new level of material comfort. A medical breakthrough put parents'
minds at ease when a vaccination was found for polio, and strides were
made in other childhood illnesses. Yet nothing changed Americans' lives

more than television. This revolution was so complete that by 1960 more homes had TV sets than indoor plumbing.

Trends noticed previously in the Rockies continued. The federal government's active economic role helped stimulate and sustain the expansion. Washington seemed to be involved everywhere, from education to space exploration to farm subsidies and road building. The Rocky Mountain states and much of the rest of the country would benefit from military expenditures that came with the cold war and the Korean War, but the entire West benefited most. The government, larger and more invasive in people's lives than ever before, also intruded on local and state governments.

Water became a major issue or perhaps a more stressful continuing issue. As the population expanded, new industry arrived, tourism grew, and a host of other demands appeared, water grew more critical by the year. The generation's best Colorado poet, and arguably the state's finest ever, Thomas Hornsby Ferril, understood this. In his poem "Here Is a Land Where Life Is Written in Water," he wrote these words, which appear on the rotunda of the state capitol building:

Here is a land where life is written in water,
The West is where the water was and is,
. . . .
Look to the cloud that gives the oceans back,
Look to your heart and may your wisdom grow
To power of lightning and to peace of snow.[1]

Postwar water matters proved Ferril's message. The hopes of the Missouri River Authority, with its planned dams and federal development of the Missouri Basin, died during the war, and Montana never gained what the Tennessee Valley did from the Tennessee Valley Authority. Montanans did not seem particularly concerned at the time, but Indian water rights, increasing demands on water resources, downstream rights on the Missouri River, and pollution soon became serious issues.

The struggle over Colorado River water stretched back a generation and journeyed right into the postwar West. Wyoming and Colorado, plus the other upper and lower Colorado River basin states, were involved in a 1948 compact dealing with water allotment for the Upper Basin. Colorado gained 57.75 percent, and Wyoming 14 percent, of the water, with the rest going to the remaining Upper Basin states. Arizona was allotted an extra 50,000 acre-feet of water per year as well. A sweeping series of dams was planned for the rivers feeding into the Colorado River.

Did this 1948 Upper Basin Compact finally solve long-term problems? Unfortunately not. The underlying problems of water shortage, water needs, and quarrels among the basin states continued.

The agreement, in addition, opened the final disposition of unappropriated waters of the Little Snake and Green rivers. Utah's Flaming Gorge Dam on the Green backed water almost to the town of Green River, Wyoming. The dispute among Nebraska, Colorado, and Wyoming over the North Platte River, as mentioned, had finally been resolved in 1945. Unhappily, in the years that followed, Wyoming's hopes for increased irrigation failed to justify earlier expectations. Interstate compacts additionally divided up water in other rivers in the state, including the Snake and Yellowstone. With each new compact, the federal government's role increased locally and elsewhere.

After the wartime boom, agriculture nationally and in the Rockies slipped into the doldrums. At the same time, the average farm continued to increase in size, while farmers specialized more, equipment needs and costs multiplied, and farming became big business. This forced many out of rural, small-farm America and into the cities, in turn affecting nearby farm villages. The old refrain of more and better jobs, modern conveniences, and being where the "action" beckoned continued to lure Rocky Mountain ruralists.

Denver's suburbs also grew "like weeds," swallowing up nearby agricultural land. Soon that pattern became discernible along the entire Front Range. Mounting concern arose about the political influence of the declining rural districts, many of whose legislative representatives seemingly did not understand the problems of the cities, yet in all three states rural legislators dominated. The problem came into sharpest focus in Colorado with its jumping urban boom.

As a result of the baby boom of the postwar years, the population exploded in the late 1940s and the 1950s. At the same time, women's numbers in the workforce increased over prewar figures. Many a "riveter Jane" or WAVE returned home and became a housewife, but others enjoyed the economic freedom, responsibility, and opportunities that were becoming available to them.

The new urbanites, male and female, often did not live in the cities. They settled in the suburbs mushrooming around them, thanks to the ease the automobile granted them to commute to work, shop, and enjoy the suburban "good life." Potentially, this trend would weaken the ties of traditional communities and their neighborhoods. Without question it accelerated the flight of white Americans from the inner city, which was now looked upon as a place to work, not to live. The suburbs, with more open space, better schools, shopping centers, newer homes, neighbors of the same racial background, fewer problems than the older inner cities, and a modern lifestyle, attracted the upwardly mobile middle class. A host of problems loomed because of this demographic shift.

The automobile industry continued to play a key role, from Detroit to Cheyenne. Production topped 8 million cars in 1955, and many drivers journeyed west to see the legend and the reality, from scenery to history, and to perhaps look for a potential new home. Americans became more mobile than at any time in their history, allowing many to go to the West—Horace Greeley really said, "Turn your face to the great West, and there build up a home and fortune." They did—those veterans who had traveled there during the war, those searching for better opportunities, and those who had dreamed about moving to the western "land of opportunity."

All these trends would influence the three Rocky Mountain states, especially Colorado. Within fifteen years of war's end, the consequences would be noticeable, from town to farm and ranch. Old-timers had witnessed change and complexity in their day, but nothing like what they witnessed now.

As the war ended, Colorado stood on the threshold of unprecedented economic and population growth. Montana had just gone through a dramatic population shift—both departing and arriving. Even during the mining era, and hardly by the bust of the homestead eras, had such a development been seen. The state, at the moment, faced a less promising future. Of the three states, Wyoming had been the least affected by the war and looked to the years ahead similarly to Montana.

Politically, the Republican Party rebounded after the disastrous (for them) 1930s. Yet it never completely dominated the political landscape. In Wyoming, for example, Republicans—who were strong in the rural counties—typically controlled the legislature, won most statewide elective offices, and monopolized the state's lone House of Representatives seat. Democrats with strength in the urban areas kept things interesting, though, especially in the race for the United States Senate, where they fielded some impressive candidates, notably Gale McGee, who won in 1958. An impressive campaigner, he visited every corner of Wyoming.

The political urban-rural split became even more pronounced in Colorado. For years, it had often been Democratic Denver versus the outlying counties, a pattern that continued. Neither party could claim a monopoly on Coloradans' political allegiance. Both major parties could point with pride to victories in the postwar years, with the Democrats dominating the governor's races. Two Democratic warhorses, Wayne Aspinall in the House and Edwin Johnson in the Senate, served twenty-four and eighteen years, respectively, in Washington.

The Republicans, however, kept the state in their column during the presidential elections in the 1950s. Without question, one reason for Republican success in the fifties was the nationally popular Dwight Eisenhower, who had married a Denver girl, Mamie Dowd. Ike loved vacationing and fishing in Colorado, and Coloradans enjoyed having him publicize the state's attractions. Colorado often became the summer White House. Unfortunately, that publicity almost backfired when he had a heart attack in 1954, which some people blamed on the state's high altitude. Chambers of Commerce throughout the mountains took a deep breath and waited nervously until Ike's doctor reassured the country that altitude had nothing to do with the attack.

Conservatives dominated the 1950s in Montana, even with that old kingmaker, the Anaconda Company, retreating from its earlier political influence. When Anaconda sold its newspapers and broke with its longtime corporate partner, the Montana Power Company, an era ended that stretched back decades. Montana did maintain its tradition of sending liberals to Washington, including Lee Metcalf, James Murray, and Mike Mansfield. Conservative Republicans continued to enjoy the governor's chair and power in the legislature.

In analyzing Montana politics, the authors of *Montana: A History of Two Centuries* concluded: "One of the most refreshing aspects of Montana politics is its open, breezy, grass-roots democratic atmosphere. The state's small and unpretentious population has ready access to political leaders and political power, and local people like their politics low keyed and down to earth."[2]

The same might be said of Wyoming, but not of Colorado. Growing faster than its Rocky Mountain neighbors, Colorado's urban population dominated national elections but not state ones, where rural districts retained their nineteenth-century power. The state political legislative power continued to rest in the declining rural districts. They were not interested in surrendering that power, realizing that their destiny then would be controlled by Front Range communities stretching from Fort Collins to Pueblo. Shrewd statewide candidates aimed their message and appearances at those places where the most voters resided, a fact rural voters resented.

Overall, the mountain states remained political mavericks, even if not quite at the excitement and level of earlier times. After backing Truman in 1948, they supported Ike in 1952 and 1956, as did most everyone, with the usual party splits at the state and local levels. Personality often overrode party labels, particularly in the smaller states of Wyoming and Montana. The increasing numbers of independents carried the balance in many a close election.

Politics aroused the party faithful and many others come election time, but the big news—the postwar boom—aroused many more. America prospered after the war, and so did the Rocky Mountain states, with Colorado in the forefront.

A major reason for this ongoing prosperity came straight from Washington, with the continued need for national defense. Peace had not really come at the end of the Second World War; the apprehension and conflict only shifted to a new threat—the Communist Soviet Union and its allies. Almost as soon as the guns grew silent, astute American observers realized that the Soviet government had returned to its original idea of a world revolution. Tension between the East and West, as it became known, existed throughout the world, from divided Germany to China and eventually to Cuba and Latin America in the U.S. backyard.

On one side of the cold war stood the United States and its allies; on the other, the Soviet Union and its supporters. The two groups were opponents on most major issues, a situation made even more threatening because both sides soon stockpiled atomic bombs and other weapons. Winston Churchill ably described the situation during a speech at

Missouri's Westminster College on March 5, 1946: "From Stettin in the Baltic to Trieste in the Adriatic an iron curtain has descended across the Continent."

Although far from the "battle" front, the Rocky Mountain states soon found themselves involved in the cold war in a multitude of ways. First came the plans, then the contracts, then the construction, and finally permanent installation—each bringing money and people to the Rockies. That the mountains and prairies were generally out of Soviet missile range, had few possible targets, and included rural areas with a scattered population—thus allowing for more secrecy—made them more attractive to the Defense Department and its planners. Also, excellent universities existed in the region, and the federal government already had an assortment of offices in the Denver area.

The Strategic Air Command bolstered its Malmstrom Air Base at Great Falls and built a new base near Glasgow. Montana also gained intercontinental ballistic missile installations as tension between the two superpowers escalated. Defense spending became an important part of the state's economy, a pattern repeated in Wyoming. Cheyenne's Warren Air Force Base became a major intercontinental ballistic missile base, and more missile installations were scattered around southeastern Wyoming.

Northeastern Colorado also gained some missile sites, a small part of the defense money flowing its way. Colorado Springs' Camp Carson became Fort Carson, one of the country's most significant military bases, and it continued to grow as the Korean War and then the Vietnam conflict expanded America's military establishment. Major military medical centers were created in Denver and Grand Junction, and the Veterans Administration operated centers there as well. Military spending had only begun to benefit the Centennial State.

Ordinary westerners became involved in the cold war in a more personal way. Repeating World War II preparedness, schoolchildren practiced air-raid drills, now heightened by the atomic bomb threat. Civil defense committees and drills supposedly kept people alert, and ground defense plans prepared to repel those "un-American" communists should they dare to appear. People were given individual tasks, such as guarding ham radio operators' towers to keep communications open. Towns practiced evacuations. One in Denver turned into a mad scramble, laced with confusion; cars jammed streets and traffic slowed to a crawl as parents rushed to pick up children—any children—and head for the mountains. According to the overall plan, some residents were supposed to drive all the way to the state's southwestern corner, but that part of the practice drill remained on paper only. Those who were truly concerned built bomb shelters in their backyards, an albatross when times calmed and a For Sale sign appeared in the front yard.

By the mid-1950s this phase of the cold war had become history. In the meantime, government aid kept coming to the Rockies, profiting some towns and businesses more than others. Overall, the Rocky Mountain states had benefited more than most other states.

Colorado Springs gained the North American Air Defense Command, which, among its peaceful pursuits, would track Santa Claus's trip on Christmas Eve for the country's children. With two major military bases and its emergence as a favorite retirement home community for military personnel, Colorado Springs grew at an unmatched pace to become the state's second-largest city.

Then Colorado Springs' cup overflowed, when it was awarded the United State Air Force Academy. With the emergence of air power in World War II, the need for a military academy specializing in that area became obvious. Plans were being discussed when the Korean War broke out in 1950, turning the cold war into a shooting war. Not until 1954 did Congress authorize the creation of a separate institution. Colorado Springs became one of the three finalists for this federal plum.

In an almost unprecedented display of state, county, and city cooperation, Colorado Springs won the prize, overcoming rivals' objections that the site selected along the foothills was at too high an altitude. Construction started as the first cadet wing entered college at Denver's Lowry Field. In late August 1958, the cadets moved to the beautiful Colorado Springs campus, with its rectangular silhouettes profiled against the mountain backdrop.

By that time, $140 million had been spent, only a portion of the federal money that flowed into that section of the state. The Air Force Academy not only brought people and money to Colorado but also became a major tourist attraction, enhancing the already established popularity of the Colorado Springs area.

By the early 1950s, the military-industrial complex permeated the state's economy to a degree Wyoming and Montana never experienced.

The mountains, scenery, and climate had attracted a variety of industries and businesses to the state, and they now benefited from Uncle Sam's largesse. A brief summary indicates the scope. Martin Marietta built missiles and later rockets used in the space program, and other companies were awarded military and aerospace contracts. The Rocky Flats Nuclear Weapons Plant opened northwest of Denver in 1951 and soon mushroomed into a massive operation. The Rocky Mountain Arsenal's chemical weapons and pesticide plant was located in nearby Adams County.

All this expansion created thousands of jobs; brought people to Colorado; gave defense, energy, and space research contracts to the state's universities; and promoted Colorado nationally and internationally. Colorado continued to boom, a situation that obtained into the mid-1980s. Only agriculture sat on the outside looking in.

After World War II, the old Denver Arms Plant was converted, as mentioned, into the Denver Federal Center, with a growing group of agency offices there. Boulder benefited greatly when the National Bureau of Standards opened a branch on the south edge of town. The addition of the National Center for Atmospheric Research, combined with the existing University of Colorado, made Boulder one of the country's top research centers. Other Colorado cities were less blessed, but they had national forests, Bureau of Land Management offices, national monuments, parks, and park headquarters to brighten their economies. Some Coloradans continued complaining about Washington's involvement in the state, but they were a shrinking minority.

This postwar development separated Colorado from Wyoming and Montana in population, growth, economy, recognition, and role in the nation's affairs. The multitude of blessings Colorado received energized the economy, promoted the wonder of living there, and accentuated its urban growth. All three states had strikingly beautiful mountains, a variety of climates, and bountiful eastern prairie lands, but there the similarities ended.

When the Soviet Union exploded its first atomic bomb (1949), the two major powers now both had atomic potential, and the world's political and military stage darkened. To expand its military arsenal of A-bombs, the United States had to find more uranium. The Atomic Energy Commission, created by Congress in 1946, started searching for domestic uranium sources. Logically, they turned to the Four Corners area, where it had already been mined, and to Wyoming, where small deposits had been found as early as 1918.

Suddenly a mining rush, much like the excitement experienced in the nineteenth century, invigorated would-be prospectors all over the region. Some had experience, most had only hopes and dreams. The age-old story repeated itself—prospectors and miners thought to get rich without working. Most participants ended up working harder than they ever had.

The optimistic prospectors purchased guidebooks just as their excited ancestors had done in 1849 and 1859. They read about what to wear ("tough, relatively heavy pants and shirts") and what necessities to take (an air mattress "may be found very serviceable"), and they were given bountiful words of encouragement ("uranium has become a magic word"). Stories of rich strikes made these modern prospectors even more excited and determined. It all seemed magical, just like those long-ago days of the Pike's Peak gold rush.

Stores in Wyoming and Colorado stocked books, tools, maps, boots, and a wide variety of clothes, in what some of them dubbed the "Prospector's Corner." With their Geiger counters and scintillation counters to pick up traces of uranium, prospectors in Jeeps loaded down with camping equipment scurried over hills, plateaus, and valleys. They eagerly awaited the rapid ticking that would indicate a high-grade deposit. Some modern prospectors even used airplanes, hoping to zoom in on rich strikes. Others had burros and tramped over the terrain.

As they had a century before, a few women joined the rush, some prospecting, most trying to establish homes for their families under some primitive conditions. A few nearby towns benefited either from being a staging point or from gaining a uranium mill, but this was not an urban West as earlier rushes had been.

The Atomic Energy Commission encouraged prospecting, watched over all these activities, created guidelines, guaranteed prices, purchased the ore, and established mills. The individualism that had characterized earlier rushes was muted by Washington's continuing its wartime policies.

Wyoming's first paying discovery came in the Black Hills in 1949 when the Homestake Mining Company in neighboring South Dakota joined in the excitement and developed the claims. Other strikes followed, and

Wyomingites were caught up in a uranium frenzy. Prospectors rushed everywhere and filed thousands of claims, most of which proved to be too low-grade to be profitable, or even to be worthless. As in earlier rushes, wealth, for most, was not to be found, despite high hopes and effort. If a claim panned out as less than rich, no one eagerly stepped forward to purchase it, and the finder rarely had the resources to develop the "bonanza."

Wyoming's greatest excitement came from Pumpkin Buttes in southwestern Campbell County. After publicity in 1951 touted it as a hot spot, a great rush was anticipated; it looked as if rushers would overwhelm the county and locals. Ranchers did not want a noisy, excitable prospecting horde overrunning their range during lambing and calving season and managed to wield enough influence to postpone the opening until November. Even as winter settled in, the rush came, followed by claim jumpers and lawsuits, not the expected bonanzas.

Wyoming lacked uranium mills, which did not arrive on the scene until the late 1950s. Finally, the state, which contained over 20 percent of the country's reserves, came into its own, with Riverton emerging as "uranium capital."

Wyoming also gained a new town, Jeffrey City, near one of the uranium mills and not far from the state's first mining rush and boom at South Pass City and Atlantic City. The result was eerily similar: a 1960 population of 750 drifted away, disappointed, when the bust came, and eventually only slightly more than 100 people lived there.

The Four Corners region saw even more excitement, for fortunate prospectors found some highly profitable mines there. Furthermore, the region carried a long history of uranium excitement. Once again, a mining rush brightened prospects.

Grand Junction thrived as never before, becoming the uranium center, followed closely by Durango. Mining engineers, promoters, miners, government employees, stock salesmen, the drifting crowd, the curious, and more than a handful of shady characters arrived. If one did not want to go into the field in this hot, lonely, and generally arid region, the possibility existed of making a fortune in uranium stocks. A familiar pattern emerged. Every major western mining district had gone through a similar excitement, except this one was ignited in the twentieth century with new ways to advertise, promote, and excite the credulous.

Uranium stocks became the new, quick way to make a fortune. Again, the gullible and naive fell prey to wily promoters who offered penny-ante stock shares in companies formed even before core drill tests had been made to confirm the quantity and quality of the ore.

Meanwhile, just as occurred during the war, Washington offered price supports and other assistance. With the cold war at high tide, not until 1956–57 did the government even relax restrictions enough to allow production tonnage to be publicized. The boom peaked in mid-decade with 174 uranium mines (using the term loosely) scattered throughout western Colorado's mesas, canyons, and sand. Eastern Colorado tried to enter the mining mania, but the pitchblende deposits there proved negligible. For a brief moment, old districts such as Caribou and Central City received newspaper coverage and promotion, but they soon returned to the quiet of yesterday.

Uranium processing plants provided jobs for locals and destination points for prospectors and miners in the hinterland. Rifle, Uravan, Slick Rock, Maybell, Durango, Naturita, Gunnison, Grand Junction, and Cañon City beckoned and busily processed the ore hauled in by trucks.

As the decade ended, so did the mining excitement. Mills were shutting, prospect holes were abandoned, and once-glittering stock collapsed, worth not even the paper on which it was printed. Quiet returned to Wyoming and western Colorado; nonetheless, considerable reserves remained, awaiting another day. Man had left his tracks behind. Abandoned machinery, roads going nowhere in particular, mine dumps, fallen claim stakes, tin cans, broken bottles, a wide variety of junk—the relics of a twentieth-century mining boom scarred the countryside.

Once again the Rockies had seen the cycle of mining boom-and-bust, although this time something tangible remained. The federal government, to hasten getting ore to market, had built or improved roads throughout the region, which in western Colorado in particular provided a boost to the growing tourism business. Durango, Colorado, for instance, now had paved roads that connected it with Flagstaff, Arizona, southern California, and Albuquerque, New Mexico.

In the postwar years Wyoming and Colorado's mining cup overflowed with both states enjoying a second mining boom, this one in oil and natural gas production. This time Montana joined them, and the Rockies became an important oil-producing region just as the demand for gasoline leaped. Americans, with more leisure time, took to the road in unprecedented numbers.

Wyoming became one of the top five oil-producing states in the country. Casper emerged as the state's oil capital, with three refineries; and Park County, in northwestern Wyoming, raced out in front as the major producer. The state's tremendous natural gas potential brightened the picture further. An estimated 4 trillion cubic feet of recoverable reserves awaited development, and production soon placed Wyoming among the country's leaders.

Montana would not be left out this time. It had experienced some oil excitement back in the 1920s near Cut Bank and Shelby. Realizing the significance of promotion, Shelby hoped to put itself on the map in 1923 by staging a world championship heavyweight boxing match. The result was not what promoters had hoped. As one account put it, "They lost their shirts in the biggest flop in the history of world boxing when fewer than eight thousand people paid to attend."[3]

The Depression further dampened prospecting and production until the Second World War, when production bounced back. Interest in Montana's potential grew steadily after 1951, when the huge Williston Basin Field, stretching from western North Dakota into southern Saskatchewan and eastern Montana, was blown in. A frenzied race for leases, rivaling the contemporary uranium craze, had oil companies scrambling throughout the region. Production doubled as new discoveries came in one after another. Billings joined Casper as an oil capital with refineries and a pipeline connecting the town with Spokane. The frenzy almost rivaled the legendary 1920s Oklahoma madness; in the late 1950s, however, the excitement faded.

Montana also enjoyed a boom in natural gas production as home and business owners there, as elsewhere, realized the advantages of gas heating over coal. The demands became so great that local production could not meet the need, so Montana companies imported natural gas from Canada and Wyoming to serve customers. As with oil and Colorado uranium, by the late 1950s, production, employment, and the furor were fading.

All three states enjoyed a postwar oil boom, with Colorado's northwestern Rangely Field joined by the Denver-Julesburg Basin in the 1950s. The oil and natural gas frenzy in the southwest corner of the state caused

Durango's population to double and Cortez's to nearly triple. Neither could match the growth of neighboring Farmington, New Mexico, however, which leapt by five times. The Four Corners had never seen such excitement, even in the earlier, and now concurrent, uranium madness.

Colorado tried to follow Wyoming, but oil prospecting drilling quickly leveled off, just as it had with its neighbor. For example, in Colorado's peak year, 1955, of the 1,539 oil and gas wells drilled, 1,043 came in dry.

Natural gas might have emerged as a serious threat to coal, but King Coal continued to dominate in the Rockies. Montana had the most coal reserves of any state in the union, with 108 billion tons—nearly double its nearest competitor. Most of it lay near the surface in the southeastern and east-central parts of the state. A wartime revival had been followed by a return to stagnation during the postwar years in the state's coal regions. Hope did not die, however, since the easily strippable coal seams still held potential as the 1960s began.

Although Wyoming continued to have fairly strong coal production until the late 1940s, the future caught up with it. Local mines suffered because the railroads, their major customer and owner, shifted to diesel fuel for their engines. With that market gone, the impact of coal on the state's economy became negligible.

The shutting down of the mines in Rock Springs, Hanna, and elsewhere dislodged miners and their families. They had once been an important segment of Wyoming society, and now they virtually vanished. The ripples spread beyond the coal districts and caused a severe disruption of local economies statewide, affecting merchants, school districts, the job market, and county and state tax bases. Agriculture and tourism could not pick up the slack, and the whole state suffered.

In both Colorado and Wyoming, however, strip mining came to the rescue—in some ways. Using large steam shovels and trucks, mine owners could lower expenses and increase production. But they utilized fewer miners, exacerbating the coal-town problems just discussed. Although that seemed the best way to compete with oil and natural gas, it created the major potential environmental problems of unsightly dumps, ruined vistas, and water pollution.

The fossil fuels oil, coal, and natural gas, joined by the exotic uranium, led to another boom-and-bust cycle. They left behind, by the early 1960s, former boomtowns, indicators that man had invaded a once-pristine environment, disappointed investors, and squashed hopes. Rather than creating ongoing prosperity, the mines and boomtowns generally caused unanticipated long-range environmental problems. The Rockies once again had been exploited for their natural resources to the benefit of outside regions and companies. Now, however, some locals were raising angry voices in protest.

Strip mining also left a horrible vista for those travelers who happened upon one of the mines. That threatened the tourist industry. Tourists coming to the Rockies hoped to see that pristine environment while enjoying the comforts of postwar life. From Mesa Verde in the south to Glacier in the north, a wide variety of national parks and monuments became the destinations of visitors in their automobiles.

Everything seemed in place. Salesrooms had plenty of cars to tempt buyers, Americans had money saved from the war years, the highway system was improving every year, gasoline continued to be inexpensive, and ordinary workers and middle-class folks had more vacation time. No longer was traveling west an adventure of time, expense, and determination, as it had been a century or even a generation earlier. Americans eagerly took to the road, and the western tourist industry was ready to greet them with motels, hotels, tourist shops, restaurants, gas stations, and other services they might need during their travels.

The automobile's impact ranged widely and continued to change the tourism and local landscapes with strips of motels, drive-ins, shops, cafés, and the ubiquitous tourist traps. Larger, more distracting billboards appeared along highways, and roads and traffic steadily increased in and around towns and cities. Parking lots dotted the landscape everywhere, sometimes at the expense of tearing down wonderful examples of earlier architecture. Rural small towns suffered as travel became easier, granting local residents a much wider range of access to stores, entertainment, and a variety of opportunities. Overall, though, tourism was generating more revenue than at any time in history.

Yet part of the West's heritage disappeared when elegant Victorian and other older buildings became parking lots or modern glass and metal buildings. Poet Thomas Hornsby Ferril was one of those who had his doubts about progress. In his "House in Denver," he pointed out that the view from his home had changed since his youth:

In the morning I could stand
A long time watching my father disappear
Beyond the sunflowers which you noticed farther
In the morning. Now tall buildings interfere
In piles of shining masonry, but are there
Walls yet to come no more secure than these?
My city has not worn its shadows long.[4]

Denver had not worn its shadows long, and the city's destruction of its heritage, as well as that of its contemporaries, was viewed as progress. But it raised questions in Ferril's mind and in a slowly growing number of other Denverites as well.

Tourism advanced steadily in the economic lives of all three states, ranking behind only mining and agriculture in Montana and Wyoming and joining the federal government's impact as the wave of the future in Colorado.

Thanks to the efforts of the CCC in the thirties, the national parks were better prepared to receive the tourist influx. The downturn of visitors during the war had given the Park Service time to rehabilitate its parks—just in time before the rush came. Mesa Verde's visitation numbers jumped from the low 40,000s as its prewar peak to five times that number by the end of the 1940s. Yellowstone's visitors increased by almost the same ratio to two million as the 1950s closed, and its neighbor, Grand Teton National Park, raced to keep pace.

The increase in visitors led to familiar problems in all the parks: traffic jams, too many people crowding popular sites and trying to stay in camps, and negative impact on the wildlife. Tourists also created new dilemmas. The issues of declining air quality, commercialism versus conservation-preservation, and ecology versus visitation intensified. So did the questions of park expansion, and protected animals straying outside park boundaries and impacting nearby farmers and ranchers aroused locals and others to debate and write letters. No matter what it did or did not do, the Park Service could never resolve everyone's concerns. These problems increased as the years slipped by.

The long struggle to include Jackson Hole National Monument in the Grand Teton National Park finally succeeded. As the 1940s ended, objections started to decrease in Wyoming as the obvious benefits of tourism became more apparent. John D. Rockefeller Jr. eased the way by giving the federal government title to his Jackson Hole holding in 1949, and Congress authorized the consolidation of the monument and the park the next year. Some of the bitter feelings, however, continued before finally waning as the opponents learned to live with the new times and perhaps enjoy the good times.

The park's popularity grew in the years that followed; indeed it proved to be little short of phenomenal. Economic prosperity came to Jackson Hole and Teton County. The impact was clear when a 1959 study pointed out that 72 percent of the county's income came from tourism.

Preservation groups also became interested in national parks and national monuments. They were particularly concerned about dams and federal projects unrelated to parks, such as the Colorado–Big Thompson Project that skirted Rocky Mountain National Park, but that might impact parkland. This led to the first of what became ongoing struggles throughout the Rockies. In the 1950s fight over Colorado's Dinosaur National Monument, two proposed dams and reservoirs that would have encroached upon the monument became the issue. Conservationists successfully blocked them, but battle lines were being drawn.

Meanwhile, another old favorite, dude ranching, did not bounce back and regain its earlier prosperity. It enjoyed a brief revival of popularity after the war, but interests, travel destinations, and times were changing. Tourist families wanted to see as much as possible during their vacations, and other vacation areas offered more variety of things to see and enjoy in a short time. The old magnets of the ranches, rest and adventure, did not hold the appeal they once had. Dude ranches were slowly pushed into the background of the escalating tourist-recreation business, becoming a relic of an earlier age.

Dude ranches deserve credit, however, for helping to create interest in the West as a place to visit and to savor a western lifestyle. They were also one of the significant catalysts for the evolution of the vacation industry. Especially in Wyoming and Montana, dude ranches were a major factor in the birth of the vacation industry in many locales, and in Colorado they gave it a substantial boost.

Recreational hunting and fishing more than surpassed the economic benefits dude ranching had once provided for the three states. The impact proved truly amazing. For example, resident and nonresident hunting and fishing expenditures in Wyoming in 1955 exceeded the value of agriculture crops. As the years passed, the revenue continued to grow, although nonresidents complained about the rising costs of licenses and some residents did not appreciate having outsiders crowd their favorite fishing spots. Ranchers were also unhappy when hunters trespassed on their land or mistook a cow for a deer or an elk. Others might chuckle; the aggrieved owner did not.

When it came to tourism, Colorado far surpassed the other two states. They all had state and national parks, mountains, fishing streams, hiking trails, camping spots, historic sites, lakes, and beautiful scenery, but Colorado had the added advantages of being the easiest to reach and having more to see and enjoy. Not only did major highways tap the state, but Denver had also become a major airline hub. Wyoming and Montana offered nothing comparable, although Cheyenne had pretensions about its importance, just as it earlier had with railroad travel. Though most Americans had not flown commercially by 1945, the numbers increased steadily in the next fifteen years.

Denver experienced an increase in the number of major transcontinental airlines serving Stapleton Airfield, the region's largest. Connected to both coasts and major cities in between, Denver had a clear advantage over its regional rivals. International connections soon followed, all of which boosted the "Queen City of the Mountains and Plains" to a new height. Denver also offered a host of urban attractions—museums, orchestras, plays, hotels and restaurants, a zoo, parks, and sports teams (the minor league Denver Bears, for example) that no other Rocky Mountain rival could match for either tourist or local appeal.

As the first Rockies community to have its own television stations, Denver was on the cutting edge of the communications future. What radio had done in helping to break down isolation and bringing the three states more in tune with the rest of the country in the 1920s, TV would do visually in changing lives throughout the region. Both media provided news, sports, culture, entertainment, soap operas, and a variety of other shows. At the same time, they helped ameliorate regionalism. Westerners could instantly be kept abreast of fads, fashions, and daily events. For the children a whole new world appeared with Saturday cartoons, and particularly with *Sesame Street*, which came later, in 1969.

Denver not only pioneered television but was also the headquarters for its own airline, Frontier Airlines, Colorado's "baby" airline. Frontier, by the late 1950s, flew to local airports across the state. Frontier eventually became a major player throughout the entire Rocky Mountains region. For the novice, a trip might turn into an adventure, as planes climbed over high mountains and zoomed down into mountain-locked valleys, giving the riders a bounce or two along the way, and often a queasy stomach.

Direct flights were not initially available; a flight from Denver to Durango, for instance, stopped at Colorado Springs, Pueblo, and Alamosa along the way. Some flights were nicknamed the "vomit comet" because of all the ups and downs, but Frontier soon helped alleviate travelers' distress. It was worth the effort and higher ticket expense. One could fly from Cortez and Grand Junction to Denver in a little over an hour instead of many hours over the course of a day or so that the same trip took by car.

This progress came at a transportation cost. Railroads, once the king of travel, found passenger traffic declining and freight hauling threatened by truckers now that the roads had improved. Colorado's other "baby" line, the Denver & Rio Grande Western Railroad, had been abandoning track for decades, and that trend continued with it and the other lines in the Rockies. Not limited by rails, truckers and airplanes could service almost every town in Wyoming, Colorado, and Montana faster and more frequently than trains.

By the late 1950s, the Denver & Rio Grande's train between Durango and Silverton, through the beautiful Animas River Canyon and the rugged San Juan Mountains, carried more tourists than freight or regular passengers. Steam engines, old railroad cars, and leisurely mountain railroad travel had become tourist attractions rather than a means to reach a destination. As railroads switched from steam to diesel power, railroad buffs and others longed for the "good old days" of steam engines, passenger trains, and whistles.

It took awhile for the D&RG to realize the moneymaking possibilities of becoming a tourist attraction in the Colorado Rockies, but by the 1960s the company had joined the rapidly growing tourist industry, particularly on the run from Durango to Silverton, Colorado. No other Rockies railroad had the same advantages of scenery, history, and nostalgia, but in the years ahead, railroads in general gained more attention as they slowly faded from the scene.

Colorado was soon enjoying another bonanza, skiing. As far back as the 1880s, Coloradans had slid down mountains on twelve-foot skis after having to walk up the slopes or catch a ride partway in a sleigh to start their adventure downhill. They called it snowshoeing then. By the 1930s, skiing had gained more popularity, but then the war intervened. World War II benefited skiing in one way, because the famous Tenth Mountain Division carried out its training on skis. While skiing between Leadville and Aspen, division members realized the state's potential as a skiing destination.

As noted earlier, some of the members returned after the war and over the next two decades were instrumental in starting a group of ski resorts. The most famous, Aspen, a languishing former silver-mining town, became instantly popular. Its popularity and profits soon gave birth to rivals. The veterans did not accomplish all this alone. Starting in 1948, Walter Paepcke, a Chicago industrialist, initiated the conversion of Aspen into a health, sports, and cultural center. Combined with the winter attraction of skiing, it evolved into a year-round tourist destination.

Unwilling to let such an opportunity pass, other Colorado, Wyoming, and Montana mountain towns set about to gain for themselves a share of this winter prize and create their own skiing prosperity. That would take awhile.

Aspen also benefited from being relatively near the major population center of Denver and other Front Range cities. As roads and airline travel improved, it was not difficult to reach the ski slopes for a long weekend or a winter vacation.

Other Colorado towns dreamed of duplicating what Aspen had achieved as a tourist mecca. Even if a town were not blessed with excellent ski slopes, additional tourist possibilities existed. Central City proved that and reinvented itself. The first major gold mining town in the state, Central City's fortunes had decidedly waned after the turn of the century. Then, in the 1930s, the town experienced a cultural revival with the opening of the Central City summer opera and theater season.

After the war, Central City's reputation grew as home to one of the leading summer opera seasons in the West. The 1870s Teller Opera House found itself the center of a month-long season. Not only did the season feature operatic favorites, hoping to attract new operagoers by having them sung in English (shocking to purists!), but the Central City Opera Association also underwrote the creation of new operas. The most successful and longest-lasting of these, *The Ballad of Baby Doe*, debuted in 1956. It told the story of three legendary Coloradans, Horace, Augusta, and Baby Doe Tabor, and their love triangle. It became a standard in Central City's repertoire.

In the opera's last act, Tabor, while considering what he had accomplished, beautifully captured the spirit of Colorado in the late 1870s and the 1880s:

> How can a man measure himself?
> The land was growing, and I grew with it.
> In my brain rose buildings
> Yearning towards the sky
> And my guts sank deep
> In the plunging mineshafts.
> And my feet kicked up gold dust
> Wherever I danced,
> And whenever I shouted my name
> I heard a silver echo roar in the wind.[5]

That urban exuberance, optimism, boom mentality, and confidence was not seen again in Colorado until the postwar era in the late 1940s and the 1950s.

Abandoned mining camps, "ghost towns," and old mines also became tourist attractions. The famous four-wheel-drive Jeep of World War II was perfectly adapted to mountain travel, allowing tourists to visit the isolated mountain sites of nineteenth-century mining excitements. Western Montana also benefited from this fascination with a long-gone past as Jeepers bounced over old roads and trails to reach their destinations. Wyoming did not have much precious-metal mining history but did have military, cattle, and railroad history to share. Gold and silver mining ghost towns attracted tourists' attention, but not abandoned coal mining camps, of which Wyoming contained an abundance.

Company-dominated coal mining towns, filled with foreign immigrants laboring in an occupation that was hardly romantic, never had captured the public's fancy. The few modern uranium villages stirred little public interest either. The many more numerous abandoned prairie farm towns also drew scant attention. Few visitors found anything fascinating about a coal or farming settlement or the industries that gave birth to them. They could not match the legends of the quick wealth and adventuresome nature of the gold and silver mining camps and towns. The prosaic nature of coal and farming could never equal that legend. As had happened in 1859 and 1879, visitors rushed past the prairies to dash into the mountains.

It might have been the legendary appeal of precious-metal mining, but it also could have been the fun of hiking and driving in the mountains as opposed to prairies. Not many visitors tarried long before they reached the mountains in Colorado that the state had in spades.

Wyoming placed its focus on being the "cowboy state," certainly an attraction as the popularity of western novels and movies soared after the war. Cody and its famous namesake lured tourists to northern Wyoming, where they were not far away from another long-time tourist destination. Popular Yellowstone National Park gave the state another bonanza attraction. Montana's isolation, particularly the more scenic mountainous western part of the state, still hampered tourism. Wyoming and Montana would never have enough attractions or variety to cut into Colorado's tourist lead.

Nevertheless, for Wyoming and Montana, tourism was still a fast-growing industry. Wyoming and Montana dreamed of being ski resort destinations, but their remoteness and distance from major population centers handicapped them. To reach them, skiers had to travel past better-known ski areas. Wyoming tried, with nearly a dozen ski areas statewide, but none equaled those in Colorado.

For all the advantages of postwar transportation and other developments, nature could still play a terrifying role in the Rockies. A blizzard in January 1949 nearly paralyzed Wyoming, Colorado, and, to a lesser extent, Montana. Towns and travelers were isolated for days, trains stalled, highways were blocked, starving animals died, and people froze to death. In Wyoming's fourteen worst-hit counties, 100,000 sheep and 20,000 head of cattle died because of the storm. Airplanes dropped hay to cattle and sheep, and federal and state agencies worked to open roads, restore power, rescue stranded travelers, and try to help in any way possible. Storms raged until mid-February, making matters worse with no thaw or Chinook to bring relief.

Floods and forest fires, droughts, dust storms, and unpredictable weather in any season also plagued the West. As old-timers were apt to declare: "Wait around all day and you will see all four seasons." Westerners still had to learn to live with their environment, just as their ancestors had done.

The New Deal, the war years, and developments over the next decade and a half laid the groundwork for the remainder of the century for the Rocky Mountain states. The pluses outweighed the minuses in this rapidly changing world. Rocky Mountain folk could look around them and see the changes, and those changes came whether they liked it or not.

The interstate squabbles, urban jealousies, rural fears about the future and their urban neighbors, environmental concerns, and uncontrolled growth underlay all that was happening. So did worries about becoming a larger part of America and losing the individualism that had characterized the West.

Yet the Rockies by 1960 enthusiastically invited people to come and enjoy the western lifestyle. They could find new jobs in prosperous urban areas, visit the "untamed and legendary" West, participate in outdoor recreation, and relax and live in rural landscapes. They could do that if they did not mind traveling to the nearest city to find work. Horace Greeley's advice appeared as accurate in these years as when he had told adventuresome and ambitious young people to travel west a century before.

CHAPTER 8

The World Crashes In

The 1960s through the 1970s

Ban Mining: Let the B——s Freeze to Death in the Dark.
—*The Mining Record*, on numerous occasions in the 1970s

IT AROUSED PRAISE AND CONDEMNATION; was it a "vast wasteland" or the opportunity of a lifetime to expand knowledge and culture? Was it being used to distract and delude us, as reporter and TV personality Edward R. Murrow charged? Regardless, nothing could deny the influence that television made on Americans, urban and rural, during these decades. Nor were the Rockies' high mountain valleys or eastern plains immune to the revolution.

Television's impact on the Rocky Mountains expanded yearly during these decades; both young and old became addicted to it. Black-and-white TV transformed into color, screens increased in size, and even most of the rural West could receive television signals. From the evening news to Saturday cartoons to sports programs, Rocky Mountain folk marched right in step with their eastern and western cousins. Their lives would never be the same.

Rocky Mountain westerners watched with interest as almost nightly television showed that America in general was changing. From Birmingham to Watts, black Americans were on the move. Blacks were not the only group to push for rights and equality. Spanish Americans (many preferred to be called Chicanos, Latinos, or Hispanics) and Indians (some came to prefer *Native Americans* or tribal names) soon followed in their footsteps. Americans found that the immigration melting pot still contained some lumps. These various groups saw a few glitches in their American dream, from the use of derogatory words to describe them to a lack of appreciation for their contributions to American society. For all of them, the response of white America would determine the direction and success, or lack thereof, of their efforts and hopes.

These decades were a time of stress, confrontation, and alienation in America and the Rockies. The Vietnam War, antiwar demonstrations, the civil rights movement, "the hippies," and the impeachment of President Richard Nixon highlighted the era on the national scene. The assassinations of John Kennedy, Martin Luther King Jr., and Robert Kennedy left a sense of sadness and bitterness across the nation.

Add to this litany the cold war, urban riots, antigovernment and paramilitary groups, poverty, the decay of cities, a burgeoning crime rate, concern over nuclear weapons, and frayed race relations. A century's worth of tension and violence racked the nation in the 1960s and spilled over into the 1970s. Even an issue such as environmental concern caused a backlash. All of these challenges strained the fabric of American society, creating its worst domestic crisis in a hundred years.

At home, in the towns and cities, Americans worried about traffic congestion, underfinanced or underachieving public education, unsatisfactory public services, and unresponsive local government. Too much growth or a decline in population, religion in the schools, and such pocketbook issues as declines in agriculture and closing of factories and businesses, loss of jobs, the rising cost of living, and the cost of health care added to the uncertainties.

Morality in America became a sensitive area as well. Some thought "the Pill" spelled the end of morality for American youth and would only promote promiscuity. Others blamed Elvis Presley and the rock-and-roll era. Still others feared lowering the voting age meant trouble, whereas younger Americans worried about senior citizens having too much influence with their "old standards" on a rapidly changing world. Drugs hit the scene bigtime and shocked parents, politicians, law enforcement officers, teachers, and nearly everyone else concerned with youth. Nor were these just big-city problems; they hit small-town and rural America as hard. The "youth culture" seemed to be taking over. Television received its share of blame for almost everything from cultural decline to the sexual revolution.

In these years rural America declined in population while urban America grew. Hometown merchants in small-town America found themselves threatened by large, nationwide franchise businesses. Main streets had more vacant buildings, a situation that only became worse when interstates bypassed small towns. Meanwhile, the brighter opportunities of cities continued to lure people away from villages and towns, affecting everything from the local tax base to declines in school populations. Rural small-town America was losing its reason for existence as schools consolidated, businesses closed, churches merged, and the young people moved away.

The Rocky Mountain states missed none of this. Some issues impacted them more than others, but it had been several generations since distance and isolation provided a barrier from national and world problems.

Meanwhile, the women's rights movement gained momentum in significant ways, such as demanding equality in job opportunities and in employment advancement and wages. Socially and legally they pushed for other rights. Some women flaunted the movement's more symbolic side by not wearing bras. Many men and conservatives still argued that women should not abandon their honored status as housewives and mothers.

By the mid-1970s, Americans realized they had gone through one of the most eventful times in their history, an age of crisis and upheaval. It had taxed their ability to absorb and contain wave after wave of turbulent change. President Lyndon Johnson, himself a victim of that era, described it as the "great restlessness." Even with American society undergoing the travail of rebirth, Americans never abandoned their commitment to the goals of renewal and progress.

The Rocky Mountain states did not escape the turbulence; the days of their somewhat isolated existence had long ago disappeared. The expectations and frustrations were as noticeable in the Rockies as in New York, California, or Illinois. The unrest, a worldwide phenomenon, could be seen in Denver, Helena, Cheyenne, Billings, and the rural ranches and farmlands. Even those folks who fled to the mountains to retreat from society could not avoid it, in their hippie communes or more lavish second homes.

Continuing the postwar trend, Colorado witnessed the most dramatic changes of the three states and most clearly reflected American attitudes ranging from left to right. While all three states grew in population, the Centennial State was the most popular destination in the Rockies for restless Americans, whether tourists, job seekers, retirees, or those alienated from society or angered by the political scene.

Wyoming illustrated what happened to a state somewhat out of the American transformation mainstream. Some civil rights issues surfaced there when black football players on the university team leveled accusations of discrimination and what they perceived as racism in Laramie. The situation captured national news, shocked Wyomingites, and led to a severe backlash against the university. Loyal football fans saw their team take a beating on and off the field. Yet minorities remained scarce in the state, as did many urban problems such as slums and big-city crime. For some Americans, that made the state more attractive.

The "cowboy state" was itself tied to declining economic old-timers such as mining and agriculture. Both the cattle and sheep industries suffered in the 1960s and 1970s. Fewer sheep and cattle grazed in Wyoming valleys and prairies than at any time in the century. Prices remained low and both industries suffered as the public's food tastes shifted, more dramatically with mutton than beef.

In fact, the sheep industry received a double hit. Clothing styles and fabrics changed with severe competition from synthetic fibers. This cut into the wool market, compounded by mutton and lamb no longer being popular menu items. The federal government subsidies helped, as they did in other agricultural areas; they could help the industry survive, if not prosper. Despite these declines, that legendary cattle state Wyoming still ranked as one of the top sheep states in the nation as the decade of the 1970s progressed.

In Wyoming, cattle and coal had helped lay the foundation for statehood and economic growth. Now they were relegated more to the past than the present. Indeed, so few old-time cowboys remained that the state clung more to a legend than a reality, but the legend still helped tourism, the state's fastest-growing industry in the 1960s and 1970s. As in the rest of the country, most Wyomingites lived in cities; the 1960 census, for instance, found nearly one-third of the state's people living in Cheyenne, Casper, and Laramie. The census count also confirmed the trend of people leaving and others arriving, with only 44 percent of the residents claiming native status.

Montana exhibited some of the same trends. The 1960 census showed for the first time in the state's history more inhabitants living in urban than in rural settings. Historian Clark Spence pointed out that Montana had experienced "a sluggish overall growth rate" since 1950, and it continued into the 1970s. A 1970 study by the University of Montana School of Business described the state's economy as "relatively colorless," "with a steady erosion of the state's position relative to the national economy."[1]

New industry did not come to Montana, and mining and agriculture declined along with jobs and income. The state continued to be a producer and exporter of raw materials, not a manufacturer or processor. Previous problems remained to hamper development. Isolation from main transportation lines and remoteness from markets led to ongoing higher living costs. Strong financial institutions were absent, and unemployment remained above the national average. The ongoing out-migration of educated young people meant that both Montana and Wyoming lost valuable resources difficult to replace. The trends already noticed in the eastern counties endured, with farms consolidating, small towns declining, and rural problems multiplying.

Contrast these trends with Colorado. Its population continued to grow, reaching 2.2 million by 1970—54 percent higher than it had been at the end of the war. It was the fourth-fastest-growing state in the nation. Denver remained the region's number one city, and it along with its neighboring counties—Adams, Arapahoe, and Jefferson—remained the state's fastest growing. In population, the suburban communities around the capital city jumped ahead of almost all the large towns in the other two states.

Elsewhere in Colorado, the mountain and eastern plains counties and the Western Slope either lost population or grew far more slowly than the Denver area. In some counties, the alarming decrease caused populations to drop to nearly half their prewar figures. One trend that bucked the overall pattern was the growing popularity of second homes in the mountains, particularly around ski areas and just west of the Front Range. Politically, however, in all three states the rural areas had a tenuous grip in the state legislature, an ever-building, contentious issue.

The decrease in population was most noticeable in the agricultural counties of eastern Colorado. Familiar trends continued, with farms getting larger and more mechanized, families moving away, small towns shrinking, the tax base eroding, and political power potentially waning. The jobs and advantages of urbanization beckoned just a few miles to the west, and with water rights worth more than the land, many were tempted to sell out. The federal government stepped in with various programs to try to help, but farming in all three states suffered. By the mid-1970s, the family farm in some areas had become almost extinct.

Nature did not help either, as the ongoing cycle of drought and wet years continued. Rainmakers again tendered their services, with mixed results. Denver and California companies offered help for a price and sometimes claimed to be effective; other times, little difference was noticed. The idea of seeding winter storms with silver iodide particles or something similar promised to increase snowfall. Farmers, ranchers, and skiers were optimistic. In theory, this seeding would improve the snow-pack in ski areas and improve the spring and summer runoffs. The results proved inconclusive, however.

New business and industry poured into Colorado, mostly along the Eastern Slope of the Rockies from Fort Collins to Pueblo. That longtime population core had the most to offer. Meanwhile, tourism, except during the oil crisis, continued to soar everywhere, apart from the eastern plains.

Almost all aspects of Colorado's urban economy joined the parade. The economic base included a varied assortment of businesses and industries, such as space exploration, tea, computers, candy, skis, environmental consultants, and clothing manufacturing. The influx exacerbated the urban problems described previously.

Meanwhile, the old standby, mining, illustrated the other side of the economy. Gold and silver mining slipped further into decline, in fact, nearly vanishing by the 1970s except for small operators or as a by-product of other mining. Butte's copper mining was under mounting pressure from foreign operations with higher-grade copper and lower labor costs, newer and larger deposits, and fewer labor problems.

Uranium mining's boom faded as well. The Atomic Energy Commission concluded that it had enough ore. With that, and having misjudged the large reserves available, the AEC stopped subsidizing production in 1962 and curtailed purchases. By then uranium stockpiles exceeded military and national needs. Mills and mines in Wyoming and Colorado closed, and employment in the industry collapsed. Another mining boom had busted.

It left behind a strange and worrisome legacy. Quiet returned to the plateaus, mountains, and plains where the uranium mining had been, but few tourists came to see the scarred landscape, weathered buildings, abandoned mines, and declining towns. In fact, people complained about the scarred landscape, and some raised more serious concerns. The mill dumps in or near towns and cities with low-grade uranium ores left over, like those near Durango and Grand Junction, raised worries about whether the tailings were "hot" and what risk they posed to nearby residents. Some people were scared about the risks and had every right to be.

Reports of fish, birds, and cattle dying from the contaminated water draining from the mines indicated problems. Uranium leaching from low-grade ores left on the dumps, or in abandoned mines and pits, percolated into watersheds and streams, producing a long-range problem. Also, an increasing number of uranium miners were coming down with cancer, particularly lung cancer. These red flags did not portend a bright future for the uranium country or its inhabitants.

Not everything was gloom and despair for the industry, however. Wyoming and Montana ranked high in American coal reserves. With strip mining providing a cheaper way of production and with the use of coal as a fuel for electric power plants, coal's future looked more promising than it had in years. With the nation seeking additional fuel reserves, all three states offered the potential for energy freedom from foreign sources. This worry intensified as the Middle East, with its vast oil reserves, continually became a more volatile area on which to rely.

Americans were learning how dependent the country was on Middle East oil and its Arab suppliers. Because the United States had supported Israel during the 1973–74 Arab-Israeli war and earlier as well, the Organization of Petroleum Exporting Countries (OPEC), after a brief embargo, quadrupled their prices. With the huge amounts of oil it used, the United States was hard hit.

The oil crisis affected all aspects of western economic life — manufacturers, farmers, ranchers, homeowners, the tourist business, merchants, and transportation. Gasoline prices soared toward a dollar a gallon, car prices increased, and so did nearly everything else. The cost of living bounded upward; in addition, unemployment climbed briefly into 1975, reminding some of the dreadful days of the 1930s. Frequently faced with long drives to town and increasingly relying on mechanization, Rocky Mountain farmers suffered as transportation and work costs soared. The crisis also decreased tourism, on which so many relied. People from the Midwest and East stayed home or in the neighborhood — no long, costly trips to the Rockies.

Desperately seeking new oil sources, Washington turned to that notorious coquet, the ever-promising oil shale. Wyoming and Colorado both contained large deposits, but no one had yet figured out how to profitably refine it. The potential impact on the land worried environmentalists and others, while local communities were concerned another boom might fizzle.

Historian Richard White captured the times when he wrote that "westerners who opposed rapid energy development did so from environmental concerns and also from a resurgent sense of western domination by easterners—both corporate officials and bureaucrats." Their resentment also came from a "history of booms and busts" and "fears for the future."[2] They had every right to be resentful.

All these developments had a long-range impact on western fuel reserves. Montana and Wyoming's coal production had dropped steadily, and the industry as a whole seemed to be on a definite decline as other fuels replaced coal. In Wyoming, coal towns such as Rock Springs and Hanna lost population, the latter declining by more than half to just over 600 people. Then the industry revived, if not individual towns that had once relied on coal mining. Wyoming's low-sulfur coal, much of it not very deep in the earth and containing high BTU quality, was economical to use in coal-fired generating plants. The expansion of coal-burning steam-power-generating plants increased the need for coal. In the 1960s, strip mining became the rule.

Unfortunately for Wyoming's reputation as part of the new coal boom, the Jim Bridger Power Plant was constructed near Rock Springs. Nothing was wrong with the power plant, but the 3,000 workers overwhelmed the unprepared community. The situation grabbed national attention with every "boom problem" imaginable—not to mention a corrupt city government, open prostitution, and other questionable activities. "Sinful" Rock Springs became a symbol of what could happen to the Rockies as the energy crisis expanded and the country looked eagerly and somewhat greedily at the three states' oil, natural gas, and coal reserves.

In Montana, the industry began to revive in 1968, rejuvenating coal mining by the early 1970s. Strip mining started major operations in southeastern Montana in the Colstrip area in 1968. The coal shipped to Billings to a new coal-fired steam-generating plant, soon followed by two more in Colstrip, also traveled by large "unit trains" to Minnesota for use in electrical utilities. In the 1970s, Montana coal went as far west as the Columbia Basin, east to Illinois, and south to Texas. Increased local profits, business, and jobs, however, were counterbalanced by a host of questions.

With the new interest in coal came the old arguments about colonial exploitation to benefit outsiders. Considering where Montana coal was shipped, at least for Montanans the argument held true. A comment appeared in the *Atlanta Monthly* in September 1972 that made Montanans begin to wonder about the rest of the country: "Mining is the best thing that could happen to eastern Montana. It's just a desert, anyway. Hell, strip it."[3]

Again, natural resources were being exported from the Rockies and leaving behind scars on the land, a mess in local streams, and blighted air quality. Should others help to pay for the restoration of the land and water? Could air quality be restored? Would this be another boom and bust? How much should the federal government step in and help? Did Montanans even want Washington to intervene?

All this happened just as the national environmental movement gained a full head of steam. Interest in conservation of natural resources had existed since at least the 1890s with such organizations as the Sierra Club and the Audubon Society. In the twentieth century a fear that the country might be running out of coal focused attention on conservation, as did President Theodore Roosevelt, with his enthusiasm for the outdoors and national parks. The great oil discoveries in Texas and Oklahoma put the fuel shortage worries to rest. However, as the century passed, interest expanded beyond conservation of natural resources to environmental issues to a focus on land, water, and air.

By the 1950s, apprehensions had revived and the environmental movement was launched. Although initially small, the movement grew steadily. The elusive term "quality of life" became popular as many Americans began to realize the importance of clean air, unpolluted water, unblemished landscapes and vistas, safe local environments, and unspoiled wilderness.

The publication of naturalist Rachel Carson's *Silent Spring* (1962) took dead aim at pesticide poisoning and environmental pollution. Highly popular, the book shocked the country. Those concerns, plus rapidly growing interest in environmental issues, set the stage for the rest of the century. Two Gallup polls found that in the mid-1960s, only 17 percent of the public considered air and water pollution a major government problem; but that figure had risen to 53 percent by 1970. The movement cut across all segments of the American public, from sportsmen to naturalists, from youth to senior citizens.

Washington responded, particularly during President Lyndon Johnson's administration and his "Great Society" program. The programs ran the gamut, from the National Wilderness Preservation Act of 1964 to the president's wife, Lady Bird Johnson, leading a beautification campaign to eliminate unsightly billboards and junkyards along the nation's highways.

The movement gained momentum, carrying over into the Nixon administration; Congress responded with scores of bills to protect endangered species, reduce pollution, control strip mining, promote clean air, improve water quality, and address a host of other issues. The Environmental Protection Agency (established in 1970) became the government's largest regulatory agency within a decade. Many old-time westerners shook their heads in disbelief at what was happening.

Although the movement was focused broadly nationwide, in the Rockies it was initially aimed at mining and excessive use of water. The latter focused on dams and large-scale irrigation projects that, although popular several generations before, now drew heated criticisms. The "desert" should not be made to bloom simply to grow crops that could be grown more easily and cheaply elsewhere, many now argued. Dams also spoiled the natural environment, endangered fish species, produced silted reservoirs, and impacted stream flow.

Westerners, and Americans in general, used more water per capita than any other industrial society. The problem for the Rocky Mountain states, where streams were encumbered by interstate water compacts, focused on where to find water sources for the rapidly growing urban areas. Colorado faced that challenge first, fastest, and foremost.

The mining industry received more attention than it had at any time in its history. Throughout the Rockies unsightly dumps, scarred landscapes, polluted streams, mercury residue from smelting and milling, and community watersheds threatened by leaching minerals from mine portals and dumps, aroused environmentalists. Even those who did not call themselves environmentalists worried about their local areas and quality of life. Health issues concerned everyone.

The growing activism of the "Spaceship Earthers," as they were nicknamed, put the industry under general attack in all three states. Technology, the darling of previous generations, was challenged as a major threat to the earth. Uncontrolled technology devoured raw materials and created vast quantities of waste products. Dependent on nature and mining, man had an obligation to both. The industry, foes charged, had a moral obligation to protect the environment and to conserve that heritage for future generations.

The miner under the ground and the geologist above it had never been denounced in these philosophical terms. Values clashed against values, and mining suffered. Western mining also suffered because of the sins of others, including strip mining in Appalachia and coal mining in Pennsylvania and elsewhere. The industry could no longer rely on its economic significance to the country to sidestep such criticism, concerns, and issues.

Neither side completely understood or listened unemotionally to the other. For many people mining and miners had become environmental Genghis Khans, bowing to the great god Profit.

Mining responded initially with a bunker mentality: dig in and fight. Had not miners been the "heroes" of the past? Had not the industry helped open the Rockies, populate it with "sturdy pioneers," and develop the natural resources that had benefited the entire region as well as the nation?

The regional spokesman for the industry, Denver's *Mining Record*, responded through its feisty, braying rapporteur, "Prunes" the burro, with a variety of complaints and blistering observations:

50 years ago smoke was a sign of progress; now it's a dirty word!
—October 6, 1971

If the old-time miners had been forced to replant the trees and restock the trout streams like today, they'd never have made it!
—July 26, 1972

I want a front row seat when the Environmentalists start digging coal to satisfy their energy needs.
—March 29, 1972

Did you ever stop to think what kind of pollution problem we'd have if those 90 million cars in the U.S. were horses?
—September 1, 1972

Ask not what the government can do for you—but of what the government can do to you!

—October 10, 1973

Another of Prunes's comments, oft-repeated, even became a bumper sticker, thrown in the face of environmentalists: "Ban Mining: Let the Bastards Freeze to Death in the Dark."

The industry printed another slogan, "If it can't be grown, it has to be MINED." Neither stickers nor Prunes and his supporters' best efforts worked. Mining was dragged kicking into the late twentieth century and was forced to become environmentally concerned and involved. In a way, the criticism was not completely warranted. There had been concerned people within the industry since the nineteenth century; the majority simply overwhelmed them and their efforts. Unfortunately, the two groups worked at cross-purposes. Other industries had not exhibited concern either, but their "sins" were better hidden.

As the 1960s ended and the 1970s began, the shouting, name-calling, and public condemnation left scars on mining and shaped the industry's responses in the later 1970s. Western mining would not forget this upheaval. As Prunes repeatedly observed, "Don't make excuses—make good." In the Rockies, with mining on the wane, the industry stood on the defensive about its heritage and its present situation and found few friends beyond the portal and pit. The present did not deserve all the blame; old mines also polluted streams and the landscape as they had for years, and their owners were long gone or even dead. Who was to pay for their share of the costs? Should the government or the state step in, or should the industry in general be responsible? The question of uranium mining, which raised even more questions, haunted Wyoming and Colorado. Fortunately, few other mining states had to deal with the problem.

The answers were not found during the seventies. Some progress was made cleaning up streams and restoring damaged landscapes, but the future would still have to pay the price for the past's "sins."

Not all westerners were enraged about environmentalists and their ideas. In the late 1960s and early 1970s, Montanans became one of the most environmentally concerned groups in the nation. The coal boom, with its scarred landscapes, damaged river systems, and plant pollution, brought matters to a head. Present coal plants and leases held the promise of future expansion. The prospect of a massive energy expansion loomed, which pleased some, horrified others.

The state legislature responded with tough environmental protection laws in 1971, followed by the Montana Strip Mining and Reclamation Act (forced restoration of mined land), the Montana Water Use Act, the Montana Utility Siting Act, and the Strip Mine Coal Conservation Act, all passed in 1973. A sweeping, controversial 30 percent coal severance tax instituted in 1975 closed the era. Montana now emerged a national environmental leader with some of the country's most stringent environmental laws. Colorado also had strict laws, but they did not produce significant results. Wyoming trailed both its neighbors on environmental issues.

Montana's new state constitution (1972) guaranteed Montanans the "right to a clean and healthful environment." The old 1889 constitution had seemed out of date, and with a progressive mood sweeping the state, voters approved the calling of a constitutional convention in 1971. They also narrowly approved the new constitution, half the length of the old, the following year. That constitution strengthened the legislature and modernized the government, among other things. Surviving legal challenges, it was hailed as a "model document."

The vote over ratification of the constitution revealed a strikingly familiar pattern in the Rocky Mountain states—liberal urban voters were pitted against conservative rural voters. It also pitted the young, better-educated, and more liberal legislators against their older, more "school of hard knocks," and conservative counterparts. The pattern was familiar from earlier days, but now, with President Nixon's Watergate woes, and his resignation, liberalism stood strong.

Another major source of controversy was the Vietnam War. In the debate, the impact of television was profound. As the war continued through the 1960s and crashed into the 1970s, TV viewers could watch on the nightly news as the war expanded and victory danced elusively away. They could also see the mounting protests, as Americans both young and old became more and more concerned about why the U.S. forces were even there, the cost in human lives, and Washington's role in defending our involvement. Before the sixties had ended, the war had destroyed Johnson's presidency and affected almost every segment of American life.

In the Rocky Mountain states, as throughout the country, Vietnam became in part a generational clash between youths and older adults, liberals and conservatives, and hawks and doves, the latter joined by anti- war activists. The most active opposition surfaced in Colorado, the most liberal of the three states, but college campuses in all three states had antiwar demonstrations. This uproar created among other things con- cern about faculty and what was being taught, and conservatives attack- ing higher education.

Protests came in a variety of forms: sit-ins, antiwar demonstrations, speeches, clashes over military recruiters being on campus, teach-ins, newspaper letters and articles opposing the war, and lessons on how to avoid the draft (a hot issue). Some students went so far as to deny those supporting the war their right to speak or disrupted them when they tried to do so. In some cases, public and private property was destroyed when demonstrations got out of hand. Shocked, horrified, and disgusted patri- otic Americans, some of whom believed in "my country right or wrong," watched the rising opposition in disbelief. Unrest spread from campuses to the streets; more than college students were involved, with those opposing the war coming from all lifestyles, occupations, and regions of the country. Young men from all three Rocky Mountain states fled the country, many to nearby Canada, to avoid the draft, further antagonizing war supporters and horrifying the Second World War generation. The situation reflected a time of stress, rising anger, and frustrations on both sides.

To make matters worse, this was the age of the hippie (the "New Age"), of multicolored vans, psychedelic clothes, long-haired youth, and communes, not to mention pot smoking and free love. Drugs of a more addictive nature, although illegal, also became more commonly used. If the older generation had been shocked by the antiwar attitudes, all these developments really upset them. They despaired of what America had become and where it might be going. They tended to forget that many of their parents had been members of the flapper and speakeasy genera- tion and recalled only that they themselves had come of age during the Depression and World War II, when sacrifices had to be made. Their children had not experienced these deprivations, and they had worked hard to spare them from such problems. They could hardly believe that this was their reward.

Again, Colorado more than conservative, rural, and traditional Wyoming and Montana reflected the national scene. More urban than its neighbors, more cosmopolitan, and more liberal in its attitudes, Colorado experienced more of the hippie era. Colorado had more communes, hippies, and tolerance for different lifestyles, although both state and local officials made efforts to curb the growing drug scene. Many Coloradans, however, could not tolerate the new lifestyle and were vocal about it.

Part of the confrontation stemmed from the long-standing, serious issue of urban versus rural America. In each of the three state legislatures, as discussed, members' districts had been drawn long ago when rural districts reigned.

From the urban viewpoint, most rural legislators did not understand their problems—slums, crime, transportation, minorities, white flight, and poverty, for example. Rural legislators claimed their urban counterparts did not grasp their situation—population decline, the erosion of ranching and farming, a disappearing tax base, and being left out of many urban benefits that city dwellers took for granted. Urban politicians wanted more representation in the legislature, and rural politicians realized that if they did not defend the status quo, they would lose political power forever. They would then become, so to speak, second-class citizens.

This problem did not exist solely in the Rockies; it was discussed, debated, and fought out throughout the country. In Wyoming and Montana, rural representatives maintained a better hold, until Washington intervened. In the 1962 case of *Baker v. Carr*, the Supreme Court opened the way for reapportionment of state legislatures. The standard became the famous—or infamous, according to one's view—"one person, one vote."

This was the crucial turning point that broke rural legislators' controls. Lightly populated districts would now be consolidated so that all state legislative districts would represent, as nearly as possible, the same number of voters. In the United States House of Representatives, the urban districts gained the political power they wanted and fairly deserved. Rural districts, as they had feared, lost voice and clout. In Colorado, legislators with agricultural ties became nearly extinct. One of the most significant twentieth-century transformations in the Rocky Mountain states occurred with this change in political and legislative control.

This trend exacerbated another issue, the Eastern versus Western Slope split along the Continental Divide. With the predominant majority of Coloradans living on the Eastern Slope, Western Slopers found themselves outvoted and consigned to a decided minority. With its mountains, plateaus, mesas, and beautiful valleys, this land offered a tourist mecca. Nevertheless, on crucial issues such as roads, money for higher education, and other state financial outlays, the Western Slope had become a poor country cousin.

The big issue, however, that affected westerners from all walks of life was water. No easy delimitation put people on one side or another. Many rural people charged that "damnable" environmentalists and their urban backers did not understand the needs of the West. Urbanites pointed out that they needed water too. Critics on both sides accused outsiders of trying to place their standards and ideas on outnumbered westerners. Rocky Mountain residents clearly resented being criticized by easterners for spending taxpayers' money on "boondoggle" projects. Newspaper editorials fought back and forth, and papers carried inflammatory headlines.

In Colorado, the Western Slope had abundant water and few votes; the growing Eastern Slope yearned for water and had political clout. Interstate water compacts stopped those who wanted to get water around or under the mountains to where, in their estimation, it would be better utilized. As that old western saying pointed out, "water flows toward money."

Residents fought over the Frying Pan–Arkansas Project for transmontane storage and water division to assist the state's southeastern region. Water collected—or "stolen," depending on one's view—west of the Continental Divide would be tunneled through the mountains and then stored for use in municipal water systems and for irrigation. Western Slopers lost when the U.S. Congress approved the project in 1962. That was not the end of the struggle; Eastern Slopers had their eyes on other water.

The Western Slope did gain some of the dams and reservoirs promised under the Colorado River Compact. Local irrigation and reclamation benefited along with tourism; but as the 1970s progressed, federal water projects became harder to secure. Such issues as environmental impacts, endangered species, threats to subsurface aquifers, and Native American water rights hindered rapid planning, and expanding costs upset taxpayers beyond the mountains, who saw no benefit to them.

In Wyoming, the problem was less east versus west, or urban versus rural, than it was the failure of the long-expected benefits from reclamation projects. A 1963 Bureau of Reclamation study reported that most of the state's reclamation projects were handicapped by poor soil and high altitudes. Indeed, the government offered to buy back land from farmers on the third phase of the Riverton Project because the land was so unproductive.

Wyomingites found little cause to complain, because even if the project failed to match expectations, it temporarily benefited the state's economy. Against the few acres that might be reclaimed were such benefits as employment, flood control, dams that generated electric power, and increased recreational opportunities.

More statewide worry existed about reclamation projects undertaken nearby. Montana and Idaho projects were attacked by Wyoming's congressional delegation in the 1960s. Sen. Gale McGee, however, proved farsighted when he argued that western states must work together for regional development, something other perceptive westerners had long favored. Until such a time of regional teamwork became a reality, the Rocky Mountain states would find themselves outnumbered in Washington.

One sign of the future arrived—the conflict between urban-industrial needs and agriculture, which controlled most of the water rights. Until the mid-1950s, Wyoming laws had recognized preferred water rights, defined as water used for domestic, municipal, and transportation needs. Everything else had a lower priority.

However, uranium mills and other power-generating plants needed water too. The 1955 and 1957 legislative sessions tackled the problem and finally gave industrial purposes preferred status. Although not given the power to condemn existing irrigation water rights, they could buy existing rights and claim unappropriated rights. The future of irrigation water rights, as opposed to industrial development, now came under close scrutiny.

Montana's experiences with water during these years were less divisive. Except for a brief dispute with neighbors over a proposed dam that was never built, the state marched forward. Its Fort Peck, Hungry Horse, and Yellowtail dams provided both irrigation and power. In 1968, construction of the Libby Dam was begun; together with other smaller projects, it provided an impressive resource for the state.

Meanwhile, another issue flared, complicating the water situation: Indian water rights. The Winters Doctrine (1908) had given tribes prior (but unquantified) water rights that most had never used. That meant tribes owned the number one water right on the streams running through their lands, something that would become an important issue later in the century. Also, in the dam-building era, Native American lands had been condemned, and the government often offered the tribes inadequate compensation.

As the 1960s passed, tribes began questioning what had happened to their rights. With the aid of lawyers, some started pushing to regain what had rightly been theirs. Meantime, most reservations suffered through hard times.

Washington did not help the Natives when it approved a controversial policy of "termination," harking back to an earlier idea. Cutting off federal supervision of the tribes, a 1950s policy of relocation aimed to remove them from the reservations, where they were trapped in a situation of high unemployment. They would then be moved to an area with better job opportunities. Denver, for instance, gained an increasing number of Native Americans; in fact, they soon outnumbered the Utes living on their two reservations in the state's southwest corner. The program proved disastrous. Many Native Americans did not adjust to their new, usually urban, environments or possess the skills needed to find or retain jobs there. Fortunately, Washington, seeing its mistake, abandoned the policy in the 1960s.

On the Wyoming and Montana reservations, poverty, high unemployment, mounting welfare cases, alcoholism, and other social problems bedeviled everyone. Often located in isolated rural settings, with almost nonexistent employment opportunities, reservations offered little hope. With a few exceptions, life there generally reflected poverty and substandard living conditions.

Montana's Salish-Kutenai Reservation was one exception. Favorably located in the northwestern part of the state, it had large stands of valuable timber, a dam that generated power profits, and endless recreational possibilities in the Flathead Valley. Far to the south in the Four Corners region, the Southern Utes, headquartered in Ignacio, Colorado, prospered as well; they had natural gas and oil as benefits. With excellent tribal leadership they became one of the richest tribes in the nation.

In stark contrast, the neighboring Ute Mountain Ute Tribe frittered away money from mineral leases and remained one of the poorest of the Rocky Mountain tribes. They faced the usual problems of poverty, lack of education, a high murder rate, and a variety of social problems, including alcoholism.

Some reservations tried to alleviate their poverty by encouraging tourism, recreation, hunting, and fishing. This plan worked for a few. Isolated locations, long travel distances, poor promotion, and no nearby large urban neighbors doomed most efforts.

Meanwhile, the number of urban Indians increased steadily. Denver saw some adjust very nicely to the urban situation; others did not. Some of these Natives tended to be more radical than those who remained on the reservation. Out of this grew the American Indian Movement (AIM), which started in the Midwest and spread west. AIM brought national attention to the plight of Indians both on and off the reservation. The group's tough, flamboyant leaders ransacked the Bureau of Indian Affairs building in Washington (1972), and violence followed their occupation of the South Dakota village of Wounded Knee (1973), leading to protests from many reservation leaders, who were promptly denounced by AIM. "Red Power" advocates called them "apples," red on the outside, white on the inside, and the total Native American cause suffered.

The movement collapsed in the mid-1970s amid excesses, which included murder and local and federal repression. More constructive for the future were developments such as those at Fort Lewis College in Durango. Under a 1910 agreement with Washington, when an Indian school became Colorado property, Native students were admitted tuition-free. After evolving from a rural high school to a junior college to a four-year liberal arts college, Fort Lewis maintained its "sacred trust" and became one of the nation's leading educators of Native students.

Hispanics also started to push for their rights. Their largest numbers, among the three states, lived in Colorado. Located on the border of the Southwest, Colorado had witnessed an increasing migration of Hispanics northward. They lived in both rural and urban settings and often were the last hired and the first fired from jobs. They faced problems of discrimination, lack of skills, low-paying jobs, difficulties in the schools, language obstacles, cultural stress, and substandard living conditions. An extreme example of this existed in Colorado's San Luis Valley, where

New Mexicans had settled as early as the 1840s. Many had been migrant workers in the beet fields or had done various types of agricultural work or minimum-wage urban jobs.

As the civil rights movement gained momentum in the 1960s, Hispanics started the struggle to gain their rights. The decades-old division between Anglo and Spanish cultures—long unspoken—came into the open, initially catching the public's attention at Center, Colorado, in the San Luis Valley. Both permanent and migrant Hispanic workers lived in Center and faced the same conditions their fellow Hispanics did elsewhere. The difference was that they organized, protested, and—through the political process—gained control of the town council, secured seats on the board of education, and pressed ahead on other issues.

Elsewhere, through both violent and peaceful protests, Hispanics pushed for bilingual and bicultural education, increased numbers of Hispanic teachers in the schools, and increased awareness of Spanish culture and heritage in Colorado. Among other issues that surfaced were discrimination in the workforce, stereotyping of Latin American people, and segregation into a certain section or sections of communities. Like Americans throughout the country, Coloradans had demonstrated over the years a continual lack of awareness of and sensitivity toward these people in their midst.

Even though Denver had a sizable contingent of African Americans, nowhere else in the three states did blacks live in appreciable numbers, particularly not in the rural areas. Wyoming, however, did pass a civil rights bill earlier, in the late 1950s, being one of the first states to do so. It protected a person "of good deportment" from being denied the necessities of life or the rights guaranteed in the Declaration of Independence on the basis of "race, color, creed, or national origin."

There might not be large numbers of minorities, but the number of tourists grew as tourism continued its upward climb on the economic ladder. Except for the eastern plains, which basically captured only pass-through traffic, all over the region tourism became a fixture in the late spring into the early fall. Winter skiing held intriguing possibilities for another strong tourist season, which materialized for some communities and resorts. From Chambers of Commerce to Main Street merchants to those involved in the tourist industry, Rocky Mountain folk looked at tourists as walking dollars to be deposited. They came, saw, and left, and a growing number planned to return permanently. Some of those who feared the long-range impact of tourism pointed directly at the tourists who came back to stay as helping to spoil the Rockies and its quality of life.

By the mid-1960s, Wyoming was benefiting from out-of-state travelers, who spent over $100 million dollars in 1963, nearly triple what they had spent only fifteen years before. Grand Teton and Yellowstone parks led the way as tourist attractions, but local cities had difficulty luring these visitors to come and stay awhile. Only Cheyenne, with its Frontier Days rodeo and accompanying festivities, succeeded in doing so. Tourists came to Wyoming to see national parks and travel on, neglecting everything else, although some with historic interests did pause to visit Fort Laramie, Devil's Tower, Fort Bridger State Park, and museums scattered about the state.

Montana gained over $72 million from tourism at the same time; Colorado easily surpassed both Montana and Wyoming. Montana, however, acquired a multimillion-dollar resort complex when investors opened Big Sky of Montana on the West Fork of the Gallatin River. Still, its ski resorts languished because of the old, unresolved problems of no large urban areas from which to draw and difficulties getting to the state and the ski areas.

Skiing might be attracting more visitors to the Rockies, but the lure of the Old West remained strong. Much as writers had done earlier, a new generation of authors kept its fame alive. They captured the earlier West and through that saga its modern counterpart as well.

"What made them go was a sort of urge, a frame of mind. One man that had it would take it up the hill with him and work his guts out, while the fellow next door with the same feeling would use it sitting on his ass scheming out ways to cheat the first one." Thus Walt, a character in David Lavender's novel *Red Mountain* (1963), describes why people settled in the Colorado San Juans. A. B. Guthrie Jr. told of another Rockies trait in *The Way West* (1952): "Change was coming on change. Summers [character in book] thought it was only the earth that didn't change."[4] Both authors caught the spirit of past and present; their characters could have as easily been speaking about the twenty-first century as the nineteenth.

In the generation after the war, the literary West blossomed as never before, including such masterpieces as Guthrie's *The Big Sky* (1947). A host of prominent authors helped their readers understand historical detail and current social events.

Following in the fictional footsteps of Ernest Haycox and others, they wrote with greater historical realism and social detail. Guthrie and Lavender displayed those traits; so did Jack Schaefer, Frank Waters, Larry McMurtry, Wallace Stegner, Dorothy Johnson, Ivan Doig, Tony Hillerman, and N. Scott Momaday. They have all written about or touched on the Rockies fictionally, historically, currently, and sometimes all three.

No one, however, was more popular or more widely read than Louis L'Amour, who set a score of his stories in the Rockies. His West was the legendary West, a place of adventure, action, and good guys versus bad. What took him beyond writers of the genre was his careful historic research and detail of each book's setting, which he visited before writing. L'Amour and the others helped shape the public's view and awareness of the Rocky Mountain heartland past, present, and future.

Historians were also busy digging into its fascinating past. Scholars like Robert Athearn, T. A. Larson, Carl Ubbelohde, Clark Spence, and Michael Malone educated a generation of students, "buffs," and fellow historians. Seldom, however, did they approach the popularity or impact of the creative writers mentioned previously.

Among the poets, this author's favorite is the already cited Thomas Hornsby Ferril, who wrote in one of his prose pieces, "What it all comes down to is making something out of what we are where we are. Our most terrifying international problems are, at the core, provincial problems. Local frustration generates the plundering nomad in us."[5] Making this point just after World War II, Ferril could as easily have been describing the 1960s and 1970s.

Much as these authors influenced the image of the West, so did movies and that already discussed latecomer in the 1950s, television. They helped shape the mythological West for a new generation of twentieth-century viewers and locked the West in the nineteenth century. A wide variety of westerns hit the movie screens in the postwar era, from *High Noon* (1952) to *Cheyenne Autumn* (1964) to *Butch Cassidy and the Sundance Kid* (1969) to *Little Big Man* (1970) as Hollywood produced some of the finest westerns ever made. Durango and Silverton, Colorado—with their rugged mountains, excellent scenery, and narrow-gauge train—appeared in a variety of westerns from the late 1940s into the 1960s, including Marilyn Monroe's debut in *Ticket to Tomahawk* (1950).

Television became very popular in the fifties, with such favorites as *Gunsmoke, Cheyenne,* and *Have Gun, Will Travel.* The 1960s, however, represented the last great decade for the western. Whether novels (with the exception of Louis L'Amour's), movies, or television series, westerns lost out to the decade's cynicism, countercultures, changing lifestyles, and unrest. Americans were becoming visually oriented, and reading suffered. Further, life seemed less simple and black-and-white than often portrayed by Hollywood and TV westerns. Even though many of these movies and shows did not take place in the Rockies, the Rockies were in the West, and many people assumed the West to be what they saw and read. Visitors coming west brought that mythic West with them, and many locals willingly obliged them by making it seem that the image was reality.

Colorado continued to offer more variety of attractions, from national and state parks to cultural events to popular ski resorts to professional sports, for visitors. The Denver Broncos, with their vertically striped socks, became the Rocky Mountains' first professional major league team in 1960 when they became part of the American Football League. They forged ahead without much success in the 1960s—their best, a 7–7 season. Finally, in the 1970s, this popular and strong franchise became a winning team.

Denver also yearned to have a major league baseball team. It nearly gained one during the early expansion years. Failing there, the city continued to field one of the strong minor franchises in the nation; the Denver Bears drew very well. Their best days occurred when they were a farm team of the powerful New York Yankees. Denver also had professional rodeo and for a brief while other professional teams. Denver thus became the Rockies' only "major league" city—a goal of all cities. No other Rocky Mountain city gained that designation.

Despite having become a growing ski destination combined with its residents' love for sports and the out-of-doors, Colorado turned down a chance to host the 1976 Olympics. Initially, Denver and its business community cheered when the state was awarded the honor in 1970; such an event would only help "sell Colorado," a perennial theme.

Then the opposition surfaced. Jealousy over Denver getting so much of the state's publicity and profit heated a long-festering envy of the capital city that could be traced back more than a century. Environmental concerns joined the fray. Site selection, transportation logistics, weak leadership, costs, and poor planning raised further worries. The cause was not helped when supporters initially estimated that "only" $14 million would have to be spent by the state, a projection that escalated to $35 million within two years.

The opposition launched a petition campaign to allow Coloradans to vote on whether state funds should be spent on the Olympics. It succeeded, and a 1972 vote to prohibit expenditure of state funds passed by nearly 180,000 votes. Shocked and embarrassed supporters felt this was a blow to Colorado's reputation and image as a winter playground. Obviously, most of the electorate felt otherwise and said so.

It was not a vote against the Olympics per se as much as it was a vote in favor of protection of the environment and better use of taxpayers' money. The issues of environment, quality of life, and population growth had finally come to the forefront for Coloradans. "Sell Colorado" had been challenged, much to the dismay of its longtime supporters, the business community and Chambers of Commerce.

Despite the Olympics defeat, winter tourism offered one possibility to increase year-round visitation. The U.S. Park Service had been reluctant to open parks such as Yellowstone and Mesa Verde in off seasons because of the expense of catering to few visitors and, in the case of the former, the impact on animals. Other attractions also closed for the season, leaving resort towns with a winter depression and high unemployment.

Skiing, however, offered great promise. Wyoming's Jackson Hole and a host of Colorado resorts gained popularity and skiers as Frontier Airlines opened routes to them. Easterners and others now could fly to Denver and then on to their favorite resort in a matter of hours and in comfort unimagined even a decade before. As skiing captured Americans' attention, an unlimited future dazzled planners and investors. However, other western states also had ski resorts and expectations, and the battle for visitors and their money had just begun.

A dream Coloradans had held since the nineteenth century now resurfaced: building a tunnel under the Continental Divide to allow easier winter travel through the mountains. With some wonderful, first-class ski areas on the other side of the mountain from Denver and its airport, better access became imperative.

With modern construction engineering and equipment, the dream became feasible in the 1960s. It was helped along by the building of interstate highways in the 1950s and 1960s. Interstate 70, with its long, tedious route over Loveland Pass, needed such a boost to become a major year-round transcontinental artery. The Eisenhower Tunnel under Loveland Pass beyond Georgetown fulfilled that dream. Completed in 1973 at a cost of $1,000 per inch, it allowed ski areas in Breckenridge and Aspen and points in between to boom. A second tunnel, named for Edwin Johnson and allowing one-way traffic, brought further prosperity in all seasons. As each year passed, I-70 and the Eisenhower Tunnel carried more and more traffic, sometimes causing traffic jams as weekend travelers headed back to Denver and its suburbs.

The popularity of tourism did not always lead to the anticipated joy and prosperity, however. National parks continued to be overcrowded during the high summer tourist season. Yellowstone started closing garbage dumps and removing bears that had become "addicted" to their contents. The once-popular "bear jams" along park roads and favorite spots also disappeared, much to the displeasure of some visitors who, among other things, tried to have their children stand next to the bear or to lure them to, and sometimes into, cars for photographs. In addition, pollution from increasing automobile traffic diminished air quality and hampered the once-pristine vista.

There were no simple answers for the Park Service. Popular visitor locations not only became overcrowded, but actually suffered damage because of their popularity. The quality of visits diminished correspondingly. In Mesa Verde, structures that had stood for a thousand years were being threatened by crowds tramping by; the acid smoke from nearby power plants did not help, either, in the preservation efforts.

Many ideas floated about, such as limiting the number of people in the parks per day or charging high entrance fees. But these suggestions, in turn, raised the question about what form the parks should take and who should be able to utilize them. Mesa Verde monitored acidity of the rain, as did other parks, but little was done to resolve the problem or to define a mission statement for parks, tourists, and the future.

While the three states improved in their efforts to work toward common goals, a mounting undercurrent of jealousy and fear could also be discerned. Denver's growth and its business, banking, transportation, health, and entertainment sectors served as magnets, drawing people from Cheyenne, Billings, and points in between. There seemed little the other two states could do to stem the tide.

Each state had a love-hate relationship with Uncle Sam. Montanans, for instance, complained bitterly about encroaching federal laws and agencies. At the same time, they complained equally loudly about the closing of the Glasgow Air Base in 1969 and the termination of the anti-ballistic missile program in 1972. So did Wyomingites and Coloradans. They wanted to be left alone, except when they needed help with agriculture, mining, or some other problem. A new federal office, base, or beneficial program was usually not rejected either.

The Centennial State reached its own centennial on August 1, 1976, and Colorado celebrated with appropriate ceremonies competing with the United States, which celebrated its bicentennial. From fireworks to opera to pageants and "pioneer" picnics, Coloradans celebrated. Wyoming and Montana would have to wait their turns a few years later.

No longer were the Rocky Mountain states isolated behind prairie and mountain barriers. They reflected what was happening throughout the country and even throughout the world. The problems San Francisco, Chicago, and New York City experienced, Denver did also. The problems of a rancher in Oklahoma or Nevada or a farmer in Illinois or Ohio were understood by their counterparts in Montana, Wyoming, and Colorado. Western urbanite and ruralist faced them, if not at the same magnitude or immediacy. The breakdown of local idiosyncrasies and regionalism drew each state closer to the main current of American life.

A cynical Mark Twain observed back in 1876, just after Colorado gained statehood, "I said there was but one solitary thing about the past worth remembering, and that was the fact that it *is* the past—can't be restored."[6] Rocky Mountain westerners' past had generated an economic windfall, guided their today, and pointed toward tomorrow—a tomorrow they looked toward with renewed confidence in the bicentennial year of the United States.

CHAPTER 9

The Century Ends, Problems Remain

The 1980s through the 1990s

Here is a land where life is written in water
The West is where the water was and is
. . . .
Look to the green within the mountain cup
Look to the prairie parched for water lack
— Thomas Hornsby Ferril

As the twentieth century neared its end, the Rockies faced a variety of problems and issues, some stretching back a century, others seemingly new as yesterday. As poet Thomas Hornsby Ferril knew, water was the major problem for the Rocky Mountain heartland. Water impacted population growth in urban areas and nearby counties, as well as counties with recreational attractions. Rural areas found their water eagerly sought by developers and others. Westerners debated environmental issues, often pitting urban versus rural folk, newcomers versus old-timers. New jobs appeared and old ones disappeared, and those with highest levels of education gained the most in this world.

Rocky Mountain residents tended to be upset with the local, state, and, particularly, the federal governments. They (especially Coloradans) tended to be better educated than the average U.S. citizen, and each decade their average age crept up a little. Thus, the rising cost of health care became a major concern. Reflecting their ancestors, they continued to be conservative overall and to vote Republican. Arriving newcomers were not always welcomed, particularly some of the ideas they brought with them to their "promised land." At least in Colorado, Mexican Americans and Mexican immigrants (some illegal) were starting to make an impact in urban areas.

Times were changing faster than many Rocky Mountain residents liked to see. Montana and Wyoming fell farther behind their southern neighbor in almost all respects, however. That rugged individualism, the western trademark, became more of an image than reality. It might be good in advertisements, but not so good in the late-twentieth-century Rockies.

The international scene hit the region with a resounding crash. While looking for a mining camp site, the author was once greeted by a rancher at his gate with a rifle. He thought I was another one of the "feds" trying to take part of his range for a railroad right-of-way for a mobile missile launcher.

The tremors of the unrest of the 1960s, the Nixon scandal and resignation, the oil crisis and leaping gasoline prices, and the Vietnam War still stunned and shocked Americans well into the 1970s. A national reprieve arrived with the 1976 bicentennial celebration and accompanying festivities. The country could then take stock of where it had been and pride in what it had accomplished. For a brief moment the country took a collective breath.

In the years that followed, a conservative reaction against the protests, welfare state, changing morality, and ungodliness seized the country and became the battle cry of the Republican Party. Issues such as environmental concerns, women's rights, civil rights, and Native American rights did not disappear but received far less coverage unless something noteworthy occurred. Gay rights, however, remained a hot issue.

Not all protests disappeared. Environmentalists blamed factories, automobiles, power plants (nuclear power plants received special attention), mines, and other polluting entities for everything from haze obstructing views to health problems to declining water quality. In the West, mining took the blame and became the stand-in for the thoughtlessness and wasteful practices that resulted from Americans' desire for the cheapest and most plentiful fuel and minerals available.

One great transformation that swept the Rockies was the computer, which eventually led to the Internet. It provided unlimited access to information, changed communication, overcame distance, revolutionized education, impacted business, and offered an unlimited future. Even the most isolated ranch could tap into previously unimagined wonders. The computer also helped widen the generation gap, as youngsters took to it while their parents came aboard more slowly. More people could now work at home, changing the lifestyle of many Americans.

The nation's economy shifted to service occupations such as clerks, computer programmers, lawyers, teachers, fast-food workers, and bureaucrats. Meanwhile, the country's industrial sector, and with it union membership, declined even further. Farms and farmers' numbers waned consistently, along with agriculture profits in general—although not productivity.

The record forty-year boom without a major recession ended in the mid-eighties. Still, most middle- and upper-class Americans found that life was good and their incomes were better than ever before. They were better educated, healthier, more job-savvy about the potential for higher-paying positions, and more mobile than their parents and grandparents.

America's population growth slowed for the first time since World War II, while the country's minority populations—Native Americans, Asians, African Americans, Latinos—reached all-time highs. Minorities in particular were clustered in urban areas. The inner cities grew poorer and faced mounting problems ranging from crime to housing to education. In response, whites consistently fled to the suburbs, although some cities tried urban renewal to lure them back. The Supreme Court entered the fray, and Denver students, for instance, found themselves bused to try to integrate de facto segregated schools. The white flight to the suburbs caused much of this problem.

In the decade and a half after the bicentennial, the United States continued its transformation, which now dated back several generations. Those who had lived through most of the twentieth century had seen greater and faster change than any Americans before them.

Meanwhile, Colorado marched boldly into its second century—growing, optimistic, prospering, and keeping pace with the rest of the country. Montana reached its centennial in 1989, economically representing more plight than prospect but still retaining the western optimism that had characterized settlement of the Rockies and elsewhere in what was described as the post–Civil War frontier.

The same could be said for Wyoming, which celebrated its centennial in 1990 with appropriate ceremonies. That state ranked last in the Union in population. It had started way behind and had never kept pace. The *Wall Street Journal* described it as "The Lonesome Land," an epitaph that would have fit like a glove a century or so before. Despite some people believing that the fewer the people, the greater the charm, this distinction hurt Wyoming in political, economic, and cultural arenas. For instance, it was the least industrialized state in the nation, but it was a major exporter of its natural resources—from cattle to coal to its young people.

Politically, except for the fallout after the Nixon impeachment that staggered the Republicans, the three states continued to have dominant GOP leadership at home. The Democrats did much better in U.S. House and Senate races, winning a fair share of the congressional seats in Colorado and Montana and of Colorado governorships, holding the chair for twenty-four years starting in 1975.

Showing their longtime overall progressive attitude toward women's rights, the three Rocky Mountain states quickly ratified the constitutional Equal Rights Amendment in the early 1970s. Equality under the law would not be denied or abridged because of sex, a view Colorado, Wyoming, and Montana had long held. The nineteenth-century women who had pioneered the suffrage movement would have applauded. The feminine equal rights movement was alive and well in the Rockies. Unfortunately, it was less alive elsewhere in the country, and despite deadline extensions the amendment failed.

In spite of that defeat, women made gains. For example, they were accepted in the service academies, and the Air Force Academy welcomed its first women. There would be problems both from male cadets and from a few old-time Air Force members, but the barrier had been broken.

Following the energy crisis of the early 1970s, the Rockies became part of a frenzied energy boom to make the country "self-sufficient." This boom was different, however. America wanted no more worn-out, wasted, and despoiled coal lands like Appalachia.

Environmental impacts now became a major concern of the coal mining industry. The environmental movement had aroused and sharpened public concern, which in turn had pressured Washington into creating a group of laws, including the Mineral Policy Act, the Threatened and Endangered Species Act, the Federal Land Policy and Management Act, and the National Park System Mining Regulation Act—all passed between the years 1970 and 1976. Reclamation now became an important part of mining, with preservation of the landscape no longer taking a back seat. No more wastelands, such as those in the East and Midwest, were left behind.

In 1977, America took another step forward with the establishment of the Abandoned Mine Reclamation Fund. Congress levied a tax on coal to help reclaim over a century of waste deposited over the landscape as mining had advanced and receded.

Coal mining in Wyoming and Montana, and to a lesser degree Colorado, witnessed a major change. To satisfy federal requirements, a new group of agencies and individuals with stronger regulations descended on the coal mining towns and districts. Mining's impact on the environment, totally defined, needed to be monitored and controlled.

Archaeologists, soil scientists, wildlife biologists, historians, water-quality specialists, and a "Noah's ark full" of men and women joined mining engineers, miners, and geologists in and about the mines. They came as boom times returned, to the shock of the industry's diehards.

Women also labored as miners, something unheard-of previously. Many an old-time miner had considered it bad luck to have women visiting a mine, let alone working in one. From Colorado hard-rock mines to Wyoming coal mines and Montana strip mines, these barrier-breaking miners overcame abuse, cruel jokes, and male chauvinism to be accepted. One of the last western male bastions had fallen.

Male and female miners in Wyoming mined over 71 million tons of coal in 1979, five times the amount mined just five years earlier. The reason was easy to find. The single strip miner produced an average of one hundred tons per day, roughly nine times what an underground miner could dig out during her or his shift in the mine.

They called it a "new frontier" with a somewhat typical lack of historical perspective. It was not new to have large companies dominate Wyoming coal mining; they always had. New towns were created and old ones grew, also a familiar scenario. Boom conditions coexisted with all the familiar problems—strained social services, shortage of homes, overcrowding, red-light districts, lack of social cohesion, and crime. Everything would have been familiar to Wyomingites, or other Rocky Mountain folk, of a century before.

Gillette, in the Powder River coalfields, understood all this firsthand. From Main Street merchant to city hall to school classroom, the boom impacted everyone. Alcohol abuse, family abuse, loneliness, lack of community cohesiveness, and all the other problems associated with boom existed there. The "Gillette Syndrome," they called it, and it resembled the way loneliness and hardships had affected early settlers. This time the companies responded responsibly, however, and tried to provide more physical, social, and cultural amenities.

One problem arose in the mining communities—drugs—that reflected America in general and the easy money, changes in morality, boom-time pressures, and social acceptance of the times. Further, the quality of life was not spectacular. Trailer homes blossomed in hastily built "suburbs"; the trailers proved just as unsuitable for Wyoming and eastern Montana as they had before in cold, dusty, and windy lands.

The town of Wright burst on the Wyoming scene, a product of the "new frontier" of coal mining. Without the national commitment to energy independence and reasonably clean air, the town historian Robert Righter concluded, the community would never have existed. Further, he assumed, "the majority of Americans would not find Wright a particularly desirable place to live."[1]

Located on a broad, vacant, semiarid, treeless plain of northeastern Wyoming, Wright came to life in 1975 thanks to Atlantic Richfield, which built the town for its workers at the Black Thunder Mine. It started with trailers and evolved to include homes, malls, schools, and a post office. Within seven years the town had a "lived-in" feel. As inexperienced pioneers before them had done, the new settlers planted trees, planned parks, and implemented modern innovations such as greenbelts and bicycle paths, but they could not make the arid land blossom.

Thanks to Wright and the fact that the entire region was loaded with rich coal seams, some as thick as a ten-story building, good times and excitement returned to the Wyoming coal industry in the 1970s and 1980s for the first time in several decades. The boom slowed, but it did not bust, although the miners were laid off. It looked like the old story. The difference this time was that production increased thanks to huge strip-mining equipment and improved truck and railroad haulage. Machines had replaced humans as they had on railroads.

Meanwhile, coal production figures alone for the region were startling. In the decade between 1973 and 1983, over 681 million tons were mined, a third more than the total state coal production to that time. In 1983, 112 million tons were mined, with each miner averaging over 20 tons, an indication of what strip mining could do. Even that level of production did not threaten the state's reserves of an estimated four trillion tons of coal, of which an estimated 31 billion tons were strippable.[2] That figure seemed unbelievable to Americans, many of whom were quite willing to sacrifice the West to provide for their heating and power needs.

Low-sulfur, clean coal was needed to meet increased national environmental standards. This benefited Wyoming, because its coal represented a major source of fuel that could be burned economically to meet federal clean air standards. Thus, throughout the 1980s, Wyoming coal produced the lion's share of the state's wealth. Indeed, the state indeed was the nation's leading producer of coal in 1989.

Montana had also learned from past booms and busts and was determined not to let this one pass by without collecting its fair share of revenue. The *Great Falls Tribune* (September 10, 1975) bluntly stated that Montanans refused to become the "boiler room for the nation." There would be safeguards and a fair monetary return to benefit the state and impacted communities.

As a result, despite industry threats of pulling out of the state, severance taxes were levied against coal, oil, gas, and other mineral production. By 1979 the tax on coal had reached 10.5 percent of production. This provided money for impacted communities, highway construction, education, water and sewer projects, and other areas. The whole state benefited, and throughout the rest of the century money continued to pour into the state's treasury.

"Western coal bandits" some midwestern and other states' newspapers called this tax as it raised local fuel bills. Finally, however, a compromise had been reached about the long-range implications of boom and bust and development of finite natural resources.

While such discussions went on, the modern industrial world came to coal mining. The coal trains rumbling across Wyoming and Montana no longer had cabooses or steam engines. Diesel engines hauled long trains, which simply ended without a caboose, much to the displeasure of rail fans. Meanwhile, computers helped operate the lines, and fewer trainmen were needed in this new world.

Although coal prospered, the same could not be said for Wyoming's oil industry, which declined greatly in the 1980s. Evanston boomed for a time and was overwhelmed with growth, the biggest excitement since the arrival of the railroad and the opening of the coal mines. But as with the rest, prosperity soon waned. LaBarge experienced a brief boom that faded almost before construction of a gas processing plant was completed. The plummeting per-barrel price of crude oil, the new fuel-efficient cars, and OPEC's failure to keep prices high resulted in a return to a reliance on foreign oil, despite the traumas of the early 1970s.

A much more spectacular bust occurred in neighboring Colorado. With the disappearance of cheap energy, a desperate search for new sources accompanied the 1973–74 oil crisis. What followed over the next decade illustrated a myriad of efforts to try to make the country oil-independent.

Exploration and development underscored a "hot" Colorado econ-omy. No longer masters of their fate, however, Coloradans and others watched as Washington and international circumstances guided their destinies. Denver fared well, initially emerging as the headquarters for energy companies in the 1970s and 1980s. It quickly proclaimed itself the "energy capital." Construction of high-rise buildings changed the sky-line, and office and building rents skyrocketed right along with them. Denver's postwar boom reached new heights.

In contrast, Craig, in northwestern Colorado, and the district sur-rounding it mushroomed into a complex of jerry-built houses, strip mines, power plants, and an overwhelmed community from town hall to the schoolroom. Somewhere between the two lay a glimpse of the future. Colorado's environment and its quality of life had become pawns in the nation's strategy to satisfy pressing demands for more fuel and energy.

Colorado's coal did not equal Wyoming's tonnage, but it topped the state's previous record with 20 million tons mined in 1980. As with its neighbor to the north, however, most of the coal went to utility compa-nies to generate electricity. Coal again reigned as the king of the state's energy industry. The major producer—strip mines primarily in Routt and Moffat counties—had the same old reputation for environmental devastation, however, despite a new emphasis on reclamation. All three states faced similar problems as the twentieth century neared its end.

As exciting as this coal development was, it did not hold Coloradans' attention long. Oil shale, far more exotic and exciting, soon pushed coal off the front page. It was touted as the means of relieving the country's energy pressures. Exxon, the world's largest oil company, envisioned pro-duction that would reach a stunning 8 million barrels of oil a day by the year 2010. Meanwhile, people talked of a new western Colorado city that might approach 100,000 people by that time.

Once again Garfield and Mesa counties in northwestern Colorado became the focus, with their vast shale deposits. Neighboring Grand Junction envisioned itself an oil shale capital soon to be second only to Denver in population. Other regional communities saw a bonanza right around the corner. The old problem, before any bonanza days, remained the same, however: could oil shale be cheaply and successfully refined?

In 1980, amid great excitement and amazing forecasts, the Colony Project started. The Exxon company predicted that over one million Coloradans would eventually be mining, transporting, retorting, and doing other jobs related to developing and producing oil. The plan, if developed, however, would open a Pandora's box of troubles with unprecedented staggering sociological, ecological, and economic implications. Nevertheless, at the same time, it would also create jobs, bring in income, and create a boom in a traditionally depressed region. People from all over the country rushed to Grand Junction looking for work. The housing market became tight, rents went up, trailer courts blossomed, schools were crowded to the seams, and social problems multiplied in all communities near the Exxon project. An all-too-familiar scenario greeted the newcomers and communities.

Not everyone saw a promised land. An editorial in the June 29, 1980, issue of the *Denver Post* warned that the state had failed to prepare adequately for the development: "A surging shale industry doesn't have to do simply with oil. A surging shale industry involves roads and schools, law enforcement and medical services, domestic water supply and pollution control—a myriad of human concerns, all of which are Colorado's concerns." Gov. Richard Lamm, who had led the fight against the Olympics, had long opposed the idea, primarily because of environmental and growth concerns and the burden being dumped on the state. One had only to look at neighboring coal towns caught up in their own boom to project potential problems on a much larger scale.

Exxon, meanwhile, faced its own problems, including the familiar ones of not finding an economic solution to the retorting problems, combined with the crippling cost overruns as the project advanced. Fluctuating international oil prices did not help either; the lower they went, the bigger the gap between the price of a barrel of crude oil and a barrel of oil shale. Predictions that it would take a price of $50 a gallon to make shale oil competitive scared Americans. What that cost would do to prices at the pump and the home worried everyone.

The immediate need was to find a way to retort the shale economically. Then suddenly, on "Black Sunday," May 2, 1982, Exxon abandoned its Colony Project—2,200 people immediately becoming unemployed. An economical method to retort the shale, despite intensive scientific efforts, had still not been found unless the oil price reached $50 a barrel. So once again oil shale proved a fickle mistress.

That was just the beginning. Depressed, disillusioned, and bankrupt, former employees drifted away over the next few years. Their dreams and the dreams of the area went right along with them. Businesses closed, the small towns of Craig and Parachute slipped into a depression, Grand Junction went into a slump with an overbuilt housing market and a multitude of other problems, and the planned new community of Battlement Mesa barely left the drawing board. It did recover later—ironically, as a retirement community.

The damage did not stop there. Elsewhere in the state, oil and natural gas companies slowed exploration and drilling. They also laid off workers, and local economies suffered. The falling international price of oil showed the Rockies that they were not immune to uncontrollable outside influences.

The oil shale boom went bust to the shock of many Coloradans who had not studied the history of previous excitements. Governor Lamm accurately observed, "This is part of the boom-and-bust cycle the West has been experiencing throughout its history."[3] Western Slopers now had experienced two busts since the Second World War—uranium and oil shale—but this last time expectations had flown higher and fallen farther than before. The overeagerness to back any promised economic savior had once again led only to trouble.

Mad Coloradans blamed two of their favorite whipping boys: big business and the federal government. Their ancestors would have done the same thing, but they also needed to weigh their own responsibility.

Wyomingites became just as disappointed. Wyoming had oil shale and the federal government invited bids to develop the deposits in 1975. Glowing promises of an oil shale future proved premature: no bids were submitted. In addition to the problems already discussed, Wyoming did not have enough water to consider development, because any shale process demanded large quantities.

Montana's oil industry was affected by the same factors as oil shale, rising international productivity and national conservation. The oil crisis of the 1970s turned into a glut in the early 1980s, causing prices to plummet. The oil and natural gas industries became depressed and did not rebound during the rest of the decade.

Coal, however, continued to be strong based on future prospects. Montana, according to the United States Geological Survey, held the nation's largest reserves of minable coal, the key word being *minable*. Neighboring Wyoming claimed more reserves, but minability was more of a challenge. The two states argued about which had the most reserves, more for publicity's sake than anything else.

During the 1970s, Montana's coal industry prospered; then it ebbed in the 1980s. Montana's severance tax, 30 percent, was higher than Wyoming's, which created stiff competition. The coal companies complained that the tax was unfair. In the 1980s, Montana's production leveled at 30 to 40 million tons a year, but the future for low-sulfur, low-polluting coal remained promising. One idea fortunately never saw the light of day, the suggestion of turning Montana's Powder River Basin with all its coal reserves into a "national sacrifice area."

Another approach to generating electricity captured attention: the idea that the alternative source of using wind turbines would not sacrifice the land. Each state had an abundance of this free resource on its windy plains, and its nonpolluting benefits offered a plus. Information was being gathered by the late 1970s about costs, methods, and so forth.

Wyoming installed wind turbines south of Medicine Bow. Following a string of bad experiences, the federal government withdrew its funding. A private individual encountered no better luck when high winds in January 1994 wrecked the remaining machine. Colorado has some "wind farms," but the same problems that have dogged oil shale reappeared: costs and the need for a more efficient and economical process to generate the electricity. Potentially, nonetheless, wind turbines hold out the hope of providing at least a small percentage of needed electricity by environmentally clean means.

All three states represented national treasures, at least as the rapidly growing numbers of tourists attested. Among them, they offered almost everything a sightseer might wish to glimpse and enjoy, except an ocean.

They offered history too. In fact, if reality stood in the way, some offered the legend as gospel. From the Canadian border to the Four Corners, the Old West galloped forth. As historian Gerald Nash explained, "The mythic West continued to represent the other America—a mirror to contemporary society that served to explain Americans to themselves. For many, it represented that ideal, perfect society which served as a marked contrast to the imperfect civilization of the present." He concluded that the mythic West was a "mirror" of how "they would like to see themselves." In the end, "the mythic West still provided the Great American Escape."[4]

Montana, Wyoming, and Colorado all offered the "mythic" West or the "escape," both of which produced dollars. The Rocky Mountain states did not approach this moneymaking bonanza in quite the same fashion. Montana offered much for the sportsman and visitor, but despite its obvious attractions, the state made little total effort to build the industry. Promotion was key for all three states, although Montana lagged behind until 1987 when it established a "bed tax." Revenues from the tax would be spent on promotion.

Tourists continued to come, however, even without a great deal of promotion by the state. As the 1980s closed, the state was spending about $850 million each year on promotions, totaling about 9 percent of the economic base. Twelve thousand Montanans, or thereabouts, were employed directly in the industry, and another 10,000 benefited indirectly. Communities in the western part of the state gained the most, particularly since more people flew to that area from Denver or the East or drove northward from Wyoming. Yellowstone provided a magnet for both states. In Montana, in 1988, tourism generated a total of almost $1 billion, ranking second only to agriculture in the state's economy.[5]

Not everyone in all three states was pleased about tourism and its impact. Cars crowded the roads leading into state and national parks during the tourist season. When they were finally in the parks, visitors encountered hordes of people, car exhaust, noise, and parking problems that sometimes made their visit less than enjoyable.

Part of the problem came from the tourists themselves and what they desired to experience. Some wanted a quick visit to see the popular sites or animals, and then off they went. Others wanted to enjoy a park's quiet and solitude. These goals were not compatible.

The ongoing debate about the issue of overpopularity ruining the experience in national parks continued. Was it a wilderness experience tourists desired? If so, they would be disappointed. Yellowstone, Glacier, and Rocky Mountain national parks were not what the first visitors, or even prewar visitors, had seen. The best that could be hoped for was semipristine land, forests, streams, lakes, and, in Yellowstone's case, areas around geysers. Environmentalists and concerned park supporters became particularly aroused about what was happening to the land and the animals.

In the case of Mesa Verde National Park, popularity continued to present a threat to the millennium-old structures. Finally, to limit the crowds at popular sites, tickets had to be acquired to secure times for a visit. Meanwhile, less well known, but still spectacular, sites on Wetherill Mesa found few people touring them.

That was not true of Yellowstone. The park particularly became a touchstone in the 1980s. Winter snowmobiling offered the opportunity for tourists to see a different environment and boost local economies, but it did nothing for the ecology or the animals startled by the noise, exhaust, people, and general commotion. A heated debate arose over the need for this winter business and its long-range impact on the park, but no simple answers appeared as local businesses and interests pitted themselves against environmentalists and the U.S. Park Service.

Yellowstone and local tourism suffered a terrible blow with the 1988 fire that burned about 900,000 acres. The question of whether to let fires burn out naturally or fight them had long been an issue in the parks. Starting in 1972, naturally caused fires at Yellowstone had been allowed to burn unchecked. Under normal conditions such fires had cleared out dead timber, allowing the area to regenerate, but 1988 proved not a normal year. Severe drought conditions left the region a tinderbox, and a fire of epic proportions raced out of hand. It changed the park as nothing had since its creation and continued the debate about fires and the park's purpose.

If Yellowstone had been a touchstone about changing times and situations, nearby Jackson Hole faced similar issues. Dubbed Wyoming's "Sun Valley," skiing and tourism had transformed the community. What earlier had been a refreshing western place to live and visit evolved into something quite different. A cosmopolitan, arty atmosphere continued to replace the western ranching atmosphere. Along with it came more automobiles, buses, and traffic, plus crowds, higher-priced homes, and all the other problems associated with popularity and a growing year-round tourist skiing environment. The Park Service faced an unending fight to preserve the vistas. Expensive homes crowding nearer and nearer to the park and framing those beautiful natural vistas grew more contentious. Meanwhile, animals, long a part of this and other parks' attractions, found their ranges curtailed and their ways of life impacted.

That was not a problem just for parks. As popular mountain homes spread into the foothills, mountains, and mountain valleys, they squatted on what had been the range of deer, bear, and elk. Birds such as eagles were impacted also. To a lesser degree, the same thing happened as suburbs expanded over the prairies along Colorado's Front Range and in other urban areas, although the animals tended to be different: antelope, coyotes, and prairie dogs, not to mention rattlesnakes. Some, like coyotes, might adjust to this new world, but most animals did not. This aroused concern and worry about nature's balance, but no easy answers emerged or simple solutions surfaced. It was the age-old conflict between nature and man that would only get worse as population grew and expanded.

Meanwhile, traffic problems were not limited to national parks. Car exhaust polluted what had once been a pristine atmosphere, generating further complaints and concerns. The outsiders also received more than their fair share of the blame for littering and for general carelessness toward nature and its wonders. Until controls were instituted, signs and billboards further polluted the landscape as they promoted businesses or attractions.

Rivalries between towns over which was "the gateway" to a park extended back generations. Publicity and profit would be gained by the one that secured and held that honor. For example, communities from all Four Corner states—Durango, Mancos, Cortez, Santa Fe, Albuquerque, Gallup, Moab, and Flagstaff—all proclaimed themselves "the" gateway to Mesa Verde, offering the shortest, fastest, most scenic, and best route to the park. Such rivalries had been heated at various times throughout the twentieth century. Much to one community's dismay, another might disparage it with half-truths or complete falsehoods to tempt tourists to their town. Nothing new about all this; it had been occurring well back into the nineteenth century.

Further, the three Rocky Mountain states were not always friendly rivals, especially when financial gain was at stake. Snide comments about who had better ski slopes, the best highways, the friendliest people, and anything else an advertiser could dream up were used, to promote one state at the expense of another.

Another problem that came with the tourist industry—low-paying jobs—was particularly noticeable in ski towns but seen everywhere. Suitable housing could not be found for these underpaid workers, who might hold several jobs and live in substandard housing so they could enjoy the benefits of the ski slopes, the town, and the region. Old-timers, meanwhile, often lamented the lifestyles, dress, and political activism of these newcomers.

Conservative critics bemoaned the loss of yesteryear's quality of life, friendliness, and neighborliness, which in their estimation had been hall-marks of the Old West. They were not alone in voicing concern about the tourist intrusion and its impact. Most people, however, welcomed the visitors and the revenue they generated.

One of the continuing problems Colorado, Montana, and Wyoming faced was their isolation, even with air connections. Most tourists, how-ever, continued to drive, often amazed at the distance in the West. As the price of gasoline began a steady climb upward, unease mounted right along with it. Initially the higher prices had little impact, except during an economic downturn in the mid-1980s. The soaring price caused some people to crowd as much as possible into a short time, thereby limiting the quality of their experience and the time of their stay in one place. This alarmed locals, who wanted them to stay longer and spend more.

Improved air connections somewhat alleviated the time factor. Also, more Americans were flying, particularly folks coming for ski vacations, and some areas benefited immensely from that development. But the air-lines were not immune to troubles. Colorado's "own," Frontier Airlines, went bankrupt as a result of expanding too fast as a regional carrier, poor management, and the government's deregulation of airlines, which brought low-priced competition. Some of its officers and others later revived the name, and it became a national carrier that still served some of the larger Rocky Mountain cities.

United, Continental, Delta, and other airlines stepped in to fly passengers to major terminals, where either a smaller feeder airline took them farther or a rental car offered a means of transportation to another destination. Unfortunately, some small towns either lost out completely or found their daily flights curtailed. Passengers, meantime, worried about the rising costs of tickets.

Railroad traffic played only a meager role in the tourist business, as it did in the economy of the Rockies. In one area it held its own, carrying coal from the Western Slope of Colorado to the Front Range or from a Wyoming or a Montana field to a market or power plant.

Reflecting what was happening elsewhere as the industry consolidated, the one home railroad—the Denver & Rio Grande—disappeared into the dustbin of history. Merged with other companies, the railroad lost its name even as its tracks still carried transcontinental freight and Amtrak passengers. Its branch lines into the mountains had long since been abandoned and torn up.

With tourism picking up the slack as mining and agriculture slumped (they represented only about 3 percent of the Colorado workforce by the mid-1980s), the late 1970s and the 1980s generally featured a growing economy. Wyomingites and Montanans might have desired a more robust one, but Coloradans could not complain. Their state was enjoying a four-decade boom, with only a few dips here and there. Then came the mid-1980s.

The nation hit an economic wall with a scandal involving savings and loan banks. Deregulated by the federal government, they had expanded vigorously—some with too little thought or direction. Inadvisable loans, poor or corrupt management, shady or at best shoddy practices, "creative accounting," and staggering debt loads brought some down, and the ripples affected the entire industry. Colorado became a symbol of everything that happened when Denver's Silverado Banking, Savings & Loan went down.

This high-flying institution had become an icon of Colorado and Denver's good times. During its decade-long meteoric rise, Silverado's leaders had emerged as movers and shakers, and the institution as a pacesetter in helping build Denver up during the energy crisis. Oil and mineral companies arrived to make the town their headquarters; high-rise buildings were interjected into the skyline, and fancy homes dotted plush suburbs.

But everything started to unravel in 1986, and late in 1988 the federal government took over Silverado after a revealing investigation. Its "creative bookkeeping," shady practices, and overly ambitious adventures became the talk of the town. Like its guilty counterparts elsewhere, Silverado collapsed, leaving taxpayers holding nearly $300 million in bad debts. It created a national stir in part because Vice President, later President, George Bush's son Neil served on Silverado's board. Not until after the century's turn was the mess cleaned up.

That marked the end of Denver and the state's good times, and the slide of the postwar boom—Colorado's longest—into history. Not until the early 1990s would the good times return. The crash proved devastating to a generation that hardly remembered the 1930s depression. Bankruptcy petitions peaked in 1989, and even a year later, 2,077 businesses failed. The construction business, a former state pillar, crumbled, with employment dropping by nearly a third to 61,000 workers in three years. The situation did not immediately improve despite hopes. Many Coloradans who had arrived since 1945 wondered where the good times had gone and if they would return. Experienced old-timers knew they would return and questioned the crybaby attitude of those who had been attracted by the times and "land of milk and honey" anticipations that came with it and thought they would never end.

Nothing better revealed Denver's and its suburbs' growing role in the state than the Silverado collapse. Denver and its neighbors continued to hold the state's economic future in their hands, to experience a population explosion, and to guide the state's political destiny. But they were also vulnerable to forces outside their control.

Beyond Denver, few folk had heard of Silverado until it failed and affected their lives and gave the state a bad image. The economic slump that had hit the energy business, the savings and loan failures, and the collapse of regional railroads and airlines all had their roots in outside influences and actions. Clearly and dramatically, westerners, as in earlier times, did not control their fate to a large degree. Their Populist and Progressive ancestors had known that, and now a new generation learned it. Such events were further examples of what Governor Lamm and others had long warned: the Rockies were becoming a "colony of the East."

The same held true throughout the Rockies. Whether they lived in Durango, Jackson Hole, Glasgow, or anywhere else, the New West residents found themselves in some degree of colonial status.

Historians and economists studied and discussed this New West, with its urbanization, tourism, national and international ties, and the increased role of government agencies—local, state, and national—in the region and the lives of its people. They debated the implications and impacts of these developments for the present and the future and reached a variety of conclusions.

Once again, of the three states, the significance of the issues was most clearly shown in Colorado. In 1990, government agencies employed 14 percent of the state's workforce. No mountain state could match Colorado's 53,000 federal employees—an impressive figure, but only a third of the number employed by local governments. Montana and Wyoming might not match those levels, but the trend was obvious everywhere. Conservatives in all three states shuddered at such government control and involvement on all levels and feared the increasing taxes needed to support those programs.

Meanwhile, in the regional economy blue-collar jobs declined and white-collar and service jobs increased. Industry left the Rockies, with the Exxon oil shale project just one example. Such onetime giants as the Anaconda Copper Mining Company and Colorado Fuel and Iron joined their smaller counterparts in being absorbed by another company or closing, with a loss of jobs. Butte and Pueblo, the respective homes of those once-powerful corporations, were now depressed and desperately trying to find something to replace what had been lost economically.

What happened to Anaconda, once Montana's premier industry, illustrates much of what occurred throughout the mining West. The problems had multiplied for the company. Chile nationalized Anaconda's rich mines, the ore grade declined in Butte, and the company cut operations and laid off workers everywhere. Anaconda became a prime target for a takeover. Atlantic Richfield, flush from the rising gasoline prices, did just that in 1977. Atlantic Richfield's management might have known the gas business, but it did not know mining; first it closed the Anaconda smelter, and in 1983 mining ended in Butte. Copper mining in Butte left behind an environmental disaster waiting to happen as the huge Berkeley Pit began to fill with toxic groundwater.

Denver had once been a mining center; now it benefited from the increase in white-collar jobs, as did Cheyenne and Helena. High-tech, space industry, and similar occupations required more experience and training—along with, probably, education—and paid higher wages.

Unfortunately, service-job wages, particularly those tied to tourism, remained low. This area grew the most rapidly in the 1980s and beyond, as restaurants, motels, the ski industry, tourism, chain stores, and similar businesses expanded and offered jobs, albeit at lower wages. Especially in and near popular destinations such as ski areas, national parks, and mountain villages, the cost of living rose quickly, and the service workers fell further behind in trying to live where they worked.

In towns such as Vail and Aspen, Colorado, Jackson Hole, Wyoming, Whitefish, Montana, and their ski contemporaries, a wealthy, often absentee upper class and an "underclass" became the norm. "Ski bums," as some called them, were either old-timers or newcomers who had come to ski. To do so, they took one or more low-paying jobs and found themselves marginalized in this world of glitter.

They could barely afford to live, let alone purchase a home, in the resorts. Housing options were not available for them or for many members of the middle class, who simply moved away. Further, the wealthy newcomers were not particularly welcome either. Reporter/writer Molly Ivins observed that "wealthy Texans buying real estate in Aspen" and elsewhere were "about as popular in Colorado as white colonialists in black Africa."[6]

Meanwhile, in places like Aspen, Jackson Hole, Telluride, Vail, and Breckenridge, people crowded together, or moved into less pricey suburbs where low-cost housing might be available, or spent more time traveling to their workplaces. Disruption of home life, stress, and a marginalized lifestyle resulted. That was all part of the bargain to work in, and "enjoy," life in this segment of the New West.

The same trend affected everyone, including college and university staff and teachers, in popular communities such as Durango and Boulder and Missoula and Bozeman, where soaring home prices far outstripped salaries. As the 1990s began, the trend continued, and what buyers had once considered higher home prices now became average. When average prices threatened to top a million dollars, a new day had arrived. It was becoming increasingly costly to live in "paradise," as well as more crowded and contentious.

Some Rockies folks joined other westerners in what was aptly termed the "sagebrush revolt." Tired of Uncle Sam's regulations and bureaucracy, grassroots protesters rode out of the prairies and mountains as they had done before. In public meetings, letters to the editor and legislators, and threats of a political upheaval, they presented their grievances. It stirred the hearts of conservatives and conservative legislatures throughout the mountain states and gained national publicity. According to a story in *U.S. News & World Report* (December 1, 1980), they were the "right" people to chart the future of "their" West.

The rebels argued that because of extensive federal landholdings, their states were placed at a competitive disadvantage with eastern states. By reducing federal restrictions and land ownership, development would come, the tax base would improve, and a new rural prosperity would arrive. The rebels found what little support they had in rural areas, not in the more populous urban areas. Passionate enthusiasm and rhetoric were no substitute for success, and that revolt fizzled more because of local than outside opposition.

While they argued and debated, their Rocky Mountain West was transformed around them, and the changes both helped and hindered the rebels. The computer arrived and with it went some of the ranch, farm, and mountain isolation that had characterized the region. Potentially it meant a revolution for rural, small schools that could tap into educational opportunities not previously available. Small towns could also gain advantages they never had in years before.

At the same time, however, the cities gained the most in jobs and opportunities, with, especially, Denver's suburbs' growing numbers of new residents leading the way. In both areas the youth continued to accept the revolution more willingly than their parents.

Higher education widened the gap between generations and, sadly, between ethnic groups. More young men and women saw the advantages of attending junior or four-year community colleges because of better job opportunities, higher salaries, and the benefit to their future quality of life. Graduate schools also increased enrollments as the ever more complicated world demanded more education. Unfortunately, black, Hispanic, and Native American youth seized the opportunity less readily, and they found themselves left behind in the job market. Primarily this resulted from their being unable to afford the expenses that would have to be incurred in college. Some did not have the family support needed.

The Rocky Mountain states had outstanding universities in Boulder, Laramie, and Missoula, where nationally recognized faculty taught in excellent programs. For many students, a two-year junior college was a perfect way to bridge the gap between high school and the workforce, and at less cost. Colorado led the three states in the number of colleges and community colleges, as might be expected, and the state had one of the most highly educated populations in the nation. Interestingly, it was not natives but rather newcomers settling in the state who produced this development.

Television still continued to break down barriers and isolation. Throughout the rest of the century, dishes and cable networks in small towns and on farms replaced the familiar antennas. High school and college courses could also be taken through television, which heightened the education revolution throughout the Rockies but aroused critics to question whether the students received a quality education.

Life in rural America was improving—so much in fact that urban residents moved to the country to get away from the stresses of city life. Unless retired, they commuted to work, leading to traffic congestion and demands for better roads and more urban amenities to enhance their rural experience. This situation also led to a clash of ideas with the older residents over what should or could be done about, for example, city government, local services, and law enforcement.

In the decades after the end of the war, Colorado's urbanization became more evident every year. Coloradans' reactions to a variety of matters reflected their urbanization and the loss of their rural roots. Wyoming and Montana did not share this characteristic. In neither state did 80 percent live in one urban sprawl, as did Coloradans along the Eastern Slope of the mountains. Less urbanized, residents clung to older conservative western attitudes, and neither state suffered to any great degree from unchecked growth and its corresponding problems and issues, as Colorado did. Colorado reflected more the situation of Arizona, California, and other Pacific Coast metropolitan areas than its neighbors did.

The ongoing tug of rural versus urban again rose to the fore. In some ways, the sagebrush revolt was the last stand of the former. Urbanites were more environmentally concerned, more conservation-minded, greater outdoor recreational enthusiasts, and less unhappy with Washington or, at least, with most of its activities than were their rural counterparts. They held the political and economic power that their rural cousins had long lost.

A trend noticeable throughout the century continued: the family farm and the family ranch were becoming an endangered species throughout the region. As previously noted, agriculture was not disappearing, it had simply become big business. This presented a basic problem for the rural areas, particularly those far from urban areas—a concern with no simple solution. The continued trend of rural towns losing population, schools consolidating, churches closing, and businesses shutting their doors spoke volumes about the future.

Other relevant concerns about excessive, time-consuming paperwork, useless regulations, and the irritating fact that federal employees received better pay and retirement benefits than their state and local counterparts flared periodically in all three states. Especially around election times, when an issue sparked a protest it was trumpeted in the press and in letters to editors.

Underlying at least some of this debate lay the old concern over water and the newer one over clean air. Limited water resources were now stretched to meet urban, rural, industrial, agricultural, and recreational needs. The examples were numerous: Eastern Slope versus Western Slope in Colorado, Wyoming's fight with Nebraska over the Deer Creek Dam to store municipal water on the North Platte River, ongoing disputes over the Colorado River, clean water advocates, Indian water rights, and urban versus agricultural interests—the list stretched throughout the Rockies. If, as some westerners say, "water runs uphill toward money," some attitudes, occupations, future hopes, and even lifestyles would have to change.

Farmers and ranchers could make more money selling their water rights than they could in a lifetime of work. That raised basic questions about where the West was heading. Who could blame them for selling out, and who could chastise the urbanites for wanting and needing more water? It would take great leadership in the years ahead to untangle these conflicting interests and to find equitable solutions.

It was not only scarcity but overabundance that harmed the region, as the August 1976 Big Thompson flood in Colorado made frighteningly clear. Historian Patricia Limerick, in *The Legacy of Conquest,* summarized the problem: "While water in the West usually posed a problem of scarcity, deprivation was punctuated by abundance; storms or melting snow could suddenly create floods where a dry channel had been."[7]

Native Americans made some gains, particularly the Southern Utes and a few other tribes benefiting from natural resources or entrepreneurial advantages. Sadly, overall the tribes were still overwhelmingly dependent on the federal government. As Colorado senator Ben Nighthorse Campbell, a northern Cheyenne and the first Native American in the U.S. Congress since 1929, noted, the average Indian household income fell by 5 percent in the 1980s. The 1990 census confirmed the old problem; the median Native American household income averaged less than $20,000 a year.

Yet another dilemma facing the Rocky Mountain states was how to resolve the issue of profit and progress butting heads with quality of life. Examples, large and small, dotted the landscape. With nearby power plants generating smoke, acid rain threatened Mesa Verde National Park structures that had withstood the centuries. Smog in Denver did not drift in from California but from car exhaust and industrial plants. Acid rain threatened lakes in Wyoming and Montana, as well as Colorado. Smoke from power plants near Wyoming and Montana coalfields marred what had once been pristine prairie and mountain vistas. All this raised the unanswered question of what was happening to locals' health.

Clean air became a worry, a concern, and a cause. Old-timers thought jobs and development were the keys to prosperity. They had seen both good times and bad. Many younger newcomers—better educated, more mobile, and with more money and leisure time—worried more about their quality of life and environmental issues. It seemed that the two sides would never agree, but as the 1980s progressed they discovered some common ground, at least for discussion. As the Rockies changed, the story of the future rested on finding mutuality among diverse groups with hopes and expectations for the coming years.

Still, there were those who had lived out a failed dream on the frontier. The hopes and dreams of the agrarian pioneers had fallen far short of expectations, once they tackled the plains of Montana, Wyoming, and Colorado. Farmers and ranchers of the late twentieth century, despite modern innovations, still found themselves at the mercy of the weather, the international market, and isolation from the nation's markets.

The same was true for western mining and the few industrial enterprises. Just as Grangers in the 1880s and 1890s had protested the appearance and monopolies of eastern corporate industrialization that had swallowed their homegrown businesses and markets, so did their descendants a century later. Now those same problems were compounded by the intrusions of international corporations.

Although not completely the same, history reiterated itself. Once again, Rocky Mountain residents were tired of being controlled by and from Washington. The federal government gained power at the expense of states and individuals. The old love-hate attitudes still existed in the 1970s and 1980s and into the 1990s, as they had a century before during the great agrarian upheaval.

Just as the agrarian spokesmen and spokeswomen had feared, the cities now dominated. They still seemed to be centers of crime, congestion, controversy, misery, and greed, as Populist spokeswoman Mary Lease, among others, had warned a century past. Now rural areas could no longer chart their own course, and their fate rested in the hands of city folk, who perhaps had never lived on or even visited a farm or ranch. The plight of the farmers and ranchers could be summarized in the words of the English poet Alfred, Lord Tennyson, who wrote in "Ask Me No More":

Ask me no more: thy fate and mine are seal'd:
I strove against the stream and all in vain.

Much of the old rural Rocky Mountain West found urban dominance to be its fate as it entered the last decade of the twentieth century.

Too many people had fallen victim to the legendary version of the West or hung onto a vanished era instead of recognizing the twenty-first-century vision staring them in the face. They visited the historic sites, the spruced-up mining and ranching towns, drove the Jeep trails, rode the few historic trains that gave their riders a taste of the past even to cinders and smoke, listened to legends, and imagined what it must have been like. They imagined far more than had actually happened.

Richard Lamm and Michael McCarthy argued in *The Angry West* that while that "dream lives," it "is dying." Rather, "a new Manifest Destiny has overtaken America. . . . Ways of life change forever. Values, attitudes,

customs—the core of western life—shatter."[8] Yet the future of the Rocky
Mountain West rests with its people of all opinions, ages, and walks of
life. They must come to grips with this new, ever-changing West.

A man who lived in and loved Colorado and the West for all his ninety-
two years wrote a much longer poem about land and water, part of
which introduced this chapter. Denverite Thomas Hornsby Ferril,
Colorado's late poet laureate and one of his generation's major poets,
concluded the poem (found in its entirety in the Colorado capitol
rotunda) with these prophetic words.

> Beyond the sundown is tomorrow's wisdom,
> Today is going to be long long ago.[9]

CHAPTER 10

Into a New Millennium
The Twenty-First Century

> Turning water into gold: Cities' desperation creates crazed markets for
> a precious resource and saddles newcomers with the costliest hookup
> fees in the land.
> —*Denver Post*, November 20, 2005

THE WEST AND THE UNITED STATES as a whole experienced a dramatic
demographic change in the 1990s and the early twenty-first century.
During the 1990s nearly 10 million legal immigrants arrived, nearly surpassing the all-time record of 10.1 million during the years 1905–14. Of
these, nearly 40 percent settled in the West, unlike the earlier period,
when the Northeast received the largest percentage. Estimates of illegal
immigrants settled in the Rocky Mountain states ranged as high as 50
percent. No one knew definitely what that number might be, but public
concern was rising about their impact on everything from welfare to the
job situation.

Slightly over one-third of the immigrants—illegal and legal—came
from Mexico and Central America and another 25 percent from Asia.
The lure: the United States had once more become the land of opportunity, the promised land of western legend. The American economy
recovered in the early 1990s as inflation declined, investment increased,
unemployment fell, the job market greatly increased, and productivity improved. American companies embarked upon a wave of mergers,
large corporations swallowing smaller ones. Once again the urban Rocky
Mountains boomed, but not the rural areas.

Most upper- and middle-class westerners prospered as the economy
soared. Yet not all Americans shared in the good times. Many of the
available jobs paid little more than minimum wage, and those workers
had a difficult time making ends meet, continuing the familiar Rocky
Mountain pattern that stretched back over a century. Minority groups,

whose numbers grew throughout the decade, faced the toughest time of all. The gap between rich and poor westerners widened. It could be seen socially, financially, culturally, and educationally in almost every Rocky Mountain community, visible especially as the wealthy purchased second homes in the beautiful mountain valleys.

Then, in 2001, the economy faltered and continued to do so. That decline, compounded by the September 11 terrorist attacks on New York City and Washington, D.C., put Americans in a pessimistic, anxiety-filled, fearful mood. The U.S. adventures in the Middle East had also proven less successful than hoped, despite optimistic pronouncements from the White House. As 2006 drew to a close, the struggle in Iraq drew haunting parallels to Vietnam thirty years before.

Environmental issues and the worry about global warming continued to make headlines. Western winters warmed, and ski areas suffered. As the price of oil and natural gas continued to move upward, more people looked longingly at the natural resources scattered throughout the West, bringing environmentalists to the barricades once more to defend the land and animals. Western tourism seemed less secure with gas prices soaring to unprecedented levels.

As the century ended, Americans were graying, older than at any time in United States history as the century ended. "Gray power" advocates joined minorities, gay rights advocates, and women fighting for equality. Many of all ages shook their heads in disbelief at the antics of the youths and their culture.

America was changing as was the world around it. No longer was anyone isolated from the world economy, world politics, and world problems, a reality that brought new outlooks and worries to the Rockies almost daily. The international market now set the price for gold, silver, and other minerals. Farmers had to look at the total international picture to see what their crops might bring. Ranchers worried about mad cow disease and a quarantine of American beef. High-tech industries worried about the international market, and workers found their jobs being outsourced to countries with cheaper labor and other economic benefits. The same competition faced local industries as they struggled to survive, along with merchants on Main Street, whose chief challenges came from the national megabusinesses that often relied on foreign-made products.

Colorado in particular had taken pride in its high-tech industry along the Front Range. High technology seemed to have boundless potential, but with the national economic downturn in the early years of the twenty-first century, workers found themselves as vulnerable to losing their jobs as those in more traditional industries. They, like the coal miners, railroad workforce, and steel workers before them, found themselves on the outside looking in at the American dream. The trend had become obvious in the 1990s and gained momentum in the new century.

Another 1990s heritage, the troubles in the Middle East, spilled over the turn of the century. The Iraq war vexed Montana in an unexpected way. In March 2005, Gov. Brian Schweitzer asked the Pentagon to return some of the 1,500 Montana National Guard troops and aircraft from Iraq, particularly helicopters. Eventually, they did come back, but with the continuing tragic war, National Guard members were increasingly called to duty while volunteerism for the military services dropped steadily.

Montana wanted its Guard members back because of the continuing drought, a shortage of mountain snow, high temperatures, and tinder-dry forests. The state was a powder keg of potential wildfires and needed troops and equipment to fight fires. The Guard was often called to supplement fire crews. Montanans clearly recalled the year 2000, when 3,955 fires in the state burned almost 948,000 acres and destroyed 320 homes and buildings at a cost of nearly $1.6 billion.

The governor's request did not please everyone. It appalled Linda Anderson, executive director of the Glacier County Regional Tourism Commission. She exclaimed, "With those kinds of statements going out right now, right in the key planning times, the message goes out to people thinking about bringing their families to Montana, and they say 'Let's go to Colorado!'" Heaven forbid such a fate, in her eyes. She continued, "If the national press is saying Montana is dry and already on fire, we can kiss the tourism season goodbye."[1]

Like so many problems facing the Rockies, no simple answer appeared. The public generally disliked the idea of letting fires burn, of tree thinning, and of spending so much money fighting fires. Yet over the past century the combination of forest management, logging and grazing, and fighting fires, or not fighting fires, had left the Rocky Mountain forests in highly unnatural, crowded conditions. Man versus nature had come to a crucial point.

In spite of the fires, Montana survived, and the entire region continued to grow. The 2000 census confirmed postwar trends in the Rocky Mountains. Colorado topped 4.3 million in population, an increase of slightly over 30 percent in ten years. Most of the newcomers, as well as old-timers, lived in the Front Range urban strip from Fort Collins to Pueblo, including Greeley slightly to the east. Colorado now ranked as the twenty-fourth-most populous U.S. state, up from twenty-sixth in 1990. Even the economic dip of the 1990s had only briefly slowed down the inflow.

Montana with 902,000 people and Wyoming with 494,000 ranked forty-fourth and last in population, respectively, although both had shown a nearly 10 percent growth over the past ten years. Colorado's far greater population pointedly showed why it dominated the Rocky Mountain region. Colorado had 41.5 people per square mile, Montana 6.2, and Wyoming 5.1. Denver alone had a larger population than Wyoming, and the combined populations of Denver and Colorado Springs surpassed that of Montana. In the years from 2000 to 2003, Colorado's growth slowed to 3 percent, while both Wyoming and Montana lost 1 percent of their population.

Although statistics can be dry, they do paint a portrait of the three Rocky Mountain states. All residents were predominantly white, ranging from Colorado's 72 percent to Wyoming's 95 percent. Hispanics, the only significant minority group in any of the three states, tallied 19.5 percent of the population in the Centennial State.

Colorado faced the largest illegal-immigrant problem of the three states. In the ski country, where low-paying entry-level jobs needed to be filled, they appeared in large numbers. They worked as housekeepers, janitors, and busboys—jobs many residents hesitated to perform because of low pay and difficult working conditions. For illegals, arrests and deportation did little good, and no reasonable solutions to the problem of illegal immigrants were found in the 1990s or the early years of the next century.

Ski areas also continued to grapple with a high cost of living and expensive land and homes, and workers not being able to live in or, in many cases, even near the resorts. Everything except workers' salaries spiraled upward. The socioeconomic gap between residents and workers widened.

Another group often found itself marginalized as well. All the land from the plains to the Rockies had once been theirs; now Native Americans were vastly outnumbered in their homeland. The 2000 census found they constituted a high of only 8 percent of Montana's population and 2 percent of the populations in the other two states. They still lived mostly on reservations or in the Denver area. Only the natural-resource-rich Southern Utes continued to enjoy prosperity on their reservation. With strong leadership, they parlayed their advantages, from oil and natural gas to gambling, into a bonanza. Other tribes, such as the Northern Cheyenne and Sioux, did not have such advantages, and they found themselves dropping even further behind their white neighbors.

Wyoming's Northern Arapahoe, fearing loss of part of their heritage, are working hard to preserve their language. At the Wind River Tribal College in Ethete, Wyoming, a program is starting to preserve and grow Arapahoe fluency and an Arapahoe curriculum in schools. Other tribes are planning or have similar projects under way. Unfortunately, one of the major problems facing most tribes is education and keeping their students in school.

Colorado ranked first nationally in the number of individuals who had graduated from college (22 percent) and the number with graduate or professional degrees (12 percent), both higher than the national average (17 and 10 percent, respectively). Montana came in second in the Rocky Mountain states, with 18 percent and 8 percent respectively, and Wyoming trailed with 16 percent in the first category and tied Montana with 8 percent in the second.

A further study of the census data by the Population Reference Bureau revealed that Colorado has the fourth-best-educated workforce and the highest percentage of residents in the workforce of any state in the nation. Thirty-six percent of its working-age population (ages 25–54) had earned a college degree, against the national average of 28 percent. The report went on to state that "younger, more educated women [in Colorado] are more likely to be working."

Wyoming, with 22 percent of its population working at some level of government, far surpassed the 15 percent national average. In Montana, the corresponding figure was 19 percent, and in Colorado 14 percent. All three states were lower than the national average of 12 percent of the population working in manufacturing, and higher than the slightly less than 2 percent involved with agriculture and mining.

The eastern rural areas of all three states continued to lose population, along with a corresponding decline in towns and villages, job opportunities, and their role in the states. Rural areas suffered from a multitude of problems, including limited health care, generally higher unemployment, lower levels of education, and more people living below the federal poverty level. Colorado's San Luis Valley was the most extreme example. The only "rural" areas bucking this trend were those near Colorado's Front Range, where farmland was rapidly becoming suburbia.

Colorado in 2004 had the highest median family income of the three states at $55,000, placing it 10 percent above the national average of $50,046. More Coloradans found higher-paying white-collar jobs, and fewer lived below the federal poverty line, than their two neighbors. Montana's median income was $40,487, and Wyoming's $45,685. All these amounts were up from 2000—Wyoming's by 13 percent, Montana's by 10 percent, and Colorado's by 6 percent. Coloradans' higher incomes helped offset their higher home costs, their higher rents, and a higher cost of living than for residents of the other two states.

This thumbnail sketch of the region highlights some of the reasons Colorado had far surpassed its two northern neighbors and continued to lure more newcomers. Some Montanans and Wyomingites pointed out that Colorado's growth had led to traffic congestion, social problems, loss of open land, overcrowding, Eastern versus Western Slopes political fights, intrastate water fights, and a host of other tribulations that impacted the quality of life.

The popular national parks faced familiar problems. Overcrowding and congestion at highly popular viewing spots, bumper-to-bumper traffic jams, the need for repairs, too little financial support, litter, wildlife protection, airborne pollution, public safety, urbanization crowding in, and general wear and tear all decreased visitors' enjoyment and appreciation of the wonders of nature. Various plans, from limiting visitation, to tour buses replacing cars, to an aerial tram bringing visitors to Mesa Verde, were advanced. The problem always remained of how to maintain quality of the visits against the needs of the parks. The government had too many priorities and too little money to address these needs. Too little money for popular parks—what a sad commentary on the times!

The importance of Yellowstone and Glacier parks to Montana was clearly shown in a 2005 report of the National Parks Conservation

Association. The two parks attracted 60 percent of the state's summer visitors, resulting in $226 million in revenue for the gateway communities each year. The report also stated that some park visitors liked the parks so much that they moved to Montana, thus producing both short-range and long-range benefits.

Yellowstone rebounded from its disastrous fire, but Mesa Verde suffered several bad fires early in the new century. Fortunately, not one of the major sites was damaged, and one small blessing occurred, as the fire uncovered hundreds of sites on the mesa tops. Nearly 60 percent of the park suffered fire damage in a five-year period, and visitors driving into Mesa Verde clearly saw a charred landscape all around them. In the arid southwestern climate, it would take decades, if not a century, to restore the piñons and cedars.

New problems, yet old problems, bedeviled the Park Service. Montana ranchers complained about diseased buffalo from Yellowstone ranging beyond the park and infecting their cattle. They wanted to kill the buffalo wherever they found them. Wolves coming out of the park were no better liked either, in Wyoming and Montana, by sheep men and ranchers. Mesa Verde had earlier had problems with mountain lions that seemed invariably, at least to owners, to select the park's neighbors' most prized bull or cow to kill and eat. Again, no easy solutions appeared.

The Yellowstone fight over snowmobiles raged on from the 1990s into the twenty-first century. West Yellowstone, Montana, which bills itself as the "hub of Yellowstone country," provides a case study. In need of a solid winter economy, it capitalized on the popularity of snowmobiling in the 1980s and 1990s. It worked well until protests mounted at the turn of the century.

It pitted nearby businessmen, who needed to attract winter visitors and enhance their profits in a slow off-season, against the park and its goals. Opponents labeled a proposed ban on snowmobiles "un-American." They also did not want to limit the number of snowmobiles. The battle was fought from the Rockies to Washington, or as the *Denver Post* (May 21, 2000) described the debate, it was a case of "Noise vs. Nature." Snowmobile opponents made steady headway.

West Yellowstone's visitation dropped from over 50,000 to less than half that by 2003, sending, as one report noted, "a wave of terror through the town almost as thrilling as snowmobiling itself."[2] Efforts are being made to find a balance and ways to diversity the economy, but this situation exemplifies winter problems for the non-skiing Rocky Mountain towns.

The 2005 report by the National Parks Conservation Association placed Yellowstone's maintenance and repair backlog at an estimated $22 million, whereas Glacier, too often ignored, faced a $400 million backlog. Delays not only were frustrating, but also meant more costs in the long run. Glacier's Going-to-the-Sun Road for years had needed relatively inexpensive repairs. With nothing accomplished, however, the problems multiplied and resulted in a huge $150 million repair project. These parks also had personnel shortages. Glacier had no fisheries biologist, and Yellowstone, with 121 geothermal features, had only one geologist. With park staffs stretched to the limit, the parks presented fewer visitor programs. The same was true for Mesa Verde and Rocky Mountain national parks and national monuments scattered through the three states.

Despite the Bush administration's promise to devote billions of dollars to meet these needs, the money appropriated was nowhere near that figure. The outlook was neither rosy nor bleak, particularly as interest groups and the public rallied and put pressure on Washington.

Local and state economic interests looked at the national parks one way and the American public in quite another, leading to a variety of challenges. Without question, parks were closely wedded to economic interests. Without Rocky Mountain National Park, towns such as Grand Lake and Estes Park would find their prospects limited and Colorado's major tourist attraction less appealing. The same was true for the towns around Glacier, Yellowstone, and others with nearby communities relying on the parks, forests, or historic sites to attract tourists. From local to county to state governments, nobody wanted to kill the golden goose that generated millions of tourist dollars and publicity.

Visitors' appreciation and desires varied. A few wanted just to race through the parks and check off another place visited on their hurried western tour. Some wanted a vacation with all the modern conveniences at hand. Others wanted to flee urban pressures and return to nature or experience something mystical in nature. Some actually thought they could step back into a wilderness paradise that their frontier forefathers had "possessed." Each in his or her own way looked for a special experience of a special place.

The harassed and often criticized Park Service was expected to meet all these expectations—an impossible task. The massive human intrusion put at risk the very wilderness and park experience each visitor expected to enjoy.

As the twenty-first century began, less and less of the Rocky Mountain region fit the definition of a true wilderness. Once the first visitor left footprints there, that experience had started to erode. Now a new generation stampeded by the thousands, seeking a lost Camelot.

Crowds and impacts on nature's magnificence were not alone in presenting problems for the park service. An intriguing conflict arose over where George Custer and five companies of the Seventh Cavalry were overrun and killed by the Sioux and their allies back in June 1876 along Montana's Little Big Horn River. More than a hundred years later, the Plains Indians and the whites again stood at odds over the site and what it meant.

The result proved less disastrous to the losers this time around. First, the name "Custer's Last Stand" was changed to "Battle of the Little Big Horn." Then a monument to the winners was erected, over the protests of a diehard group of the losers, who objected to a variety of issues besides the renaming. They argued over tourist facilities at the battle site, and even the Crow and the Sioux could not always agree on what was to be done or said. The latest skirmishes included the outrage at the Native American superintendent's allowing modern Indians to "desecrate" the mass grave of the troops who had died on that June 25.

Finally, at long last, as the twenty-first century progressed, peace finally seemed to have come to the valley and hills of the Little Big Horn. As Tolstoy observed in *War and Peace*, "The strongest of all warriors are these two—Time and Patience."

On a less contentious note, the Confederated Salish and Kootenai Tribes in Montana have gained management responsibilities for the National Bison Range. They were the first Indian group to designate a tribal wilderness area, and now they took on additional responsibilities. "This agreement represents a success for all people involved, one that will bring a traditional way of life back to the native people of the Flathead Reservation and a high quality of stewardship in the management of bison."[3]

Tourism remained strong, despite the typical ups and downs that hit the entire region or individual localities. Colorado suffered a setback in

1993 when conservative voters, upset over rising state expenditures, voted to end funding for the state tourism board. Since that time, a variety of other methods have been tried to fill the gap. That decision hurt Wyoming as well, because the board had promoted both states, so Cheyenne was forced to spend more money on tourism.

Some tourists came and stayed. Whitefish, Montana, attracted a group of them, an unusual group, mostly millionaires. Threatening to become another wealthy enclave like Telluride, Aspen, or Jackson Hole, Whitefish's natural beauty, recreational activities, wide-open vistas, and the Big Sky Country provided the appeal. The result was predictable—land values skyrocketed, keep-out signs multiplied, trophy homes occupied choice locations, taxes went up, and the less affluent moved elsewhere. As one Montanan stated, "Montanans are afraid to death that little towns are going to become like Aspen or Vail, where the billionaires chase out the millionaires, and employees have to live 45 to 50 miles away [and] drive to work."[4]

Former residents of Telluride, Aspen, Jackson Hole, and even non-ski towns like Ouray, Boulder, and Durango, Colorado, had witnessed the same pattern. New residents rush in eager to settle in their promised land. With them come money and old-timers smelling profits, greatly increasing the price of their land and homes. All this is accompanied by complaints about higher taxes, a heavy demand for services, and a higher cost of living. Less fortunate people depart or work two, sometimes three, jobs in order to stay in "paradise."

With so many attractions and tourist meccas beckoning visitors, it remained imperative that the Rocky Mountain states promote and advertise their region. Otherwise, they could experience a decline in interest and attendance, even if they had a variety of tourist attractions that few other states could match. This fear lurked in the minds of Chambers of Commerce, visitors bureaus, and other promotional groups. To sit back and assume visitors would come spelled problems for large and small communities, counties, and all three states. To make matters more complex, jealousies still existed among owners of tourist attractions.

Overall, though, the picture was bright. Tourism had become more of a year-round industry than ever before. Particularly in the mountains, many people continued purchasing second homes and using them during desirable times of the year, such as the ski season and in the summer.

Nothing comes without outside impacts, and this trend created problems as well as revenue, including absentee owners, lack of interest in local issues, and the nouveau riche.

Many tourists came for one reason, the legendary frontier West. It had never ridden into the sunset, and it continued to lure travelers. Even though the age of television westerns might have faded back in the 1960s, the generation that grew up with them now came west to see for themselves the land of their imagination. Cheyenne billed itself as the "Old West," with its famous Frontier Days, now grown into one of the major American rodeos, as the main attraction. That event lasts only a frenzied week or so in July, so Cheyenne needed more attractions. Thus, in 2002 the city launched a "beyond the rodeo" campaign. A strong emphasis was placed on the community's historic tourism and "high tea," perchance reflecting the nineteenth-century days when Cheyenne served as the headquarters for English nobility's second sons who were trying to be "cowherders."

Virginia City, Montana, promoted its days as an 1860s gold-mining town and territorial capital, including the escapades of Henry Plummer and his gang and the town's vigilante response. Those who ventured over South Pass could visit where westward-moving wagon trains once traveled and mines at South Pass and Atlantic cities. Fort Laramie, Wyoming, and Fort Garland, Colorado, highlighted the military era, and various Indian reservations emphasized their heritage and culture. Montana benefited from the Lewis and Clark bicentennial throughout 2004–6 and Colorado's Bent's Fort took visitors back to the fur trapping and trading days. All three states had mining "ghost towns" to visit and speculate on what had transpired in these now-abandoned sites.

Other communities promoted whatever they could. Homesteading and farming (a rebuilt sod house or a recreated nineteenth-century farm) attracted few visitors, but they represented an important part of a vanished West. Once again, the scenic mountains lured more tourists than the plains' historic attractions. Understandably, considering the image of the nineteenth-century West, mining-camp denizens, outlaws, explorers, fur trappers, and soldiers seemed more romantic than farmers and plains towns. Only the romantic cowboy rode the range, and when he wanted to "whoop 'er up," he galloped into town. Few scattered plains communities could capitalize on this legend, however.

Wyoming found a way to benefit from its history, from fur trappers to farmers and even its long driving distances. A special supplement to *American Heritage* (2005) promoted Wyoming: "Where the Past Meets the Future." It continued, "With so much to see on the road to Yellowstone, you'll suddenly remember that getting there is half the fun."

Suddenly, though, that image of the legendary, rugged West—so cherished in all three states—took a hit, along with the celebrated cowboy. Montana had long been Marlboro Country, with cowboys puffing on cigarettes while working in the beautiful Big Sky Country. The advertisements' viewers assumedly smoked Marlboros and dreamed about a life they would never experience. Then reality tarnished the legend as medical science exposed the dangers of smoking.

A 2005 study indicated that residents of Wyoming and Montana chewed tobacco at a rate far above the national average, with Wyoming the number two state in the country. A mixture of advertising and the "cowboy culture," heavily marketed to the rodeo, rancher, and outdoorsman set, was blamed. Wyoming's Department of Health launched a campaign to make the public aware of the health dangers involved, but it faced an uphill struggle.

Montana went further. The would-be westerners could still dream about the old smoke-filled West of saloons, dance halls, and gambling "hells," but after 2005 they would not find a smoky atmosphere if they came to Montana. The 2005 legislative session banned smoking in all enclosed public places. The state became one of ten states to ban smoking on such a widespread scale. Colorado had cities with smoking bans, but no statewide ban was in effect until 2006. No longer does the Marlboro man ride the range, or smoking seem part of the western heritage.

Other kinds of smoke had been a major problem in earlier Rocky Mountain communities because of coal-burning furnaces, smelters, industrial plants, and the nineteenth- and early-twentieth-century urban atmosphere. An industrial mining city, such as Butte or Leadville, surrounded by the wear and waste of an exploitative business and a variety of environmental problems, did not excitedly tempt many travelers. Yet, in their own industrial way, they had done more to open, develop, and settle the West than the cowboy who had ridden into legend. Their problem was they had not been featured as widely in fiction and film, nor were they likely to be.

The long-ignored coal-mining era also failed to bring back fond memories of yesteryear or to produce a tourist bonanza. The immigrant coal or copper miner working for a corporation and the underpaid American gold or silver miner laboring in a similarly dangerous underground situation failed to draw much more interest in the twenty-first century than they had in the twentieth. The prospector, prostitute, and promoter seemed much more romantic.

However, an industrial town with some other attraction beyond a few historic buildings might overcome that fate. Deadwood, South Dakota, for example, gained limited-stakes gambling and showed what profits could be made. The example was not lost on Colorado. For Central City, Black Hawk, and Cripple Creek, gambling was the answer. If the mine owners and miners had gambled on nature's "whims" in locating profitable mineral deposits deep in the ground, their descendants faced even longer odds around the gaming tables and the one-armed bandits in more glittering surroundings. In 1990, Colorado voters approved limited-stakes gambling in those three depressed mining towns. Of the three, Black Hawk, with a huge nearby population base to draw from in Denver and its suburbs, clearly came out the big winner and the big loser. It had more space for parking and casinos than did Central City (only a mile away but hemmed in by a canyon) or the more isolated Cripple Creek. To reach Central, gamblers, with money briskly burning holes in their pockets, needed to drive through its once-smelting-town neighbor. Many could not resist the initial temptations and glitter and did not journey further to Central.

Other Colorado communities looked on with envy; they too could use an economic boost. They hoped to cut in on the gambling profits by allowing mom-and-pop stores to offer limited gambling opportunities and, even better, by opening casinos in their towns. Colorado voters said no to their efforts, however, so Manitou Springs and other communities were left out in the cold.

Not entirely, however. In a related issue, the federal government, once again, played a key role. Under the 1987 Supreme Court decision (*California vs. Cabazon*), any Indian reservation in a state that allowed gambling could also offer gambling. The Southern Utes and Ute Mountain Utes promptly opened casinos at Ignacio and Towaoc. Their hoped-for bonanza failed to materialize, however, hindered by the lack of a large population base in the Four Corners region.

Meanwhile, Black Hawk did not lose gambling patrons and money like its neighbor Central City; it simply lost its identity and its heritage. One reason gambling passed was that the state benefited from the profits, as 28 percent of the gaming revenue went to preservation projects. Colorado preservation was aided except in Black Hawk, where nineteenth-century facades remain surrounded by gigantic twentieth- and twenty-first-century casinos. Both Central City and Black Hawk also lost their businesses when slots and tables promised a better return. An upturn in property values throughout the communities meant higher taxes, a double whammy for small businesses and homeowners.

To a lesser degree, the same problem hit Cripple Creek, which never achieved its expected bonanza. Outflanked, many Central City casinos closed as gamblers could not get through Black Hawk without testing their luck. Not until 2003, when a privately constructed road (thanks to Central's merchants, gambling interests, and others) took gamblers directly from I-70 up a beautiful but steep and winding road, did the town start to rebound. Fortunately, through all this, Central City still had the opera as a summer attraction.

For Black Hawk and Central City, gambling was a mixed blessing. Not only did the cost of city government skyrocket, but sewage problems had to be addressed, taxes increased, traffic problems and parking bedeviled everyone, and people left as social problems and crime mounted and the quality of life declined.

Gamblers raced to Black Hawk over dangerous, narrow, winding roads that often slowed them with construction projects and were never meant for such heavy traffic. Both Colorado and Montana had difficulty maintaining their roads. Colorado was hampered by the ill-conceived 1992 state constitutional amendment TABOR (Taxpayers Bill of Rights), which strictly limited the state government's expenditures. Backed by economic conservatives, the amendment seemed logical to a majority of voters, but it turned out to be an albatross around the state's neck. Education, roads, and poverty programs all suffered as a result. Montana did not have a problem like the TABOR predicament—just the usual repair and maintenance issues weighed against the numerous demands on the state's budget. Wyoming, thanks to its oil and gas revenues, did not suffer the same fate.

As traffic increased on all major highways and roads in the Rockies, the number of vehicle-animal confrontations also mounted. Night driving in the mountains and on the plains presented risks to locals and visitors alike. Few drivers slowed down unless a dead animal lay on the road making the danger abundantly clear.

In 2005, near Pinedale, Wyoming (which had the most vehicle-wildlife collisions in the state), a new system was initiated. Sensors along the road, triggered by deer and antelope moving through, activated flashing lights to alert motorists. Seventy miles north at Jackson Hole, traffic engineers considered building wildlife underpasses in places where a known migration route existed.

Both Montana and Colorado have the same problems with roadkill as traffic puts more pressure on the animals' territory. Colorado has another even more serious problem: its mushrooming mountain subdivisions are pushing animals off their summer and winter ranges. Western Montana is heading toward the same situation.

Still another problem haunts the West, pollution. Pollution drifts into Colorado from as far away as California, and nearby power plants in northern New Mexico threaten Mesa Verde National Park and its irreplaceable architectural and historical heritage. Colorado and Wyoming mountain lakes are becoming acidic because of airborne pollution, and Montana is close behind. Pollution is also home-grown. Another energy boom developed, putting more pressure on the scenic and animal West. It involved two old-timers: natural gas and coal. Wyoming and Montana garnered the most attention. In 2001, the government announced a national energy policy, whose goals were to increase domestic production to supply growing demand and reduce dependence on foreign sources, a familiar refrain. To reach these goals, according to the Bush administration, some environmental regulations needed to be relaxed, some protected lands opened to development, and the permit process streamlined. Rocky Mountain folk had heard it all before.

What did that mean for the Rockies and nearby states? Recent studies estimated that the region contained nearly 2 billion barrels of proven oil reserves, 186 billion cubic feet of proven natural gas reserves, and enough coal to supply the country for the next 120 years. Those staggering figures pointed toward coming changes. No other region of the United States is equally endowed.

During 2004 a series of conferences and summits were held encouraging clean and diversified economic development. The problems were many; they included shocked landowners finding out that they might own the surface rights to their land but not the subsurface mineral rights. The latter, by law, are legally dominant over surface holdings. This impacted both individuals and communities.

The lingering questions of access and damages to land hung over everything. Proponents of the status quo argued that mineral property rights owned by companies and/or individuals were harmed when surface owners required compensation for physical damage or lost real estate value. They also opposed the government rules and regulations that had to be met before mining could start. After all, in their estimation they were working what they considered to be their own property. Both sides argued about compensation.

On the other side were those who took a longer and broader view of the situation. They argued in favor of the surface owners' rights and the larger issue of to whom these resources really belonged—not individuals, but the heritage of American people in general.

In the background lurked the environmental impact of coal and natural gas plants. Montana and Wyoming contained relatively few, but Colorado had nearly two dozen. Despite the best equipment and efforts, air pollution continued and once-spotless vistas were becoming hazy. Air pollution became the first widescale environmental effect of the West's energy boom touching everyone's lives.

Another part of the problem involved wells. The Wattenberg Oil Field, located along Colorado's Front Range, has about 12,000 wells—more than Saudi Arabia. Rising ozone levels in nearby communities led the Colorado Health Department to check emissions coming from the field. The concern proved to be both real and pressing. The department determined in 2000 that vapor coming from storage tanks floated about 150 tons of volatile organic compounds into the air each year.

Moving quickly, the state required oil and gas operators in the nine-county Front Range region to install emission-control equipment. By 2003, the decision seemed to be paying off; the Denver-area ozone measurements dropped from earlier levels. Oil and gas operators, however, were less confident about the causes and additional costs versus the results.

Wyoming had the same concerns and problems with its Jonah Field, which has more than 1,000 natural gas wells. Located 130 miles south of

Yellowstone, Jonah's pollution had already affected that region. The issue did not solely involve the environment and vistas; local ranchers and others were worried about what it would do to their land and lifestyle. The 29,000 miles of new roads, more than 20,000 miles of pipelines, and 30,000 miles of utility lines could not help but have an impact. The Jonah Field, with 13.5 trillion cubic feet of gas reserves, could produce an estimated $6 billion in taxes for local, state, and federal governments, plus jobs and other local income, during its lifetime. No easy answers were available.

In a nod to the past, Rock Springs, Wyoming, boomed again, with its two "world-class natural gas fields." Rock Springs had witnessed it all before—housing shortages and higher prices, increased numbers of businesses, soaring tax revenues, greater demands on social services, pressure on roads, school issues, and a resurgence of drug problems and prostitution. Newcomers think this boom will last, but old-timers know better. Wyoming, meanwhile, remained an export state.

Except for diehard "againers," Rocky Mountain residents realize that they have to be part of the answer to the nation's energy future. That is not the main issue for them. Rather, the manner in which energy resources are developed is the crux of the matter, because the pace of exploration and development will pick up in the Rockies in the years ahead. There can be no more "rape and run" mentality, no more concern about profit over the environment. Further, more planning, development, and financing for the after-the-boom benefits needs to occur. Having been down this road before, westerners have every right to be skeptical.

Mining continued to be both a blessing and a curse for Montana, Wyoming, and Colorado. Sometimes the industry proved its own worst enemy, as in the case of the Montana gold mine right next door to Yellowstone. Pollution from the mine threatened the park and raised an outcry throughout the country. Mining finally stopped, but the mine left behind an ugly legacy.

Another Montana case involved the Zortman-Landusky gold mine, operated by the Canadian company Pegasus Gold. Hailed as the first large-scale open-pit cyanide heap-leach gold mine in the country when it opened in 1979, the operation required fifty tons of ore to recover one ounce of gold!

Over the next twenty years a continuing series of cyanide leaks, spills, and acid drainage contaminated streams and the land. Neither the state nor the federal government required the company to test for acid drain-age, which by the 1990s had contaminated streams with heavy metals and acid. As a result, in 1995 Pegasus Gold paid $36 million to settle federal, state, and tribal lawsuits. To make matters worse, promised sur-face reclamation did not meet the standards established by law. In 1998, Pegasus Gold's directors transferred remaining assets to a new company they created, Apollo Gold. Then Pegasus Gold went bankrupt, leaving Montana and Uncle Sam with a mess—including water treatment that may stretch into perpetuity.

Even worse, in some respects, was the high-handed manner in which mining occasionally dealt with its responsibilities. The Summitville, Colorado, disaster gained state and regional headlines. As with the Yellowstone and Pegasus cases, the cyanide process was the chief villain; unlike the former, it caused major environmental and water problems that were not as yet resolved in 2006.

Summitville, a long-ago gold mining district, was resurrected in the 1980s and 1990s because of its low-grade deposits, which could be profit-ably worked using open-pit mining and cyanide. Summitville reportedly contained a mountain of gold. Although easy to use, cyanide has a built-in problem—operators need to carefully monitor the process to keep it from leaching into the surrounding land and streams.

The Canadian firm operating at Summitville, Galactic Resources, misjudged everything. The area received heavy snow (well over thirty feet a year), hampering its mining and refining operations from the start. Then the company planned its operation poorly and found less gold than expected, and Galactic used environmentally unsafe procedures in set-ting up its heap-leach system. Winter weather wreaked havoc as well. In 1992, the company declared bankruptcy, closed the mine on less than a week's notice, and abandoned the area, as cyanide leached into a nearby stream, threatening people as far away as the San Luis Valley and threat-ening to spill into the Rio Grande.

Galactic fled, leaving Colorado and its taxpayers with staggering cleanup costs running into the hundreds of millions of dollars. Neither the company's bond nor the $28 million the federal government extracted as part of a bankruptcy settlement covered those costs. The ongoing prob-lems related to this disaster, as mentioned, continued into the twenty-first century.

Such examples of hard-rock companies facing heavy cleanup costs and declaring bankruptcy angered the public. So did their setting up dummy companies to take the blame. The industry could do little to control such ventures, particularly when foreign companies were involved. The predictable result bred even more bad press and demands for stronger environmental laws and their vigorous enforcement on both the state and federal levels. Pressured, frustrated, and faced with continuing bad press, mining companies moved elsewhere, away from the Rockies—some to Nevada's open-pit mines, others to foreign countries.

These examples of "rape and run," particularly those involving cyanide, hurt the industry throughout the Rockies and beyond, leading to antimining attitudes and stricter environmental monitoring. A worldwide twenty-first-century study of the industry confirmed these developments. Increased environmental regulation, public attitudes, uncertainty about future designation of wilderness land and parks, and taxation combined to rank Colorado as the "fifth-worst mining location in the world." Wyoming and Montana did not get such a ranking, but they too now watched the industry much more carefully. The old freewheeling days disappeared forever.

With numerous abandoned mines in all three states (an estimated 20,000 in Montana alone), the problem was almost insurmountable and costly, stretching who knew how far into the future. The majority of the mines had no surviving owners, or their owners were too poor to reclaim them. Taxpayers, unless faced with an immediate crisis, seemed unwilling to foot the cleanup bill.

Understandably, such examples as these put all three states and their citizens on their guard, with Colorado the most vigilant. As the Rocky Mountain energy boom took hold in the early years of the new century, they were ready. In 2003, for example, ranchers, landowners, and activists demanded more data on the planned developments in the Powder River Basin. So did Wyomingites about plans to extract methane gas under and around their properties.

In dealing with these emotional and interrelated dilemmas, politicians confronted a difficult task in planning for the future, caught up as they were with other pressing matters. They spent much time posturing, worrying about party issues, and focusing on their reelections. All reasons rated low in the public's estimation.

The political scene changed little in the years after 1990. The three states backed President George Bush twice, including the hotly debated outcome of the 2000 vote, the closest presidential election in history. Overall, Republicans won more in state elections, although Colorado Democrats made a surprising sweep in the 2004 election. For the first time in forty years, they controlled both the House and the Senate. Montanans continued their general trend of backing conservatives in state elections and sending liberals to the United States House and Senate. The more liberal western counties battled the conservative eastern ones for control, as they had for years.

This conservative-liberal split reflected a general pattern. Rural Americans tended to be more conservative, urban Americans more liberal. Rural westerners followed a long tradition of not wanting Uncle Sam to tell them what to do. Contrarily, they did not bristle at accepting federal money. Perhaps it would be fair to say that Rocky Mountain folks tended to be independent-minded and fiscally conservative.

The three states carried little power in Washington, although occasionally they received some ill-gotten fame. Montana Republican senator Conrad Burns, for one, gained national notoriety and questions at home when he observed that living in Washington "is a hell of a challenge." Many Montanans might have agreed with him, except he said it in the context of responding to a question about living among so many blacks. Colorado's Rep. Tom Tancredo also garnered a measure of attention by calling for finding ways to stop illegal immigrants, primarily Mexicans coming across the border, warning that they are "stealing jobs, destroying American culture and killing police officers."[5] From fences along the border, more border patrols including armed civilians, to rounding up and deporting illegal aliens, Tancredo hardly found anything he did not favor.

In 2000, Colorado gained a seat in the House as a result of its growth and the reapportionment that came with the new census, leading to a fight between the parties over district boundaries. The courts finally had to settle the redistricting matter. Montana was threatened with the loss of one of its two House seats. Wyoming had no worry; it could not lose the only seat it had.

Women made political progress in the last quarter of the twentieth century. Colorado elected several women to the U.S. House of

Representatives, the best-known and most influential, Pat Schroeder, who served from 1973 to 1997. It also had a female lieutenant governor, and Montana elected Gov. Judy Martz. The *New York Times* (April 21, 2001), in an article about Martz, reassured its readers about a change in Montana. The governor's aides had noticed that other governors had bodyguards and felt Montana should be up-to-date as well. It became up-to-date. Women were often found in the legislatures, county governments, and city councils, and serving as mayors. Politically, the fight for equality had made significant gains. Women not yet achieved equality in wages, jobs, and other areas, however.

Slow progress had also been made on crucial water issues in a race among needs, demands, growing population, and limited, allotted resources. The issues grew more complex and costly every year.

In southeastern Montana, for example, the Tongue River runs along the eastern border of the Northern Cheyenne Reservation. The state sold water needed to develop nearby natural gas leases it had previously sold to Colorado's Fidelity Exploration & Production Company. Montana insisted it owned the entire riverbed, but the Northern Cheyenne claimed that at least half the riverbed belonged to them. The question of who owned what ended up in court in an ongoing litigation, with the state, the tribe, and the company all defending their claims and positions.

Meanwhile in Colorado, water had turned to gold; the old alchemist's dream that water could be turned to gold had triumphed. Growing cities along the Eastern Slope desperately needed water. As the *Denver Post* (November 20, 2005) reported, "Cities' desperation creates crazed markets for a precious resource and saddles newcomers with the costliest hookup fees in the land." Continuing its four-part series on water issues, the *Post* (November 22, 2005) reported that "Colorado is [a] notoriously expensive place to shop for water," with some cities paying farmers as much as $20,000 per acre-foot, or the amount of water required to cover an acre of land with a foot of water (about 326,000 gallons). The state ranked near the top of the United States' price chart for water.

Towns that had earlier wisely secured water supplies charged new-home hookup fees ranging from $4,000 to $9,000. The higher range, for communities that lacked such foresight, ran from $19,000 to $24,000. Such a fee, of course, added substantially to the cost of a home at a time when, throughout the booming region, housing costs were already skyrocketing. In comparison, Tucson charged $1,600—and that mirage in the desert, growing Las Vegas, $5,400—for water taps.

Water literally joined the commodity market, not only because semi-arid Colorado had no more unappropriated water and little reservoir space remaining that environmentalists and others were not fiercely protecting. Proponents for dams and reservoirs just as ardently stood their ground. The situation was worse in Colorado than in the other two states, because of the larger base population and faster growth. Water had also become pricey because "water is property, and in much of the state, somebody already owns a right to use every gallon," as one water expert described the situation. Additionally, much of the available water runs through the beautiful Western Slope, across the Continental Divide, and Western Slopers are reluctant to let it go to the needy, booming Eastern Slope.

A May 19, 2003, story in *U.S. News & World Report*, "Water Fights: How Drought Is Changing the American West," clearly described the problem: "This time around, however, it is not just farmers and ranchers who are hard pressed for water. Now the agrarian West must compete with the New West's burgeoning suburbs and even with endangered species that depend on stream flows." Continuing, the article pointed out how the past failed the present. "Until recently, Westerners could avoid this looming problem. Lulled by nearly two decades of above-average precipitation that preceded the current drought, cities like Aurora [Colorado] failed to acquire the water supplies needed to keep pace with their booming populations." It was not just urbanization that caused the problems; declining rural American carried a longer share of the blame. "Even less frugal are many western farmers," noted the Denver Post (September 7, 2004), "whose crops consume about 90 percent of the region's water supply. Blessed by their forefathers with first dibs on cheap water, subsidized in part by huge federal water projects, most have had little incentive to install water-saving technologies."

Everybody joined in the debate in all three states, with urbanites and ruralists bickering with each other. Urbanites glared at other urbanites. For example, Denver and its suburbs quarreled with each other and with the remainder of the state over controversial water matters. Farmers fought for their water. Conservationists demanded a share for fish and other wildlife, and urban areas needed more water because they were growing. The demand overwhelmed the available supply.

The ripple effect of this expansion and its consequent demands is clearly shown with water running uphill toward money. It is reminiscent of the bright city lights attracting rural residents for generations to come to enjoy a better life, which was exactly what water would provide for the expanding urban sprawl along the Front Range. With their water rights sold, farms have declined. Colorado, for example, lost 1 million acres of farmland from 1997 through 2002, the third most in the country. Interestingly, the number of properties classified as farms in the state rose over the same period, because of the creation of residential "ranchettes" and small farm properties (for "gentleman farmers") in the urban developments consuming these once agricultural lands.

As farming declines in Montana, Wyoming, and Colorado, nearby communities are also threatened; one visitor described a plains hamlet as a "bunch of derelict buildings." The residents differed, of course, but the drift of time was against them. In truth, little may remain to provide a tax base, people for church membership, students for the school, or consumers for Main Street merchants. Once the school closes, many believe the village doomed. Life as it was once known disappears. That downward cycle proves difficult to stop. The decline of Crowley County, Colorado, for instance, where farmers sold their water rights back in the 1970s, clearly showed that pattern by the twenty-first century.

Cheyenne saw the same thing happening, but to a lesser degree, in its neighboring counties. Meanwhile, on the eastern plains of Wyoming and Montana the continuing decline of agriculture produced similar results, without the benefits of oncoming urbanization to provide economic relief. Some plains communities tried to promote themselves as retirement havens, with varied results, generally none too successful, or tried to encourage industry to locate there.

Not only the agrarian and urban Rockies have had their eyes on water; so have conservationists. Lawsuits have forced farmers and developers to surrender some of their water to meet the needs of rare fish and other wildlife.

The problem became further complex and litigious when it pitted farmers with senior water rights ("first in time, first in right") against those who drill wells for irrigation. Colorado water regulators had long granted extraordinary yearly permits that enabled some farmers to sidestep the seniority system; however, the well users were placed behind those who took water directly from the river. The issue came to a head when drought hit early in the twenty-first century as the Eastern Slope population continued to grow.

The dispute ended in court, and in 2003, the Colorado Supreme Court, in a pair of rulings, protected the senior rights and compelled the state engineer to enforce the seniority system. In 2005, some 1,500 wells on the South Platte River were shut down and others pumped at reduced rates. This hurt agriculture and bankrupted farmers and others who had depended on the wells. The rural exodus continued. However, the rulings helped those who owned the rights, many of whom were "water brokers" who had purchased the rights, as well as the cities and residential areas that needed the water for today and tomorrow.

Never has that old western expression "Whiskey is for drinking; water is for fighting over" been more true in Wyoming, Montana, and Colorado. The fighting over water will only intensify in the years ahead. As Richard White pointed out, "Water became the center of many battles between western municipalities." He continued, saying that "the huge cost of western projects, the growing budgetary difficulties of the federal government, and the increased competition for water" promised to make the future interesting.[6]

What this means for the future is unclear, but trends are already apparent. Farmers and ranchers near the booming metropolitan areas find it much more lucrative to sell their water rights than to continue with agriculture. Agriculture then declines as urbanization grows. Further questions will be raised about the best use of water and whether agriculture should even be undertaken in the western Great Plains.

Water sales are cheaper to accomplish than building more dams and reservoirs, so that will likely be the most feasible way to go. High profits will be made by those who gain control of water rights, and communities with water have an invaluable resource. Surface water is addressed first, then the issue of aquifers, those deep underground streams—likely leading to further disputes and lawsuits in all of the Rocky Mountain states.

Colorado's Western Slope will have to be continually on guard against schemes and plans to send its water over the mountains. Water lawyers will make money, and cases will be tied up in the courts for years. Downstream users in all three states have to be equally vigilante against pollution in receiving their share of this irreplaceable treasure. Thomas

Hornsby Ferril titled one of his poems, "Here Is a Land Where Life Is Written in Water." He caught the whole story in one line, "The West is where the water was and is."[7] Water, indeed, had become gold.

In a different arena, professional sports gained ascendancy in the Rocky Mountain region, as throughout the country. Denver had all the region's major league teams: football, baseball, hockey, and basketball. The Denver Broncos, probably the region's only real "home team," finally won a Super Bowl on their fourth try (1998) and then proved they could do it again by winning a second title the next year. Bronco game day, with its parties and other social events, became their fans' highlight of the week. The Colorado Rockies reached baseball's playoffs in their third year, and then poor trades and mismanagement kept them near or at the bottom of the National League's Western Division. The Avalanche brought further local fame by winning the Stanley Cup in 1996 and 2001.

Sports fans did not need to fret if they could not see their team or sport in person; they had bountiful choices to see almost any sporting event they wanted, thanks to cable and dish television systems. They could live in the promised land and not be out of touch in any respect.

While winning or losing is a major worry of the sports fans, more serious difficulties face the region. The problems challenging the three states in the twenty-first century are as varied as their landscapes. Colorado is booming, while Wyoming and Montana are generally holding their own. The eastern plains remain depressed except along the interstate highways, whereas the mountains are thriving. Urbanism has taken hold in Colorado, but less so in the other two states.

Change has brought conflict in a variety of ways. As photographer and Wyomingite Richard Gilbert explained, "Although cattle have almost been venerated as gods (revered more than in India—believe me), we are learning that they can erode precious streambeds, denude pastures of viable grass cover, and pollute waterways." He stated that today, "strip mining for coal and [drilling for] methane gas and natural gas are hot issues. It seems that when economic profit and land ethic along with a fragile ecosystem are brought into tension—money continues to speak loudly."[8]

True in all respects. Two of the three states are still major exporters of their resources, and only Colorado has recently emerged less so. The boom-and-bust syndrome remains alive and well in the Rockies.

Tourism is booming, but it is changing, and profit can turn to loss almost overnight. The Old West's legacy lives on—revived, debated, venerated, and despised. The New West's impact gains a similar stature—cursed, debated, and promoted. Environmental issues and pollution affect every corner of the region. International and national issues and problems are closing in on the Rockies faster than at any time in history, and regional independence is vanishing, to be remembered and cherished but perhaps not to be seen again.

Have the region and its people learned from the past generation's developments? Mark Twain, who saw part of his generation's transformation from a stagecoach window as it lumbered west to Nevada, was alternately impressed and depressed by what he encountered as he crossed Wyoming, heading into Utah.

> Toward dawn we got under way again, and presently as we sat with raised curtains enjoying our early morning smoke and contemplating the first splendor of the rising sun as it swept down the long array of mountain peaks . . . we hove in site of South Pass City. The hotelkeeper, the postmaster, and blacksmith, the mayor, the constable, the city marshal and the principal citizen and property holder, all came out and greeted us cheerily, and we gave him a good day.
>
> We left the snowy Wind River Mountains and Uinta Mountains behind, and sped away, always through splendid scenery. . . . [A grave appeared.] It was the loneliest land for a grave! A land given over to the coyote and the raven—which is another name for desolation and utter solitude.[9]

Modern visitors might have had the same thoughts as they sped along the interstate in the eastern part of the three Rocky Mountain states or raced across I-80, the nearest interstate to where Twain once jostled to and fro. They might have wondered why anyone would live, work, and try to survive there. Perhaps they reflected on what history would tell about the struggle to subdue this land and call it home. Contrast that with the prospering, growing urban Rockies West. Twain had something to say about all of this as well. "One of the most admirable things about history is, that almost as a rule we get as much information out of what it does not say as we get out of what it does say."[10]

Epilogue

LIKE THEIR LONG-AGO ANCESTORS of that chilly January 1, 1900, readers opened their January 1, 2006, newspapers to a variety of local, national, and state news.

> Think back to Jan. 1, 2000, it is hard to believe how much Cheyenne and Laramie County have changed. The community has come a long way thanks to progressive leadership both in and out of government. [Wishes for 2006: affordable housing, higher wage scale, needed services like health care, day care, and heating subsidies.]
> —*Wyoming Tribune-Eagle* (Cheyenne), January 1, 2006

> BOOMING CRISIS
> We're not prepared for the upcoming wave of baby boomer retirements.
> —*Missoulian* (Missoula, Montana), January 1, 2006

> [We are] concerned about the importance of protected public lands around our region in making this an attractive place to live. Positioning the Great Falls [Montana] region to be a center of energy production, diversity and research.
> —Guest editorial, *Great Falls Tribune*, January 1, 2006

> 2006: A NEW YEAR, NEW OPPORTUNITIES
> Each new year brings a sense of optimism, of hope. . . . Just by turning a page on our calendar, we're given a new year, a fresh outlook and another chance. [Among the things the *Post* said it would like to see in the new year were gains in medicine, compromise in politics, a state water policy, and an end of corporate greed.] . . . Here's to 2006!
> —*Denver Post*, January 1, 2006

Harking back to the predictions of January 1, 1900, universal themes remained in evidence—peace, prosperity, water, growth, quality of life, a fresh start, and the world situation. The end of corporate greed would have been a familiar tune to Rocky Mountain residents in 1900. So would improvement in medicine, a calmer world situation, and less political bickering. Worrying about "baby boomers," or their 1900 equivalent, was new and so also protecting the public lands, affordable housing, day care, and heating subsidies. Wyomingites would have been stunned to see their state with a billion-dollar surplus, but then so would residents of forty-nine others in 2006. Rocky Mountain folk, on that chilly January 1, 1900, would have been pleased with the optimism of their descendants as they entered a new year.

This twenty-first-century generation is much more passionate about their quality of life, and they define it differently in some ways. Prosperity is fine, but today if it threatens the environment, objections will appear from both rural and urban westerners. Once praised (perhaps even *honored* is more correct), the idea of growth is now contentious in some quarters.

The world crashed in on Rocky Mountain folk more personally and visually in 2006. Their 1900 ancestors would probably be stunned to see how completely their descendants have become part of the national and international scene. That trend was under way in January 1900, however; America had just been through the Spanish-American War and now read about the nasty war in the Philippines. What had happened to their independence and their mythical western Camelot? Both generations would have recognized colonialism, though, however different the form in which it appeared.

Those 1900 westerners also would have recognized the problems involving water. Ever since settlement, water had been of paramount concern. A child of that generation, Bernard DeVoto, maintained when discussing the West, "American ingenuity, will power, and energy were spectacular qualities, but, against the fact of rainfall, they simply didn't count."[1] The problem did not go away but only amplified as the decades passed. The increased demands that came with population growth put water at the top of current concerns by 2006.

Perhaps the one thing that made all the difference between the two days is something that both generations enjoyed and, in some ways, feared.

Nothing endures but change.

—Heraclitus

Nothing in the world lasts save eternal change.

—Honorat de Bueil, Seigneur de Racan

Two thousand years passed between the Greek philosopher's observation and the French poet and writer's comment. While another 450 years would slip away before the twenty-first century, the comment remains as apropos now as then. The Rocky Mountain states may have barely moved into their second century, but change has been, and will continue to be, a constant, perhaps the only constant.

America in 2006 obviously is not the America of 1900 or 1950. Neither are the three Rocky Mountain states. Times change, people change, only the land remains—although even it has changed in some respects.

Interstate highways crisscross the land; shopping malls dot the landscape; urban development has spread into the countryside, river meadow, and mountain valley; and trophy homes dot mountainsides where elk and deer once roamed. These animals are now traffic hazards where they long ago ran free. Crowds of people can be found almost everywhere except on the prairies, pressuring a fragile environment and impacting everyone's experience. Automobiles allow families to race through the countryside, polluting as they go, and traffic jams in and around cities and suburbs and on mountain highways in ski season and tourist seasons are commonplace. Colorado's Front Range in particular has fallen victim to vehicle pollution.

Those interstate highways provide corridors that create an economic boom. Life in the Rocky Mountain West has never been fair, and a town's proximity to an interstate greatly affects its chances for prosperity. Sundance, Wyoming, has the good fortune to sit astride I-90, while nearby Upton does not. Both have similar economies, but Sundance has the county courthouse. The economic advantage goes to Sundance.

One economic windfall has remained constant throughout the decades: state and federal government largesse. As in the case of Sundance, communities selected as a county seat, or those that corralled a state or federal institution, survive and often avoid the worst of a boom-bust cycle while their neighbors fail. Rico, Colorado, for example, lost the county seat designation and stagnated, along with its mining decline. Some westerners believe the government is an "eternal resource." This is the love in the love-hate relationship, although history does not necessarily follow a pattern.

Rivers no longer run free, and pollution contaminates what not long ago were pristine streams. Toxic waste sites are reminders that humans once mined, worked, and manufactured nearby. Somebody or something lays claim to every drop of water. Puny man tries to manage forests, parks, wildlife, streams, and prairies while the thoughtless litter. Even the wind brings in smog and pollution to corrupt unspoiled vistas, damage nature, and endanger health. People point fingers, states bicker, attempts are made to correct the problem, and still the problem persists.

Like southern California's urban areas, Colorado's Front Range faces a growing ozone pollution problem. The infamous "brown cloud" settles over Denver, besmirching the area's reputation and threatening sanctions from the Environmental Protection Agency. Criticism is pointed at vehicle emissions and smokestack industries, but the problem goes deeper than that, delving into lifestyles, neighboring communities and even states, economic impacts, and cost worries.

More people crowd into the region every year, yearning for the western lifestyle, freedom, and open space of the Rockies. Meanwhile, the quality of life in many prime locations declines correspondingly, and pollution drifts across mountains and plains. At least in the case of Wyoming and Montana, an out-migration of young residents (particularly in eastern counties) seeking more profitable work and job opportunities elsewhere promises challenges for the future. As Pogo, that cartoon friend of Walt Kelly, explained, "We have met the enemy and he is us."

Prairie homesteads, long abandoned, show little sign that humans at one time lived, worked, and loved there. Nature has reclaimed sites where farm villages and mining camps, along with their people, once struggled for existence. Lonely, abandoned graveyards mark the passage of earlier generations.

For 150 years, the Rockies have lured the adventuresome, the hopeful, the promoter, and the desperate-to-come. Each one of them, doubtlessly unintentionally in many respects, helped produce today, with both its good and its troublesome sides.

Despite longings, one cannot go back. Nor would one want to, considering realistically what life was like then. Again, to quote DeVoto, who cautioned the mythmakers: "The West is the loveliest and most enduring of our myths, the only one that has been universally accepted. In that mythology it has worn many faces. It has meant escape, relief, freedom, sanctuary. It has meant oblivion. It has meant Death. But whatever else it has meant, it has always meant strangeness. That meaning may serve to reconcile the incompatibles."[2]

Progress, along with change, has been the most persistent and salient current of the twentieth and twenty-first centuries. That optimism formed the bedrock of 1900, as it does 2006, and it is a hallmark of the region. These westerners still seem willing to innovate and experiment.

Fortunately, twenty-first-century Rocky Mountainites display more concern for the environment than their great-grandparents did. That trend augurs well for the future. An indication of this is the "green power" movement. It has gained support as alternate sources of energy are looked for, particularly cleaner, renewable energy. Wind farms with large wind "turbines" dot prairie land. There exists an endless source of potential energy blowing about the mountains and prairies. Slowly, people and companies are realizing the potential, including Colorado's Vail Resorts. One of the challenges facing the twenty-first century is how to cut the cost of wind power, which is roughly 23 percent more per month than power generated by coal or natural gas. A cleaner environment, less pollution, and a healthier region ride on the outcome of this and other, similar experiments. In this search for a better quality of life, the westerners follow in the footsteps of their predecessors.

Twentieth-century Rocky Mountain residents faced unprecedented challenges to their day-to-day existence and quality of life. They grappled with the Industrial Revolution, urbanization, economic depressions, the energy crisis, and the Internet. They fought in two World Wars and several smaller ones, worried about the nuclear age, and survived the cold war and two Communist scares. Reform came in spurts—progressiveness, the New Deal, "making the world safe," education, women's, civil, and gay rights, and many other issues over which not everyone agreed.

Looking back, they could see that massive cultural changes had taken place. Critics bemoaned the breakdown of the traditional family, the deterioration of popular culture, the ubiquitous consumerism, the

decline of neighborhoods and small towns, the slipping of public education, and the waning of traditional religious faith. Regardless, the cultural
evolution marched ahead.

Westerners watched their country become a superpower, and several
immigration surges changed the complexion of their cities and countryside. Like their counterparts in the rest of the country, they enjoyed
an unprecedented prosperity and standard of living. Their grandparents
and great-grandparents would have been amazed and, perchance, a little
pleased that they helped bring it all about.

The Rocky Mountain West of the twenty-first century would astound
the old-timers of 1900, especially the newcomers who have arrived, hun-
kering down for a stay and making stunning demands. These "city slickers," now in their rural homes planning on enjoying country life, wonder why the road is not plowed, the trash is not picked up, and big city
services are not available. A Gallatin County, Montana, planner placed
it all in perspective: "A lot of newcomers don't understand that a rural
county like this doesn't have the resources to provide the services they
might be used to."

In response, counties throughout the region have developed codes of
the West to help ease the transition. Some of these would be funny if not
for the seriousness behind them. Two from Colorado illustrate the point.
Gunnison County's code points out that "occasionally, cattle may get
out on the road. Avoiding hitting an animal is healthy for both you and
the animal." Then there breathes the basic issue of barnyard smells that
Larimer County's code deals with: "Animals and their manure can cause
objectionable odors."[3]

When the Rockies started worrying about barnyard smells, an era had
ended. As Charlie Russell observed nearly a century ago, "The west is
dead, my friend." Old-timers bemoaned the changes that had come and
feared those that might be coming.

More significant, however, from Durango, Colorado, to Bozeman,
Montana, and beyond, rocketing housing costs are making some attrac-
tively located communities enclaves for the affluent and often their trophy homes. Affordable housing for ordinary workers continues to be a
problem in these areas. No easy solutions appear. Parts of Russell's west
that are disappearing are family ranches and farms. They are disappearing
in part because of urban involvement in the rural lifestyle. The Colorado

State Fair has lost money year after year, and the La Plata County Fair tried to convince newspaper readers that "Urban or Rural, Together, we're PLURAL!" It did not help; each year the number of exhibits and visitors goes down. Nor is Colorado alone; county fairs are disappearing or suffering throughout the Rockies.

The Old West is not quite dead in some respects; for one, it still serves as a refuge for societal misfits, just as it did a century or more ago. The *New York Times* (August 7, 1998) noted that Montana "is the last best place that attracts unbalanced loners." Each of the Rocky Mountain states, over the past generation or so, has had problems when such people act violently. In western lore, these people often became legends; the modern versions are not to their contemporaries. In reality, a hundred or so years ago, they were not so legendary either. That came later.

Despite the egalitarianism, so highly praised by writers and scholars, that emerged from the nineteenth-century West, the modern Rocky Mountain West has easily identifiable social classes and housing subdivisions. The haves, the have-less-es, and the have-nots live and work throughout the region, noticeably in mountain and resort towns. Racial, monetary, educational, lifestyle, social, housing—the divisions are there for all to see. Despite various attempts to equalize people's situations, lasting solutions have been hard to come by.

Environmentally, all three states are suffering from the heritage of previous generations—toxic wastes, abandoned mines and settlements, industrial sites, despoiled forests, worn-out soils, polluted water systems, and, in some cases, the unintentional introduction of pests that now bedevil agriculture, humans, and the environment. Awareness has not produced total salvation throughout the region. Future generations will have to build upon the awareness and progress the late twentieth century achieved to build a future that will transcend the present. It is a race against negating the quality of life that has been a hallmark of the region.

The Old West is not quite dead in another respect; its high expectations for more mining booms. Two, in fact, made news as 2005 faded into 2006. The energy crisis spurred them both. Uranium, with all its problems, is making a comeback, now that the price has tripled since 2004 to $36 a pound. That could stir another rush of prospectors, development, and mining if the lessons of the past have not been learned.

Oil shale, America's legendary twentieth-century ace in the hole, also revived and made news. When fuel prices go up, interest in this rock, which "contains hydrocarbon energy as kerogen," has historically soared. The world's richest oil shale deposits still reside in Colorado, Wyoming, and neighboring Utah. Throughout the twentieth century, they promised much but delivered little. Will this be the time? No, concluded mining scholar and writer Steve Voynick: "Not in this generation. In fact, not until Big Oil has pumped its last barrel of crude. Until then, oil shale will do nothing more than what it's always done — make us feel good."[4]

Regardless, both oil shale and uranium seem to be making a comeback. With prices going up and needs increasing seemingly daily in 2006–who knows? — the Rocky Mountain states may make a comeback as well.

Just like in the Old West, the New West beckons as a more promising place for those with few prospects back East. Wyoming's sizzling energy economy, including the coal-rich Powder River Basin, brings workers from depressed states like Michigan, where the decline of the automobile industry is helping bring a skilled workforce to Gillette and Campbell County. They came with needed mechanical, construction, and engineering abilities, all adaptable to needs of the boom. The dry, sagebrush country is quite a change for them, like the family who killed three rattlesnakes in their front yard or another that had to drive 350 miles to metro Denver for "hands-on" shopping for baby clothes, rather than using the Internet.

With the aforementioned exceptions, the old extractive industries — mining and forestry — have but a pale shadow of their previous significance. They have left environmental problems in some areas for today and tomorrow to resolve at a cost that has not as yet been fathomed.

The key question is, Have we learned anything from the past? The German philosopher Georg Hegel cynically assumed not: "What experience and history teach is this — that people and government never have learned anything from history." The Rocky Mountain westerner has always looked more optimistically to the past and hopefully toward the future with more confidence than that.

Montana did learn something from the past and gave the first posthumous pardons in the state's history. In 2006, Gov. Brian Schweitzer pardoned seventy-eight men and one woman who, during the World War

I anti-German hysteria, were convicted of sedition. Said the governor, the state was "about 80 years too late. This should have been done a long time ago."[5]

Two Wests exist in the Rockies, the urban and the rural, both dating back to the opening of the region. Rural westerners tend to be more individualistic, conservative, and often distrustful, or they are trapped in a love-hate relationship with the federal government, as previously noted, a pattern that stretches back well over a century. Outvoted, less influential, often languishing outside the mainstream, and shrinking in numbers, they watch their way of life decline, particularly in Colorado. Their situation also reflects the depressing plight of agriculture in general.

Urbanization is triumphant in Colorado and nearly so in Montana and Wyoming. You might recall that in their very earliest days, thanks to mining, that had been true in all three. Agriculture then came to the forefront, before receding against the relentless urban tide of postwar America.

Of the three states, Colorado is the richest per capita, the most urbanized, the fastest growing, the most prosperous, and the most crowded, and is faced with the most "modern" tribulations; it also has the second-highest percentage of college-educated residents in the country. That reflects the surge of outsiders with college degrees, but interestingly, not a high increase among locals graduating from college. The Centennial State is the eighth-youngest U.S. state, although its average age is increasing—a noticeable trend throughout the Rockies.

Denver and its suburbs, the metropolitan heart of the Rockies, are the center of the region's service-based and technology economy. As it has been for over a century, it is the region's banking, transportation, medical, and business nucleus.

The state has racial tensions, urban problems, crime, poor-versus-rich issues, growth concerns, financial stress, and worries about that popular term *quality of life* that are now part of the American fabric on both coasts and elsewhere. Colorado also reflects the new immigration pattern, with a large increase in the Hispanic population. As elsewhere, the major population growth has occurred in urban areas, mostly in Denver and its surrounding counties.

Colorado, unfortunately, is also home to some of the bitterest feuds in the Rocky Mountains between liberals and conservatives on issues ranging from the political to the social to the religious. El Paso County and its county seat, Colorado Springs, are the most conservative twosome in the state and, perchance, of the whole region among larger communities. They are also the heart of the religious right in the Rockies. A few religious right representatives in the state legislature have earned the reputation as contentious, doctrinaire, right-wing politicians.

The apprehension over population and growth's collision with the mountain and valley environments is seen everywhere in Colorado and also in Montana and Wyoming's Yellowstone country. What impact this will have on tourism, downstream residents, animals, water, and nature in general mirrors what is shaping Colorado's and, to a lesser degree, Wyoming's and Montana's futures.

To live in the mountains, to enjoy the mountains, is to love the mountains. No matter what we as individuals think about what we once were, are today, or may become, everyone, no matter what their differences, works together to preserve the wonders of nature. The future rests in the hands of the present.

Wyoming, with an abundance of coal and natural gas royalties, has gained a budget surplus to finance education, government, local programs, and other projects. It is booming now, but based on the age-old pattern a bust will happen unless public planning for the future proves better than it has in the past.

At least part of Wyoming also has another modern problem despite the state budget surplus. The prairie around Cheyenne, in Laramie County, is being subdivided at an alarming rate—13,000 acres in 2005—leading to the usual problems of uncontrolled growth and demands for roads, fire protection, mail service, and law enforcement. This low-density development generates less tax revenue than such services cost, forcing the county to take limited financial resources from somewhere else. "It's exploded, it's uncontrolled and it affects everyone's lifestyle," acknowledged Laramie County Regional Planning Commission chairman Mike Dowling.[6]

Both Wyoming and Montana face environmental issues as a result of the coal and natural-gas booms. How the two states handle such problems will tell much about their future. As author Phil Condon dryly observed about the return of the oil and gas "hounds": "But they're back again this century, nosing through the Overthrust, blind to the Blackfeet medicine, deaf to the irreplaceable grizzly habitat, numb to the needs of newer generations for at least one island where the wild prairie meets wild mountains."[7] Such sentiments have echoed down through the past two generations, in urban homes and rural farmhouses.

No question exists about the impact on water of such developments. Colorado, Wyoming, and Montana all face similar dilemmas. Montana's Bitterroot Valley is confronting the issue of agricultural versus domestic use for the growing population of non-farmers and non-ranchers. The water the valley receives, from lakes, rivers, and wells plus rainfall, is a finite, limited amount and will eventually become only marginally adequate as growth expands. Any decline in the snowpack or increase in the number or length of dry seasons will bring the matter to a head. The same threat exists for areas of Colorado and Wyoming, especially nearer Cheyenne and around the Tetons and Yellowstone.

The need for water will shape the future as rural and urban representatives square off to protect or gain this precious commodity. Eighty percent of Rocky Mountain water goes to "inefficient agricultural uses," as some define the present situation. Although both groups practice better water conservation, the cities get more "bang for the buck" in using their water efficiently.

Some water-hungry companies and individuals covet the deep underground reserves that flow under the states. The issue of ownership of water potentially pumped out of aquifers already has caused interstate conflicts and also more localized ones. The financial cost of such drilling raises a big question. More significant, it is not really known what the long-range environmental impact of such activities might be on the land and subsurface area.

If limited water resources have created tension for today and tomorrow, drought has shown that it still plays a significant role despite dams and reservoirs. Frail man has not tamed nature despite a century and more of effort. Drought has forced the abandonment of farms throughout the eastern parts of all three states, with Montana perhaps the biggest loser. Nor have any miracle "cures" been found to turn that phrase hated by plains residents, "the Great American Desert," into that long-desired agriculture paradise.

The timeless American dream of a new land and a new life that DeVoto, among others, claimed had died may in some respects have only been resurrected in new forms or new interpretations. In the depths of the Depression, DeVoto preached, "Westerners . . . first understood that there are other limits than the sky. To that extent, they led the nation. It may be that to the same extent they will have a better adjustment to the days ahead."[8] They made some of those adjustments, refocused themselves, and moved on. That is part of the plains and mountains epic.

Rocky Mountain residents also tend to be somewhat polarized, a not unusual situation in twenty-first-century America. The growing split between pro- and anti-growth factions could produce some interesting results if each side would listen to the other. So might discussions between old-timers and newcomers, urban and rural westerners, environmentalists and standpatters, and traditional lifestyle advocates and champions of other lifestyles. Part of the problem in the new century, though, is that people are often not listening to another, but posturing, shouting, swearing, and demanding.

How might one describe these Rocky Mountain westerners? They are contentious, caring, challenging, controversial, and concerned twenty-first-century individuals. They enjoy "doing their own thing," whether in dress, language, or life, one may claim, even more so than their predecessors of 1900. These traits, however, in one form or another, go back further than a century.

Looking over the Rocky Mountain region as the twenty-first century marches forward, a good argument can be made that it is the most modern place in America. It exhibits to one degree or another both the pluses and minuses of a country and a people in transition, complexity, and change. The past two generations of Rocky Mountain westerners have been impacted by swift socioeconomic transformations that have changed the nature of their region's society and economy.[9] The people, the issues, the goals, the hopes, the aspirations, the successes, the failures, and the achievements reflect America and Americans of this new millennium.

Rocky Mountain westerners craft their identity by their geography, the mountains, the river valleys, and the wide-open spaces, or as Montanans say, the "Big Sky Country." At the same time, most people crowd into an urban setting, a paradox that shapes regional history.

These Rocky Mountain folk honor the seasons of the past that reflected the best and the worst of the American saga. The mountains, prairies, deserts, and plateaus, along with the people who called them home, witnessed it all. The American dream had reached reality here if it had achieved that goal anywhere.

This dream may be defined as a concept of place, which, combined with that feeling for the past, shapes the present and potentially will the future. Like the wind that blows through the mountains and across the prairies, it is always noticeable and unstoppable and can be a blessing or a curse, depending on the time and place.

Charlie Russell was right, the Old West of his youth might be dead, but not the idealism, expectations, and desires. For better or worse, they have charted the course of a century, on into a new millennium. To return to Branch Rickey's observation quoted in the prologue, "It is not the honor that you take with you but the heritage you leave behind." That heritage—its joys, sorrows, successes, failures, contributions, mistakes, and good times and bad—all have their places in the book of the history of the Rocky Mountain heartland.

One western historian, Hal Rothman, described the New West as "terrible paradox. Our collective desire has created a split between where people tend to settle and the land that surrounds them."

He further observed,

It has glitter and glitz, leisure and at least a measure of security. Yet we pine for the old West as we live in the new.

The West is the most densely urban part of the country; it is also home to the most glorious and spectacular open spaces available in the Lower 48. The two abut one another, but they rarely intersect.

Rothman concluded his article: "The New Old West is a meaningful idea, because it's somehow where we all live, wrapped between demography and geography."[10]

Each generation has written a new chapter in the history of Montana, Wyoming, and Colorado. New chapters yet to be written will reflect back to all that has transpired as well as chart new courses.

To return to George Santayana: "Those who cannot remember the past are condemned to repeat it." Whether everyone agrees about those seasons of the past, they provide lessons for those who come later. It will be up to future generations to interpret and build upon what has transpired.

Those seasons have a fine story to tell, one that needs to be told and retold, to twenty-first-century Rocky Mountain westerners as they move forward into the unknown seasons of the future.

It has been said that to know Colorado, Wyoming, and Montana is to know America. Whether one agrees or not, the three states reflect much that was and is America. Both the good and the bad, the hard luck and good luck, the success and failures, and the overriding confidence and optimism that has characterized the American spirit.

In a way, the optimism of the West has never changed as it moved forward toward the unknown. That is perhaps the one western trait above all others that promises hope for the future. The 2006 New Year's editorial in the *Durango Herald* expressed it compellingly. "On many fronts there will be growth in quality and quantity during 2006. La Plata County residents have shown they care about the former as well as the latter. That is what makes this county such an appealing place to live. Happy New Year."

Notes

Prologue

1. *New York Times,* January 1, 1900.

2. Thomas C. Reeves, *Twentieth-Century America: A Brief History* (New York: Oxford University Press, 2000), 7.

3. Alex Ayres, ed., *The Wit and Wisdom of Mark Twain* (New York: Harper & Row, 1987), 107.

Chapter 1

1. Frederick Jackson Turner, *Frontier and Section: Selected Essays* (Englewood Cliffs, NJ: Prentice-Hall, 1961), 37.

2. These and the following quotations are from Mabel Lux, "Honyockers of Harlee, Scissorbills of Zurich," in *Cowboys and Cattlemen: A Roundup,* ed. Michael S. Kennedy, 336–38, 342–43 (New York: Hastings House, 1964).

3. Clara Hilderman Ehrlich, "My Childhood on the Prairie," *Colorado Magazine* (Spring 1974), 119, 132, 139.

4. Colorado Bureau of Labor Statistics, *Eighth Biennial Report, 1901–1902* (Denver: Brooks, 1902), 383.

5. L. W. Trumbull, *Atlantic City Gold Mining District, Fremont County* (Cheyenne, WY: S. A. Bristol, 1914), 73–74.

6. *Report of the State Coal Mine Inspector, 1909–1910* (Denver: Smith Brooks, 1911), 138–39.

7. Alex Ayres, ed., *The Wit and Wisdom of Mark Twain* (New York: Harper & Row, 1987), 35.

Chapter 2

1. Robert Athearn, *The Mythic West in Twentieth-Century America* (Lawrence: University Press of Kansas, 1986), 271, 10. See also chapter 1.

2. R. Kent Rasmussen, ed., *Mark Twain: His Words, Wit, and Wisdom* (New York: Gramercy Books, 2001), 241.

3. Thomas J. Noel, *Denver: Rocky Mountain Gold* (Tulsa, OK: Continental Heritage Press, 1980), 97.

4. Lyle Dorsett, *The Queen City: A History of Denver* (Boulder: Pruett, 1977), 138.

5. T. A. Larson, *History of Wyoming* (Lincoln: University of Nebraska Press, 1965), 315.

6. Frank Mondell, "Autobiography," quoted in T. A. Larson, *History of Wyoming* (Lincoln: University of Nebraska Press, 1965), 315.

7. Owen Wister, *The Virginian: A Horseman of the Plains* (New York: Harper & Row, 1965), xviii.

8. Athearn, *Mythic West*, 166. See also 163–65.

9. Quoted in William C. Everhart, *The National Park Service* (New York: Praeger, 1972), 21.

10. A. J. Mokler, *History of Natrona County, Wyoming* (Chicago: R. R. Donnelly & Sons, 1923), 60–61.

11. Walter Lippmann speech, May 27, 1965 quoted in John Bartlett, *Familiar Quotations* (Boston: Little, Brown, 1992), 677.

Chapter 3

1. All Woodrow Wilson quotes are found in John Bartlett, *Familiar Quotations* (Boston: Little, Brown, 1992), 572.

2. K. Ross Toole, *Twentieth-Century Montana: A State of Extremes* (Norman: University of Oklahoma Press, 1972), 139.

3. Quoted in ibid., 140.

4. *Wyoming State Tribune*, July 2, 1919.

Chapter 4

1. Charles Dickens, *A Christmas Carol and Other Christmas Stories* (New York: Signet Classic, 1984), 57.

2. T. A. Larson, *History of Wyoming* (Lincoln: University of Nebraska Press, 1965), see 301–4, 347–59.

3. Quoted in Montana Writers' Project, *Copper Camp* (New York: Hastings House, 1943), 2.

4. Michael P. Malone, Richard B. Roeder, and William L. Lang, *Montana: A History of Two Centuries*, rev. ed. (Seattle: University of Washington Press, 1991), 252.

5. Bernice Ketchum, quoted in A. Dudley Gardner and Verla R. Flores, *Forgotten Frontier: A History of Wyoming Coal Mining* (Boulder: Westview Press, 1989), 133.

6. Brian W. Dippie, "The Visual West," in *The Oxford History of the American West* (New York: Oxford University Press, 1994), 694.

7. Robert Athearn, *The Mythic West* (Lawrence: University Press of Kansas, 1986), 274; see also 265–68.

8. Frederick Lewis Allen, *Only Yesterday : An Informal History of the 1920's* (New York: Bantam Books, 1959), 255.

Chapter 5

1. Copies of these interviews may be found in the Center of Southwest Studies, Fort Lewis College, Durango, Colorado.

2. Quoted in Richard Lowitt and Maurine Beasley, eds., *One Third of a Nation: Lorena Hickok Reports on the Great Depression* (Urbana: University of Illinois Press, 1981), 294, 296–97, 332, 334.

3. Sherm Ewing, *The Range* (Missoula, MT: Mountain Press, 1990), 91, 97.

4. Roosevelt quotes were all taken from John Bartlett, *Familiar Quotations* (Boston: Little, Brown, 1992), 648–49.

5. Quoted in Richard Lowitt, *The New Deal and the West* (Bloomington: Indiana University Press, 1984), 205.

6. Quoted in ibid., 204.

7. Quoted in ibid., 22.

8. CCC Interviews, Mesa Verde National Park Archives, except Thompson, which was done by the author.

9. Nikki Ducheneaux, "Flathead and Sioux in the Civilian Conservation Corps," senior seminar paper, December 15, 2003, Fort Lewis College, Durango, Colorado.

Chapter 6

1. Quoted in Clark Spence, *Montana: A Bicentennial History* (New York: W. W. Norton, 1978), 161.

2. Quoted in T. A. Larson, *Wyoming's War Years, 1941–1945* (Laramie: University of Wyoming Press, 1954), 165.

3. Quoted in Robert G. Athearn, *The Coloradans* (Albuquerque: University of New Mexico Press, 1979), 300.

4. Michael P. Malone, Richard B. Roeder, and William L. Lang, *Montana: A History of Two Centuries*, rev. ed. (Seattle: University of Washington Press, 1991), 309.

5. The statistics are found in Gerald Nash, *The American West Transformed: The Impact of the Second World War* (Bloomington: Indiana University Press, 1985), 218–23.

6. Fourth inaugural address, January 20, 1945.

Chapter 7

1. Thomas Hornsby Ferril, "Here Is a Land Where Life Is Written in Water," in *Thomas Hornsby Ferril and the American West*, ed. Robert C. Baron, Stephen J. Leonard, and Thomas J. Noel (Golden, CO: Fulcrum, 1996), 36.

2. Michael P. Malone, Richard B. Roeder, William L. Lang, *Montana: A History of Two Centuries* (Seattle: University of Washington Press, 1991, rev. ed.), 381.

3. Ibid., 335.

4. Thomas Hornsby Ferril, *New and Selected Poems* (New York: Harper, 1952; Westport, CT.: Greenwood Press, 1970), 133. Citations are to the Greenwood Press edition.

5. Douglas Moore, *The Ballad of Baby Doe. Vocal Score*. Libretto by John Latouche (New York: Chappell, [1956] 1958).

Chapter 8

1. Clark Spence, *Montana* (New York: W. W. Norton, 1978), 181; "Montana Economic Study," quoted in Spence, 181.

2. Richard White, *"It's Your Misfortune and None of My Own": A History of the American West* (Norman: University of Oklahoma Press, 1991), 564–56.

3. James Conaway, "The Last of the West: Hell, Strip It!" *Atlantic Monthly* (September 1972), 98.

4. Sources for the two quotes: David Lavender, *Red Mountain* (Garden City, NY: Doubleday, 1963; Ouray, CO: Western Reflections, 2000), 577. Citations are to the Western Reflections edition; A. B. Guthrie Jr., *The Way West* (New York: Bantam Books, 1971), 137, 218.

5. Thomas Hornsby Ferril, "On the Oregon Trail, November 3, 1945," in *Thomas Hornsby Ferril and the American West* (Golden, CO: Fulcrum, 1996), 14.

6. Quoted in R. Kent Rasmussen, ed., *Mark Twain: His Words, Wit, and Wisdom* (New York: Gramercy Books, 1997), 206.

Chapter 9

1. Robert W. Righter, *The Making of a Town: Wright, Wyoming* (Boulder: Roberts Rinehart, 1985), 9, 96.

2. Figures in A. Dudley Gardner and Verla R. Flores, *Forgotten Frontier* (Boulder, CO: Westview, 1989), 213.

3. Richard D. Lamm and Michael McCarthy, *The Angry West* (Boston: Houghton Mifflin, 1982); see chapter 2, "The Rock That Burns."

4. Gerald D. Nash, *Creating the West: Historical Interpretations* (Albuquerque: University of New Mexico Press, 1991), 257.

5. Figures cited in Michael P. Malone, Richard B. Roeder, and William L. Lang, *Montana: A History of Two Centuries* (Seattle: University of Washington Press, 1991 rev. ed.), 342.

6. Molly Ivins, "Aspen Is Wary of Takeover of Ski Slopes," *New York Times*, January 31, 1978.

7. Patricia Limerick, *The Legacy of Conquest: The Unbroken Past of the American West* (New York: W. W. Norton, 1987), 319.

8. Lamm and McCarthy, *Angry West*, 326, 4.

9. Thomas Hornsby Ferril, "Here Is a Land Where Life Is Written in Water," in *Thomas Hornsby Ferril and the American West* (Golden, CO: Fulcrum, 1996), 36.

Chapter 10

1. *Denver Post*, March 6, 2005.

2. Hecox, Holmes, and Hurlbutt, *State of the Rockies Report Card* (2005), 27.

3. Ibid., 81.

4. *Denver Post*, September 23, 2005.

5. *Denver Post*, June 6, 2005. Comments such as this appeared frequently in Denver's and other cities' newspapers in 2004–5.

6. Richard White, *"It's Your Misfortune and None of My Own""*: *A History of the American West* (Norman: University of Oklahoma Press, 1991), 553, 557.

7. Thomas Hornsby Ferril, "Here Is a Land Where Life Is Written in Water," *Thomas Hornsby Ferril and the American West* (Golden, CO: Fulcrum, 1996), 36.

8. Richard Gilbert, letter to author, April 21, 2005.

9. Mark Twain, *Roughing It* (1872; New York: Penguin Books, 1980), 84, 88.

10. R. Kent Rasmussen, ed., *Mark Twain: His Words, Wit, and Wisdom* (New York: Gramercy Books, 2001), 127.

Epilogue

1. Bernard DeVoto, "The West: A Plundered Province," in *Forays and Rebuttals* (Boston: Little, Brown, 1936), 63–64.

2. Ibid., 48.

3. *Denver Post*, September 7, 2004.

4. Steve Voynick in his "Writers on the Range" article, *Durango Herald*, January 1, 2006.

5. *Denver Post*, April 4, 2006, 8A.

6. Mike Dowling, quoted in the *Durango Herald*, January 3, 2006.

7. Phil Condon, *Montana Surround: Land, Water, Nature, and Place* (Boulder: Johnson Books, 2004), 182.

8. DeVoto, "The West: A Plundered Province," 64.

9. Richard W. Etulain, *Beyond the Missouri: The Story of the American West* (Albuquerque: University of New Mexico Press, 2006), xi–xii, 444.

10. Hal Rothman, "Welcome to the Conflicted West," *Silverton Standard & the Miner*, September 14, 2006.

Suggested Readings

The reader is heartily encouraged to continue studying the Rocky Mountain Heartland. This region has always attracted historians and others to examine and discuss its fascinating history. The region and its history have so much to say to Americans of all walks of life.

The purpose of this bibliography is twofold: first to indicate the sources consulted; second, and perhaps more importantly, to lead the readers on to books that will take them deeper into topics that may interest them. Each volume has a bibliography that will then introduce books old and new; thus, the prospecting through history will become endless.

For this reason, the majority of the books date from the past sixty years and will be easier to find in libraries or bookstores. In no way does this demean earlier studies that paved the way and built the foundation on which subsequent researchers and authors relied. See also the books cited in the footnotes.

The reader is urged to consult the historic journals published by the Colorado, Wyoming, and Montana historical societies. They provide a potpourri of articles about more localized and specialized subjects. The topics are as wide-ranging as the mountains and prairies themselves. These historical societies also have wonderful collections of primary and secondary material, as do smaller local historical societies and museums, for those who desire to dig even deeper into Rocky Mountain history.

Newspapers from communities in all three states contain a wealth of information on an infinite variety of topics, as do an assortment of local, state, and federal documents. As Sherlock Holmes exclaimed, "The game is afoot." Go forth and become hooked on a fascinating—one might say bewitching—history of three Rocky Mountain states.

General and State Histories

Abbott, Carl. *The Metropolitan Frontier: Cities in the Modern American West.* Tucson: University of Arizona Press, 1993.

Abbott, Carl, Stephen J. Leonard, and David McComb. *Colorado: A History of the Centennial State*. Boulder: University Press of Colorado, 2005.

Armitage, Susan, and Elizabeth Jameson, eds. *The Women's West*. Norman: University of Oklahoma Press, 1987.

Athearn, Robert G. *The Coloradans*. Albuquerque: University of New Mexico Press, 1976.

———. *High Country Empire: The High Plains and Rockies*. New York: McGraw-Hill, 1960.

———. *The Mythic West in Twentieth-Century America*. Lawrence: University Press of Kanas, 1986.

Baron, Robert C., Stephen J. Leonard, and Thomas J. Noel, eds. *Thomas Hornsby Ferril and the American West*. Golden, CO: Fulcrum, 1996.

Billington, Ray Allen. *America's Frontier Heritage*. New York: Holt, Rinehart & Winston, 1966.

Bragg, William F. *Wyoming: Rugged but Right*. Boulder: Pruett, 1980.

Burlingame, Merrill G., and K. Ross Toole. *A History of Montana*. New York: Lewis Historical Publishing, 1957.

Burton, Jeffrey, Mary M. Farrell, Florence B. Lord, and Richard W. Lord. *Confinement and Ethnicity: An Overview of World War II Japanese American Relocation Sites*. Seattle: University of Washington Press, 2002. First published 1999 by Western Archeological and Conservation Center.

Duncan, Dayton. *Miles from Nowhere: Tales from America's Contemporary Frontier*. New York: Viking, 1993.

Etulain, Richard W. *Beyond the Missouri: The Story of the American West*. Albuquerque: University of New Mexico Press, 2006.

———. *Re-imagining the Modern American West: A Century of Fiction, History, and Art*. Tucson: University of Arizona Press, 1996.

Faragher, John Mack, Mary Jo Buhle, Daniel Czitrom, and Susan H. Armitage. *Out of Many: A History of the American People*. Upper Saddle River, NJ: Prentice Hall, 2005.

Federal Writers Project, WPA. *Montana: A State Guide Book*. New York: Viking Press, 1949. First published 1939 by Viking Press.

———. *The WPA Guide to 1930s Colorado*. Lawrence: University Press of Kansas, 1987. Originally published 1941 by Hastings House.

———. *Wyoming: A Guide to Its History, Highways, and People*. New York: Oxford University Press, 1941.

Fritz, Harry. *Montana: Land of Contrasts*. Woodland Hills, CA: Windsor, 1984.

Hecox, Walter E., Frank Patrick Holmes III, and Bryan Hurlbutt, eds. *The 2005 State of the Rockies Report Card*. Colorado Springs: Colorado College, 2005.

Hendrickson, Gordon O., ed. *Peopling the High Plains: Wyoming's European Heritage*. Cheyenne: Wyoming State Archives, 1977.

Hurt, R. Douglas, ed. *The Rural West since World War II*. Lawrence: University of Kansas Press, 1998.

Jameson, Elizabeth, and Susan Armitage, eds. *Writing the Range: Race, Class, and Culture in the Women's West*. Norman: University of Oklahoma Press, 1997.

Kennedy, David, Lizabeth Cohen, and Thomas A. Bailey. *The American Pageant: A History of the Republic*. Boston: Houghton Mifflin, 2006.

Kittredge, William, and Annick Smith, eds. *The Last Best Place: A Montana Anthology*. Helena: Montana Historical Society Press, 1988.

Lamar, Howard R., ed. *The New Encyclopedia of the American West*. New Haven: Yale University Press, 1998.

Lamm, Richard, and Michael McCarthy. *The Angry West: A Vulnerable Land and Its Future*. Boston: Houghton Mifflin, 1982.

Lang, William, and Rex C. Myers. *Montana, Our Land & People*. Boulder: Pruett, 1989.

Larson, T. A. *A History of Wyoming*. Lincoln: University of Nebraska Press, 1978.

Lavender, David. *The Penguin Book of the American West*. New York: Penguin Books, 1969.

Limerick, Patricia Nelson. *The Legacy of Conquest: The Unbroken Past of the American West*. New York: W. W. Norton, 1987.

———. *Something in the Soil: Legacies and Reckonings in the New West*. New York: W. W. Norton, 2000.

Limerick, Patricia Nelson, Clyde A. Milner II, and Charles E. Rankin. *Trails: Toward a New Western History*. Lawrence: University Press of Kansas, 1991.

Malone, Michael, ed. *Historians and the American West*. Lincoln: University of Nebraska Press, 1983.

Malone, Michael, and Richard W. Etulain. *The American West: A Twentieth-Century History*. Lincoln: University of Nebraska Press, 1989.

Malone, Michael P., and Richard B. Roeder, eds. *The Montana Past: An Anthology*. Missoula: University of Montana Press, 1969.

Malone, Michael P., Richard B. Roeder, and William L. Lang. *Montana: A History of Two Centuries*. Rev. ed. Seattle: University of Washington Press, 1991.

McLellan, James. *History of Montana, from Wilderness to Statehood*. 2nd ed. Edited by Merrill G. Burlingame. Portland, OR: Binfords & Mort, 1970.

Milner, Clyde A. II, Carol A. O'Connor, and Martha A. Sandweiss, eds. *The Oxford History of the American West*. New York: Oxford University Press, 1994.

Moulton, Candy. *Roadside History of Wyoming*. Missoula, MT: Mountain Press, 1995.

Nash, Gary, Julie Roy Jeffrey, John R. Howe, and Peter J. Frederick. *The American People: Creating a Nation and a Society*. New York: Pearson Longman, 2004.

Nash, Gerald. *The Federal Landscape: An Economic History of the Twentieth-Century West*. Tucson: University of Arizona Press, 1999.

———. *World War II and the West: Reshaping the Economy*. Lincoln: University of Nebraska Press, 1990.

Noel, Thomas J., Paul F. Mahoney, and Richard E. Stevens. *Historical Atlas of Colorado*. Norman: University of Oklahoma Press, 1994.

Riegel, Robert E., and Robert G. Athearn. *America Moves West*. New York: Holt, Rinehart & Winston, 1971.

Roberts, Phil, David L. Roberts, and Steven L. Roberts. *Wyoming Almanac*. Laramie, WY.: Skyline West Press, 1996.

Sodaro, Craig, and Randy Adams. *Frontier Spirit: The Story of Wyoming*. Boulder: Johnson Books, 1986.

Spence, Clark. *Montana: A Bicentennial History*. New York: W. W. Norton, 1978.

Toole, K. Ross. *Montana: An Uncommon Land*. Norman: University of Oklahoma Press, 1959.

———. *Twentieth-Century Montana: A State of Extremes*. Norman: University of Oklahoma Press, 1972.

Ubbelohde, Carl, Maxine Benson, and Duane A. Smith. *A Colorado History*. 9th ed. Boulder: Pruett, 2006.

White, Richard. *"It's Your Misfortune and None of My Own": A History of the American West*. Norman: University of Oklahoma Press, 1991.

Wyckoff, William. *Creating Colorado: The Making of a Western Landscape, 1860–1940*. New Haven: Yale University Press, 1999.

Agriculture

Baker, Don, and Gerry Keenan. *Ghost Towns of the Montana Prairie*. Boulder: Fred Pruett Books, 1998.

Bell, Edward J. Jr. *Homesteading in Montana, 1911–1923: Life in the Blue Mountain Country*. Bozeman: Montana State University, 1975.

Burlingame, Merrill G. *The Montana Frontier*. 1942. Reprint, Bozeman, MT: Big Sky Books, 1974.

Decker, Peter R. *Old Fences, New Neighbors*. Tucson: University of Arizona Press, 1998.

Dick, Everett N. *The Lure of Land: A Social History of the Public Lands from the Articles of Confederation to the New Deal*. Lincoln: University of Nebraska Press, 1970.

Dunbar, Robert. *Forging New Rights in Western Waters*. Lincoln: University of Nebraska Press, 1983.

Frink, Maurice. *Cow Country Cavalcade: Eighty Years of the Wyoming Stock Growers Association*. Denver: Old West, 1954.

———. *When Grass Was King: Contributions to the Western Range Cattle Industry Study*. Boulder: University of Colorado Press, 1956.

Hargreaves, Mary W. *Dry Farming in the Northern Great Plains*. Cambridge: Harvard University Press, 1957.

Harris, Katherine. *Long Vistas: Women and Families on Colorado Homesteads*. Niwot: University Press of Colorado, 1993.

Howard, Joseph K. *Montana: High, Wide, and Handsome*. 1943. Reprint, Lincoln: University of Nebraska Press, 1985.

Jones-Eddy, Julie. *Homesteading Women: An Oral History of Colorado, 1890–1950*. New York: Twayne, 1992.

Probst, Nell Brown. *Uncommon Men and the Colorado Prairie*. Caldwell, ID: Caxton Press, 1992.

Schlebecker, John T. *Cattle Raising on the Plains, 1900–1961*. Lincoln: University of Nebraska Press, 1963.

Spence, Clark C. *The Rainmakers: American "Pluviculture" to World War II*. Lincoln: University of Nebraska Press, 1980.

Wohl, Ellen E. *Virtual Rivers: Lessons from the Mountain Rivers of the Colorado Front Range*. New Haven: Yale University Press, 2001.

Vichorek, Daniel. *Montana's Homestead Era*. Helena: Montana Magazine, 1987.

Wood, Nancy. *The Grass Roots People: An American Requiem*. New York: Harper & Row, 1978.

Extractive Industries and Transportation

Amundson, Michael A. *Yellowcake Towns: Uranium Mining Communities in the American West*. Boulder: University Press of Colorado, 2002.

Athearn, Robert G. *Rebel of the Rockies: A History of the Denver and Rio Grande Western Railroad*. New Haven: Yale University Press, 1962.

———. *Union Pacific Country*. Chicago: Rand McNally, 1971.

Calvert, Jerry. *The Gibraltar: Socialism and Labor in Butte, Montana, 1895–1920*. Helena: Montana Historical Society Press, 1988.

Gardner, A. Dudley, and Verla R. Flores. *Forgotten Frontier: A History of Wyoming Coal Mining*. Boulder: Westview Press, 1989.

Gulliford, Andrew. *Boomtown Blues: Colorado Oil Shale, 1885–1985*. Niwot: University Press of Colorado, 1989.

Malone, Michael. *The Battle for Butte: Mining and Politics on the Northern Frontier, 1864–1906*. Seattle: University of Washington Press, 1981.

Margolis, Eric. *Western Coal Mining as a Way of Life: An Oral History of the Western Coal Miners*. Boulder: University of Colorado Institute of Behavioral Science, 1984.

Martin, Albro. *James J. Hill and the Opening of the Northwest*. New York: Oxford University Press, 1976.

McCulloch, Robin. *Mining and Mineral Developments in Montana*. Butte: Montana Bureau of Mines and Geology, 1989.

Mercier, Laurie. *Anaconda: Labor, Community, and Culture in Montana's Smelter City*. Urbana: University of Illinois Press, 2001.

Miller, Charles. *The Automobile Gold Rushes and Depression Era Mining*. Moscow: University of Idaho Press, 1998.

Miller, Jeff. *Stapleton International Airport: "The First Fifty Years."* Boulder: Pruett, 1983.

Overton, Richard C. *The Burlington Route: A History of Burlington Lines*. New York: Alfred A. Knopf, 1965.

Ringholz, Raye C. *Uranium Frenzy: Saga of the Nuclear West*. Logan: University of Utah Press, 2002.

Scamehorn, Lee. *High Altitude Energy: A History of Fossil Fuels in Colorado*. Boulder: University Press of Colorado, 2002.

———. *Mine and Mill: The CF&I in the Twentieth Century*. Lincoln: University of Nebraska Press, 1992.

Smith, Duane A. *Mining America: The Industry and the Environment, 1800–1980*. Lawrence: University of Kansas, 1987.

Smith, Phyllis. *Once a Coal Miner: The Story of Colorado's Northern Coal Field.* Boulder: Pruett, 1989.

Spence, Clark. *The Conrey Placer Mining Company: A Pioneer Gold-Dredging Enterprise in Montana, 1897–1922.* Helena: Montana Historical Society Press, 1989.

Suggs, George Jr. *Colorado's War on Militant Unionism.* Detroit: Wayne University Press, 1972.

Toole, K. Ross. *The Rape of the Great Plains: Northwest America, Cattle and Coal.* Boston: Atlantic Monthly, Little, Brown, 1976.

Voynick, Stephen M. *Climax: The History of Colorado's Climax Molybdenum Mine.* Missoula, MT: Mountain Press, 1996.

Whiteside, James. *Regulating Danger: The Struggle for Mine Safety in the Rocky Mountain Coal Industry.* Lincoln: University of Nebraska Press, 1990.

Wolfe, David A. *Industrializing the Rockies: Growth, Competition, and Turmoil in the Coalfields of Colorado and Wyoming, 1868–1914.* Boulder: University Press of Colorado, 2003.

Government and Conservation

Brosnan, Kathleen A. *Uniting Mountain and Plain: Cities, Law, and Environmental Change along the Front Range.* Albuquerque: University of New Mexico Press, 2002.

Cronin, Thomas E., and Robert D. Loevy. *Colorado Politics and Government: Governing the Centennial State.* Lincoln: University of Nebraska Press, 1993.

Fowler, Loretta. *Arapahoe Politics, 1851–1978: Symbols in Crises of Authority.* Lincoln: University of Nebraska Press, 1982.

Garrett, Ruth A. *A Look at Wyoming Government.* Jackson, WY: LWV Publications, 1998.

Hobbs, Gregory J. Jr. *Citizen's Guide to Colorado Water Law.* Denver: Colorado Foundation for Water Education, 2004.

House, Verne W., and Douglas J. Young. *Trends in the Montana Economy and Taxation.* Bozeman: Montana Extension Service, 1986.

Hundley, Norris Jr. *Water and the West: The Colorado River Compact and the Politics of Water in the American West.* Berkeley: University of California Press, 1975.

Lopatch, James J., ed. *We the People of Montana: The Working of a Popular Government.* Missoula: Mountain Press, 1983.

Lorch, Robert A. *Colorado's Government: Structure, Politics, Administration, and Policy.* 6th ed. Niwot: University Press of Colorado, 1997.

McCarthy, Michael. *Hour of Trial: The Conservation Conflict in Colorado and the West, 1891–1907.* Norman: University of Oklahoma Press, 1977.

Peirce, Neal R. *The Mountain States of America: People, Politics, and Power in the Eight Rocky Mountain States.* New York: W. W. Norton, 1972.

Pisani, Donald J. *Water and American Government: The Reclamation Bureau, National Water Policy and the West.* Berkeley: University of California Press, 2002.

Waldron, Ellis, and Paul B. Wilson. *Atlas of Montana Elections, 1889–1976.* Missoula: University of Montana Publications, 1978.

Wright, John B. *Rocky Mountain Divide: Selling and Saving the West*. Austin: University of Texas Press, 1993.

Tourism, Entertainment, and Sports

Bartlett, Richard A. *Yellowstone: A Wilderness Besieged*. Tucson: University of Arizona Press, 1985.

Borne, Lawrence R. *Dude Ranching: A Complete History*. Albuquerque: University of New Mexico Press, 1983.

Buchholtz, Curtis W. *Rocky Mountain National Park: A History*. Boulder: Colorado Associated University Press, 1983.

Coleman, Annie G. *Ski Style: Sport and Culture in the Rockies*. Lawrence: University Press of Kansas, 2004.

Fry, Abbot. *A History of Skiing in Colorado*. Ouray, CO: Western Reflections, 2000.

Guthrie, Carol. *All Aboard for Glacier: The Great Northern Railway and Glacier National Park*. Helena: Farcountry Press, 2004.

Johnson, Charles A. *Opera in the Rockies: A History of the Central City Opera House Association, 1932--1992*. Denver: Central City Opera Association, 1992.

Pomeroy, Earl. *In Search of the Golden West: The Tourists in West America*. New York: Alfred A. Knopf, 1957.

Rothman, Hal K. *Devil's Bargains: Tourism in the Twentieth-Century American West*. Lawrence: University Press of Kansas, 1998.

Smith, Duane A. *Mesa Verde National Park: Shadows of the Centuries*. Rev. ed. Boulder: University Press of Colorado, 2002.

Smith, Duane A., and Mark Foster. *They Came to Play: A Photographic History of Colorado Baseball*. Boulder: University Press of Colorado, 1997.

Stokowski, Patricia A. *Riches and Regrets: Betting on Gambling in Two Colorado Mountain Towns*. Niwot: University Press of Colorado, 1996.

Whiteside, James. *Colorado: A Sports History*. Niwot: University Press of Colorado, 1999.

Young, Allen. *Opera in Central City*. Denver: Spectrographics, 1993.

Urbanization

Dobbs, Joanne W. *They All Came to Pueblo: A Social History*. Virginia Beach, VA: Donning, 1994.

Dorsett, Lyle W. *The Queen City: A History of Denver*. Boulder: Pruett, 1977.

Eberhart, Perry. *Ghosts of the Colorado Plains*. Athens, OH: Swallow Press, 1986.

Emmons, David M. *The Butte Irish: Class and Ethnicity in an American Mining Town, 1875--1920*. Urbana: University of Illinois Press, 1989.

Field, Sharon, ed. *History of Cheyenne, Wyoming*. Dallas: Curtis Media, 1989.

Gomez, Arthur R. *Quest for the Golden Circle: The Four Corners and the Metropolitan West, 1945--1970*. Albuquerque: University of New Mexico Press, 1994.

Jordan, Arthur. *Jordan*. Missoula, MT: Mountain Press, 1984.

Leonard, Stephen J., and Thomas J. Noel. *Denver: Mining Camp to Metropolis*. Niwot: University Press of Colorado, 1990.

Mercier, Laurie. *Anaconda: Labor, Community, and Culture in Montana's Smelter City*. Urbana: University of Illinois Press, 2001.

Pettem, Silvia. *Boulder: Evolution of a City*. Niwot: University Press of Colorado, 1994.

Reps, John. *Cities of the American West: A History of Frontier Urban Planning*. Princeton: Princeton University Press, 1979.

Righter, Robert W. *The Making of a Town: Wright, Wyoming*. Boulder: Roberts Rinehart, 1985.

Smith, Duane A. *Crested Butte: From Coal Camp to Ski Town*. Montrose, CO: Western Reflections, 2005.

——. *Rocky Mountain Boom Town: A History of Durango*. Niwot: University Press of Colorado, 1992.

Sprague, Marshall. *Newport in the Rockies: The Life and Good Times of Colorado Springs*. Rev. ed. Chicago: Swallow Press, 1980.

Illustration Credits

Bailey, Christine
Georgetown, Colorado, in the 1950s.

Center of Southwest Studies, Fort Lewis College
A rural school in the Rockies.

Denver Post
John Elway of the Denver Broncos.

Gilbert, Richard L.
An abandoned ranch north of Cheyenne.
A small rodeo in Encampment, Wyoming.
Hidden Lake in Glacier National Park.

Mesa Verde National Park
Cliff Palace in Mesa Verde National Park. Photograph by Gustaf Nordenskiold.
A Civilian Conservation Corps camp.

Montana Historical Society, Helena
The railroad stop at Jennings, Montana.
Homesteaders on the eastern plains. Photograph by Evelyn Cameron.

Ninnemann, John L.
Durango, Colorado.

**Wyoming State Archives, Department of State Parks
and Cultural Resources**
Cowboys in Wyoming.
A farm in Big Horn County, Wyoming. From the J. E. Stimson Collection.

Index

About the Author

Duane A. Smith was born in San Diego, California, on April 20, 1937. He received his BA, MA, and PhD degrees from the University of Colorado, where he was one of "Bob's Cubs"—the students of Robert G. Athearn. Since 1964 he has taught at Fort Lewis College, where he is Professor of Southwest Studies and History. Smith's fields of historical research and writing are the West, Colorado, mining, the Civil War, urban areas, and baseball. Among his most recent books are *Women to the Rescue: Creating Mesa Verde National Park* (2003), *A Time for Peace: Fort Lewis, Colorado, 1879-1891* (2006), and *San Juan Bonanza: Western Colorado's Mining Legacy* (2006) with John Ninnemann. His awards include Colorado Humanist of the Year (1989) and Colorado Professor of the Year (1990). Smith's wife, Gay, and daughter, Lara, helped immeasurably with the present work.